CONTENTS

Destruction of Wallasey Church By Fire	1
Battle Of The Floods	4
Warning On Dangers To Public At Tower	7
Hard Labour For Strikers	10
Coronation Buildings	27
Ship Wrecks Ferry Pier	32
Wallasey Born D-Day General Dies	36
New Factory Brings Them A New Life	38
Eiffel Tower For New Brighton	41
Fearful Explosion And Loss Of Life At Seacombe	43
The Queen Touched By Ringing Cheers	45
New Promenade Pier At New Brighton	48
Fight To Save The Avenue	52
The Last Link	55
The New Docks At Wallasey	58
A Sickening Crash	60
Escape Of A Lion : Exciting Scene	63
Anne Glassey Workshop Closes Down	65
Extraordinary Adventure Of Tommy Burns: Struggle With A Shark At New Brighton	67
News In Short	69

Bulldozers Set To Level Resort Pool	80
Father Goes To Jail For His Son's Crime	85
Coronation of King George VI	87
A New Park For Wallasey	111
A Burglar And His Yacht	116
Broken Bolts Cause Wallasey Bus Tragedy	118
The "Noah's Ark" Refreshment Rooms	127
Wallasey A Mecca Bathers	130
The Destruction Of New Brighton College	137
A Man And His Wife Drowned	142
'The Lighthouse' Has Fascinating Nautical Theme	144
Coronation of Queen Elizabeth II	149
News In Short 2	165
One-Way Precinct 'Great Success With Shoppers	181
Jobs Go As Co-op Pulls Out Of Liscard	183
On The Wall Of Thrills At New Brighton	186
Tragedy At New Brighton	189
The Great Push	191
Battle of the Brickworks	200
Gandy Belt Works Gutted	208
The Suspected Child Murder At Egremont	213
Lantern Parade At Wallasey	216
The Wallasey Pals	220
The New "Nelson"	224
Town Loses Hospital Battle	227
New Grosvenor Brewery, Seacombe	229
A Monstre Wheel For New Brighton	232
News In Short 3	234

Brighton Street Fire	255
Wallasey Men In North Sea Battle	262
Wallasey's "Pre-Fab" Dwellers Have "No Complaints"	265
Wheatland Lane Re-Development	269
Police get A 'Move Along There' Order As The Station Closes	271
The Dirt, The Noise, The Clouds Of Dust, The Plague Of Children	274
The New Brighton Tragedy: Part 1	278
The New Brighton Tragedy: Part 2	305

DESTRUCTION OF WALLASEY CHURCH BY FIRE

Liverpool Mercury

Tuesday, 3rd February, 1857

On Sunday morning the ancient church of Wallasey, so well known to all who make occasional excursions to the Cheshire side of the Mersey, was totally destroyed by fire. The particulars of the catastrophe, so far as we have been able to learn, are as follows :- About two o'clock on Sunday morning an inhabitant of the village, on looking through his bed room window, discovered smoke and flames issuing from the church, and immediately communicated the fact to the rector, the Rev. F. Haggit. The rector and several of the parishioners proceeded at once to the spot, and found that their worst fears were realised. The flames were breaking through the windows, and the fire presented an alarming aspect. A messenger was dispatched for the Birkenhead fire brigade and engine, that being the nearest place from which any effectual assistance could be had in such an emergency. In the meantime the flames spread rapidly, the persons present being unable to do anything towards arresting their progress. From every window the fire burst forth, and burnt with such brilliancy as to be visible from a distance of several miles. In a very short time the roof of the body of the edifice fell in, and then it became evident that the building must very soon be utterly destroyed. The fire brigade from Birkenhead arrived about half-past three, but even then any efforts they could make were inoperative from the want of a supply of water. After some time water was obtained and the engine got in to play, but it was then too late to make any effectual efforts towards arresting the progress of the devouring element.

Early sketch of St. Hilary's Church, c1850

The whole of the body of the church was completely gutted, and presented nothing but a heap of smouldering ruins. The tower remains standing, this portion of the edifice having to an extent been preserved by the effects of the fire brigade. The register books and some documents of value connected with the church were the only things saved from the conflagration. The handsome organ, which was erected a few years ago, and which cost three hundred guineas, was totally consumed, also a handsome font, presented to the church by Mr. Chambers. The church contained a set of six bells, which fell with a tremendous crash during the progress of the fire. Only two of the bells remain entire, the remainder being broken to pieces. The church underwent very extensive improvements a year or two ago, and a large sum of money was expended.

As for the origin of the fire, little doubt is entertained. The fires connected with the flues for heating the building were lighted as usual about eight on Saturday evening. This was the ordinary practice on that the church might be sufficiently warmed when the congregation assembled the following morning for divine service. It is supposed that some of the flues, becoming overheated, had ignited the flooring, and thus led to the results which followed. The loss is covered by insurance in the Sun Fire Office to the extent of £2000, but this, it is considered, will fall far short of the actual damage which has resulted from the conflagration. The church was one of the oldest ecclesiastical edifices in the neighbourhood. The tower bears the date of 1530, although the church itself was re-built about 100 years ago. During the day the ruins were visited by a large number of gentry on the Cheshire side, among whom we noticed Mr. D. Neilson, Mr. J.C. Ewart, M.P., Mr. Commissioner Parry, Mr. T.S. Raffles, etc., etc.

◆ ◆ ◆

BATTLE OF THE FLOODS

Wallasey Chronicle

17th January 1948

With flood-waters from the rain-swollen Birket sweeping over hundreds of acres at Moreton, Leasowe and Saugall Massie, many bungalow dwellers evacuated to stay with friends or neighbours, while a few who had nowhere else to go stayed marooned in their homes, some of which were awash.

Neighbours in waders and rubber dinghies improvised "relief" services and kept them supplied with milk and bread until the floods began going down towards the end of the week.

Roped together in pitch darkness and driving rain on Tuesday night, N.F.S. waded through four feet of water to 19 Birket Road and gave first aid to 60-year-old Mr. Charles Pierce, who had seriously sprained his ankle trying to reach dry land to get help.

Mr. and Mrs. Pierce, with their dog Prince, were evacuated in a dinghy next day by Police Sergeant Reece and Constable Bird, and went to stay with a daughter in Liverpool.

Report from flood zone yesterday:- Water down nearly 3 ft. Birket still bank high, over at points. Ditton Lane area a foot deep. Fields of root crops still under, fencing broken. Flood trail of crockery, bottles, wood, and other debris.

Roads Impassible

Worst flooding was in the Ditton Lane area, between Pasture Road and Reeds Lane (writes reporter Frank Murphy). I found several by-roads and lanes were impassable except by boat.

With the water lapping her front step, and still rising rapidly as the heavy rain drove down, continuously, Mrs. Gladys Jeffrey, of 3 Hospital Cottages, told me: "We get used to this kind of thing every year, but it has not been this high for some time.

"Some 'new' people round about got pretty scared and moved out."

Wearing thigh boots borrowed from Mr. Jeffrey, and guessing the centre of the lanes – with the risk of a six-foot ducking in a ditch if one guessed wrong – I found some of the marooned bungalows.

Round Bedposts

At 'Highfield' I found Mrs. E. Preston in bed with the furniture stacked up and water round the bedposts. A dog half-jumped, half swam to the door. Outside a cat crouched in a box on a table which seemed on the point of floating away.

"We're hoping to be all right, and stick it out," she said. "My boy Richard – he's 15 – waded out yesterday and got us some food in. It can't last forever – can it?" she added just a little doubtfully.

On the way out I noticed that the cat had decided it was safer on the roof.

Letters and parcels which could not be delivered were kept at Moreton Cross P.O. to be called for.

Among the evacuated families were Mr. and Mrs. Duncan, with Patricia, aged 5, and Catherine, 3, of 'The Nook,' Ditton Lane.

On Sunday, just before he went back after 14 days' leave from the Navy, 21-year-old Billy Jeffrey took them by dinghy to Pasture Road, and they have been sleeping on the floor at Orchard Road, where they are staying with Mr. Duncan's mother, Mrs R. Duncan.

Hoylake Road

For a time water covered the main Hoylake Road junction, Saughall, but traffic was able to plough through. After high tide the river fell a little, only to rise again later, swamping the road edge on the lower side.

At Saughall bridge (Bermuda Road) the Arrowe Brook, looking more like the Dee, had inundated fields and was at the back doors of several houses. Water was just low enough to keep the road clear.

There was also extensive flooding near Birket Avenue and Reedsville Grove, and at Bidston.

Sequel to the floods is likely to be a renewed demand for a speed-up in operation of the Rivers Fender and Birkett Catchment Board, which holds its first meeting next month.

❖ ❖ ❖

WARNING ON DANGERS TO PUBLIC AT TOWER

Wallasey NEWS

11th April 1969

Preparatory work has begun on the demolition of the charred shell of the New Brighton Tower building. Since fire gutted the interior and caused some of the exterior to crumble last weekend there has been the constant fear that the remaining gigantic blackened red-brick walls might collapse. By Wednesday the rubble heap inside had cooled down enough for an examination to be made, but this was not possible because of the extremely dangerous condition of the ruined walls.

Managing Director of the New Brighton Tower Company, Mr. Leon Davies, told the 'News' yesterday: "The building must obviously come down as soon as possible. It is in an extremely dangerous state and I am worried stiff about children who might venture near and get killed or hurt.

"I appeal most strongly to parents to make sure that their youngsters keep well away from the site. If a wall came down the debris could fly over a considerable areas".

The cause of the fire is still not known. Although an investigation by the Chief Fire Officer, Mr. E.E. Buschenfeld and senior police officers and forensic experts is under way it could be several weeks before any conclusions are reached.

Close Investigation

The investigation will follow closely each stage of demolition. It will also be some time before the assessors are able to estimate the cost of the damage. Demolition alone is likely to be very costly.

It was about 5 am on Saturday morning, the day after the Tower had opened for the first time this season, that the fire was reported by Constable Edward Brimage, who was on patrol in the area.

Within minutes the Wallasey Fire Brigade arrived on the scene, followed by brigades from Birkenhead, Liverpool, Cheshire County and Lancashire County.

Over 150 men with twenty pumps and four turntable ladders were soon in action and at 7 am the Wallasey Fire Chief sent for five more pumps.

Explosion Fear

The Promenade was a tangle of hoses snaking from the various supplies, including the Marine Boating Lake, of the thousands of gallons of water the firemen used to beat the blaze. There were fears of explosion when it was known that there were a number of unreachable oxy-acetylene cylinders in the building. But two blasts caused no injury to the fire-fighters.

Just after 9.30 am the fire was brought under control but damping down went on throughout the holiday weekend. The fairground is, of course, closed until further notice.

And what of the future? It is too soon to think of anything beyond demolition, Mr. Davies told the 'News'. His board would be meeting in the very near future to consider the situation, he added.

◆ ◆ ◆

HARD LABOUR FOR STRIKERS

Wallasey NEWS

15th May 1926

The Corporation attempt to institute a bus service at Wallasey on Tuesday afternoon proved successful, although the windows of one bus were shattered and six arrests were made.

At four o'clock, when the first bus left the shed, there was a considerable number of policemen and special constables in the vicinity. As the vehicles emerged from the sheds into Seaview Road, a large crowd surged towards it. A plank, picked up from excavations in front of the Tramway Offices, was thrown across the front of the bus by strikers, and volleys of stones were thrown at the windows. The cab of the bus was protected by wire netting, and, the mechanism being uninjured, the bus proceeded along Seaview Road, followed by a car conveying police constables.

Almost simultaneously with the smashing of the windows, the arrests were made, and a crowd of nearly 200 people were dispersed. A woman fainted. Subsequent buses to leave the depot were not interfered with, and during the evening there were three on service.

On Wednesday the bus service was almost normal, the windows being protected by strong wire netting, whilst a uniformed constable sat beside the driver and special constables were passengers.

Men In Court

There was a crowded court on Wednesday morning, when the men arrested by the police on Tuesday appeared before the magistrates. All the public seats were occupied. The accused were:

Francis Roberts (44), tram-driver, 69 Gladstone Road;
Frederick Fairclough (29), tram-driver, 39 Lancaster Road;
Robert Cartwright (34), tram-driver, 2 Tancred Road;
Francis O'Hare (35), tramway-employee, 9 Demesne Street;
Evan Thomas Griffiths (29), tram conductor, 390 Poulton Road;
Edwin James Hudson (35), tram cleaner, 30 Radstock Road;
Richard Dickson (33), 21 Percy Street;
Percy William Buck (27), tram conductor, 118 Seaview Road.

They were charged with offences under the Emergency Regulations, 1926. There were also charges of assault against Fairclough and Cartwright, and of wilful damage against Fairclough, Griffiths and Dickson.

The Bench consisted of the following : Mr. C.H. Birchall (presiding), Dr. A.Robertson, Miss. Wyers, Mr. J.Barber, and Mr. F.J. Towley.

Mr. Emrys Evans (Deputy Town Clerk), appeared for the prosecution, on behalf of the Chief Constable (Mr. P.L. Barry). The prisoners were defended by Mr.E. Lynskey, of Liverpool.

The first case was against the prisoner Roberts. He was charged first with the offence on the 4th of May - Tuesday of last week, that is. He pleaded not guilty.

Mr. Emrys Evans, in his opening statement for the prosecution, explained that the proceedings had been taken under the Emergency Regulations, 1926, section 21 (i) of which provided (amongst other things) that no person should prevent or attempt to prevent the proper running of a public vehicle.

Left Without Notice

At midnight on May 3rd, drivers and conductors employed in the tramway service of the Wallasey Corporation left their duty, without giving notice to the authorities. Most of them had been in the service of a considerable number of years. Since midnight on the 3rd May, there had been attempts to prevent the running of Corporation motor buses. For a whole week the ratepayers and public had been deprived of means to and from Seacombe Ferry. As many people in Wallasey had to go to work in Liverpool daily, the Bench would realise that such a stoppage was a very serious matter. The men who had left duty had evidently had some orders to do so from the Trade Union Congress, but they evidently did not take note of another order from that body, enjoining men to refrain from violence.

Early Violence

On the first day of the strike, a large number of the men congregated near the tramway depot. Not only did they attempt to prevent other men from going in to their duty, but they tried to stop the running of the buses, broke the glass windows, abused the volunteer drivers, and assaulted several people. There were similar occurrences in different parts of the borough.

Strike or no strike, law and order must be maintained, and the liberty of the individual preserved. It must be made clear that no one would be allowed to prevent the ratepayers of Wallasey from riding in their own buses. It was to be hoped that the sentences which the Bench would inflict upon this accusation, if the cases were found proved, would make that quite clear, and would, moreover, deter others from similar actions.

Remand Requested

At this point Mr. E.Lynskey applied for a remand, on the

ground that as the men were only arrested the previous day, he had not had any opportunity to consult the accused men, or any witnesses who might appear on their behalf.

Mr. Evans opposed any application for bail or remand, on behalf of the police. The offence on the first charge were committed over a week ago, and he himself was in the same position as his colleague. He had no objection, however, to an adjournment until the afternoon. He wished to emphasise the fact that at a time like the present, it was essential that these charges should be dealt with at once.

An Adjournment

It was decided to adjourn the case for an hour.

When the hearing was resumed, Mr. Burchall had retired from the Bench. Mr. John Barber now presided.

Seacombe Ferry during General Strike with mesh on the bus windows

Severe Penalties

Continuing his statement, Mr. Emrys Evans reminded the magistrates that the possible penalties for these offences included three months' imprisonment, with or without hard labour, and (or without) a fine of £100.

In the case of the prisoner Roberts, the facts were that on May 4th, a number of strikers attempted to stop a bus in Brighton Street, by forming a semi-circle in front of it, two of them barring the way with a plank. Instead of stopping, however, the driver accelerated, and drove through the men, who had to jump out of the way, dropping the plank. Roberts was seen by two police constables with his hand raised, as though he had thrown something. At the same moment a tinkle of breaking glass was heard, but the bus went on. P.C. Sandland caught hold of Roberts and said: "Did you throw a brick?" Roberts answered: "No, I tried to open the door of the driver's seat." If that statement was true, commented Mr. Evans, Roberts was convicted on his own showing, for he had no right to interfere with the driver at all.

In evidence, Constable Sandland said that Roberts was not one of the men holding the plank. He thought Roberts had thrown a stone, and accordingly apprehended him, and took his name and address. He was forced, however, to let him go, because of the crowd. There was no actual violence.

Mr. Lynskey: Was Roberts apart from the men with the plank? - No, he was in the semi-circle.

If Roberts had thrown a stone you would have seen him, would you not? - I saw no missile leave his hand. I could not swear that he threw a stone.

Are you quite sure that he told you he was attempting to open the door? - Yes.

If he had tried to do that, wouldn't you have seen him? - Yes; I did see him with his hand up.

Did you not step back into the gutter when the bus swerved towards him? - No; he stepped forward.

Constable Reece, who was with Sandland at the time, corroborated. He saw no stone leave Roberts's hand, he said.

Did It Swerve?

Mr. Lynskey: Did the bus swerve towards Roberts as it passed him? - No; it went straight forward.

Roberts will say that the bus swerved towards him when it passed, and that he stepped back and put up his hand to save himself: - Not at all; he went towards it.

If he had thrown a stone you would have seen it? - Probably.

Evidence of the arrest on Tuesday was given by Constable Cotton.

Fifteen Years' Service

Before calling on the prisoner to give evidence for the defence, Mr. Lynskey told the Bench that he had been in the employ of the Corporation for fifteen years, and had never before been in trouble.

In the witness box, Roberts said that he walking down to Seacombe from the bowling green at Liscard. He walked down Clarendon Road into Brighton Street, where he saw a body of tramway-men, whom he overtook. He walked along with them for about a hundred yards, but had nothing to do with their endeavours to stop the bus. After the men had dropped the plank, the bus swerved towards him. He put up his hand and jumped back on to the pavement. He said nothing to the constable about opening the door to the driver's seat.

Mr. Emrys Evans: Who were the men with the plank? - Most of them I don't know; they are new men.

You walked down with them for about a hundred yards? - Yes.

Did you know they were on strike? - Yes.

Firewood!

Didn't it enter your head that there might be trouble brewing? What did you think they were carrying a plank about the town for? - I didn't know there was a bus out. I thought they might be taking the plank home for firewood, because of the coal strike.

Were you one of the men who were standing across the road? - Yes

Why did you stand in the road? - Out of curiosity.

Whose fault would it have been if you had been run over? - My own.

Then the only part of the constable's statement you contradict is that about the opening of the door? - Yes.

John Hart, bus driver, of 20 Hawthorndale Road, said he was in company with Roberts at the time of the occurrence. He heard nothing about Roberts trying to open the driver's door on the bus.

Mr. Emrys Evans: What were you doing with the crowd? - Oh, having a talk.

What for? - To see what was doing.

Well, did you see what was doing? - Yes.

I suppose, as an old bus driver, you strongly objected to these men driving the buses? - Well, yes.

In fact, you were one of those who were trying to stop the bus? - Yes

Were you holding the plank? - Yes.

Who were the others? - I don't know.

Mr. Evans (abruptly): Thank you. Thank you. That is all.

A bus conductor named Matthew Money, of 9 Lily Grove, Seacombe, also gave evidence on Roberts's behalf, but in answer to Mr. Evans, denied having anything to do with the attempt to stop the bus.

Similar evidence was given by John McMahan, driver, of 12 St. Alban's Terrace.

The Bench found the case proved, but deferred sentence. The charges against Roberts for offences on Tuesday last were then heard.

Preparations were made, Mr. Evans said, for the running of motor buses in Wallasey on Tuesday. The effort was successful, owing to the precautionary measures taken by the Chief Constable. Before the first bus appeared, Roberts was seen in a passage behind Massey Park, picking up stones. Just after 4 o'clock the bus came out. A great number of stones were hurled at it, and several windows were broken. Had there not been wire netting around the driver's compartment, there was no doubt that he would have been severely injured. Roberts was later arrested in Earlston Road. When he was searched the lining and pocket of his coat was found to contain gravel. He said to the officer who arrested him: "You have made a mistake this time. I'm too b----- wide awake to have stones in my pocket."

P.C. Cotton, who made the arrest, gave evidence in support of this statement, adding that the accused had told him he could produce witnesses to prove he had nothing to do with the attack on the bus.

Returning to the witness-box, Roberts said that he had no stones in his pocket, nor did he throw any. The entry in which he was seen, behind Massey Park, was full of square setts, and had no loose stones in it.

Mr. Emrys Evans: After your experience last week you still wanted to be in this scene? - No; it was to keep out of the way that I went into the entry.

Isn't it true that a large number of stones were thrown? - Yes.

Do you deny there was gravel in your pocket? -Yes, I do.

This case was also found proved, and sentence was again deferred.

The next case was against Fairclough, the offences of May 4th were taken first. Mr. Evans said that Inspector Colton was acting conductor on bus No.4 the day after the strikes was declared. The bus was raided on emerging from the tramway sheds, and the prisoner was seen by Colton to break a window.

Who's That Man?

Edward Colton, of 16 Mollington Road, said that Fairclogh mounted the front of the bus and put his hand up to the window and smashed it. Then Sergt. Beere jumped up and said to him (witness): "Who's that man?" He told him.

Sergt. Beere said he saw Fairclough mount the bus and then heard a crash of breaking glass.

Fairclough, in the witness-box, denied the charge absolutely.

The charge against Fairclough of an assault upon George Hoffman, a tramway inspector, on May 4th, was then considered. Mr. Evans said that Hoffman was driving bus No.9. The bus got clear of the approach to the sheds, but at Massey Park its way was barred by a cart belonging to the Wallasey Meat Traders' Association, which was at right angles across the road. Then the strikers surrounded the bus and Fairclough hit the driver Hoffman. The engines of the bus was also disabled.

Hoffman supported this statement, averring that Fairclough gave him "a clout across the jaw."

"One To Be Going On With"

Mr. Lynskey: Did you have any conversation with him? - No; he gave me one to be going on with.

Mr. Lynskey then made some reference to some of the arrests being made a week after the offences, to which Mr. Evans retorted: "When and how prosecutions are conducted is not decided by tramway employees."

Fairclough again denied the allegations in *toto*, but another conviction was recorded.

Constable Assaulted

He was then charged with assaulting Constable Griffin, and damaging a bus on Tuesday last. Constable Reece, it was stated, saw him throw a stone at the first bus that left the depot. He followed him. There was a struggle, in which, said Constable Reece to the magistrates, "he made a savage attack on my throat with his teeth." Constable Ingram came to the rescue, and hit Fairclough on the head with his baton. Fairclough fell to the ground, but on rising kicked the constable on the leg.

Fairclough said that he saw the bus windows being smashed, and walked to Massey Park to be out of the trouble. Then a policeman got hold of him by the waistcoat and hit him over the head with a baton.

This case was proved.

Charges against Robert Cartwright, branch secretary of the Transport and General Workers' Union were then heard. He was accused of offences against the Emergency Regulations on May 4th, and with assaulting John Davies and Thomas Whittaker, on the 5th.

Mr. Evans said that the incident upon which the prosecution was based arose in connection with the departure from the depot of bus No.9 on May 4th. As had been stated in a previous case, this bus was prevented from proceeding along Seaview Road by a meat cart. Cartwright went up to Inspector Hoffman, who was driving, and said: "If you go down the road, I'll knock you silly." Hoffman said: "Don't you use abusive language!" Cartwright then told him he was risking his life, and later said he would take no responsibility for what would happen if the bus went on. When a notice was read out to the men by the General Manager, Cartwright shouted out: "The men will answer that at the proper time."

Not Afraid

Hoffman, giving evidence, said that before he was accosted by Cartwright one man said to him: "Aren't you afraid of losing your life?" He replied: "I have no reason to be; I'm not afraid of any one man."

Cross-examined by Mr. Lynskey, Hoffman admitted that Cartwright had nothing to do with the stopping of the bus.

Inspector Leigh said that there was a crowd of about a hundred and fifty strikers. When the manager read a notice to them Cartwrightsaid "The men will answer that."

Chief Inspector Roberts said that Cartwright appeared to be spokesman for the strikers. He attempted, successfully, to prevent one bus from leaving the depot.

Cartwright then entered the witness-box. He had received instructions from the strike committee, he said, to be "neutral," twenty minutes before the trouble. The General Manager read a notice to the men about handing in their uniforms. He said: "That's nothing to do with me; the men will answer that." He then walked down to the Labour Hall, and made no attempt to stop any bus. He had obeyed orders to "remain neutral" all along. Several policemen could testify that he had helped to keep the strikers under cover."

Mr. Emrys Evans: Have you succeeded?

Cartwright: Yes, in the case which Hoffman mentions, I used no threats at all. The men said: "We are going to have him out of the bus!"

He then went to the constables and asked them if they would take responsibility for the bus. He could not do so further, as the men were riotous and Hoffman was not very popular among them.

No Threats

Mr. Evans: Did you use threats? - No, not to anyone.

Were you "neutral" before this trouble? - Well, I couldn't very well be, as I was spokesman for the men.

Mr. Evans then read a letter, which Cartwright admitted he had written - at the dictation of the Strike Committee - on the notepaper of the Transport and General Workers' Union. It was dated "May 3rd, 10.15 a.m.," and expressed the desire of the committee to pass through the strike period peacefully, and to aid the policy to maintain and distribute supplies, wherever possible. There would be no violence (it continued) provided a guarantee was given that no cars or buses would be run except for food distribution, if necessary. If, however, any bus or tram was brought out for passenger purposes he would immediately call on Liverpool and Birkehead dockers, railwaymen and general workers, and if necessary the ferrymen, and if the cars and buses left the depot he would not be responsible for what might happen.

This case was found proved.

On the second charge, of assaulting two men on May 5th, the facts were that Cartwright, at 7.15 a.m., accosted John Davies, timekeeper, and Thomas Whittaker, inspector, of the Corporation tramways, who were going to work, outside the depot, and said: "Stop! You have gone far enough." On Davies endeavoring to proceed, he beckoned to a crowd of the men, but Davies got away. Then he approached Whittaker, but on the arrival of a constable, said he was only going to speak to him. It was a technical assault only, said Mr. Evans, but nonetheless serious.

Davies supported this statement in his evidence.

Mr. Lindsay: Cartwright was quite quiet? - Yes

In fact, he is always? - Yes.

Cartwright denied assaulting either of the men. He had been told the previous day that they would join the union, and approached with a bundle of cards, with a view to enrolling them.

Tried To Prevent Violence

Samuel Dodd, a tram-driver, of 3 Bishop Road, said that Cartwright had all along advised the men to keep quiet, and had done his utmost to prevent violence.

The case was found proved.

Bus On Footpath

Percy William Buck was next taken.

Buck pleaded not guilty. Mr. Evans said that on May 4th, a bus left the tram sheds, being driven by a volunteer with Inspector Colton as the conductor. When it approached the head office a striker broke the windows of the bus, and Buck jumped on and steered it into the footpath.

Inspector Colton said he was near the office about two o'clock when the vehicle ran into the crowd of strikers. He was acting as conductor. One man jumped on the side of the bus and broke the window. Another man jumped on and pulled the driver from the seat and when he had gone Buck pushed his hand through the broken window and steered the bus on the pavement.

Sergeant Beere said he saw somebody put his hand through the window, but he could not swear to who it was.

Referring to another occasion, Inspector Colland said that a wagon was drawn across the road when the bus was stopped and a number of men surrounded it. Buck jumped on before the bus had stopped, and he was closely followed by another man. He jumped on and shouted: "Now Inspector, are you coming off, or are you going to be thrown off?"

Buck: Who did? I didn't.

Wanted inspector Off

Cross-examined by Mr. Lindsay, Inspector Colland said that Buck did not interfere with the bus, but appeared to be wanting him off it.

Buck told the Bench that he had absolutely nothing to do with the steering of the bus on to the pavement. He never touched the wheel or jumped on the bus on that occasion.

Mr. Evans: You admitted that you wanted to stop the bus? - I admit that.

The Bench found the case proved.

The charges against O'Hare, Griffiths, Hudson and Dickson all related to the incidents on Tuesday afternoon and were taken collectively. Griffiths and Dickinson were also accused of doing willful damage.

Mr. Evans said that the attempt to run the service on that occasion proved successful, but not before the windows had been smashed.

P.C. Sharpies said he saw O'Hare standing near the heap of stones amongst a crowd of men, some of whom were being arrested. Witness noticed him walking threateningly towards Inspector White side. Witness never saw him throw any stones.

O'Hare was arrested and in reply said he knew nothing until he was taken in custody.

Mr. Lindsay: Apart from the fact that O'Hare was there, did he take any part in it?

P.C. Sharpies: I do not know

The Bench decided that there was not sufficient evidence to convict O'Hare, and he was accordingly dismissed.

Seen By Constable

P.C. Ingman said he saw Griffiths pick up a stone and throw it. Griffiths was alone on the footpath at the time.

Griffiths told the magistrates that there had been a meeting arranged to take place at the Labour Hall, at three o'clock that afternoon. When he got to the Hall he was instructed to go to the tram depot, and he was standing near Massey Park when the bus passed him. There was a rush forward, and he was mixed up in the crowd and his hat was knocked off. As he was bending down to pick it up he was "rushed into a motor van" and taken to the Police Station.

Mr. Evans: Who instructed you?

Griffiths: Some men who were standing at the door of the Labour Hall told me they were all at the depot. I did not know there was likely to be a disturbance at the time.

The Bench decided the case proved.

Prisoner Escapes

In regard to the charge against Hudson, Detective Payne said he was in a private car and saw Hudson standing near the Liscard end of the excavations. He saw Hudson stoop down and pick something up and after he had thrown it there was a crash of glass. When the car reached him, witness jumped out and caught Hudson. A few seconds later, however, he had to leave the car, with Hudson and the driver inside, to assist somebody else. As Detective Inspector Could well and witness were putting another prisoner in the car, Hudson dashed out the door at the other side. Witness gave chase and caught him in Thirlmere Road. When charged Hudson said he had nothing to say.

Mr. Lindsay: Did you ask him to get into the car?

Detective Payne: I didn't exactly ask him to walk in.

Detective Inspector Could well corroborated and said that Hudson threw the stone and then ran away.

Hudson, who said he had been in the employ of the Corporation since 1913, stated that he was crossing the road when two men came along in a private car, and he was taken to the station, "That was the end of me" commented witness.

Mr. Evans: It was not quite the end of you. When you got into the car did you get out by the other door? Yes I made an attempt to get away.

If you were an innocent man, why did you get away?

I did the same as any other man. There was a chance of freedom and I took it.

Prisoner pleaded that the disturbance was over when he got there, but the magistrates found the case proved.

P.C. Pickford said he saw Dickson and two or three other men pick up a plank and put it in the front of the bus. He also threw a stone and then ran across the road and was rubbing the dirt off his hands when he was apprehended. In reply to the charge, Dickinson said, "I stood in front of the bus and then stepped back again."

Mr. Lindsay: I suggest he was taken before the bus was damaged - No.

P.C. Ben field said he saw Dickinson making use of the plank and throw a stone, although he did not see it strike the bus.

"Come Along"

Dickinson said he was in the crowd but never threw either a plank or a stone. He saw the bus pass him and there had been no damage done to it. The motor car with the police came along and two offices said "Come along." He had no idea that he was being arrested. He saw the plank thrown by somebody else two or three yards further on.

The case was found proved.

The Chief Constable (Mr. P.L. Barry), said all the prisoners had previously borne good characters.

Mr. Lindsay asked that the men's length of service to the Corporation and their previous good character should be taken into consideration. Most of the men had been with the Corporation for a considerable time, Buck, who joined the army when he was sixteen, having been in the service for seven years. Roberts had been in the service of the Corporation for 15 years; Fairclough 7 years; Cartwright 7 years; Griffiths 12 months; Hudson 13 years; and Dickinson 3 years.

The Sentences

Thirty minutes after retiring the magistrates passed sentences as follows:

Fairclough - Three Months.
Roberts - One Month.
Cartwright - One Month.
Griffiths - One Month.
Hudson - One Month.
Dickinson - One Month.
Buck - 14 Days.
O'Hare - Discharged.

◆ ◆ ◆

CORONATION BUILDINGS

Wallasey NEWS

2nd April 1938

The remarkable transformation of Liscard from a district of small and old-fashioned shops into an area of modern and imposing business premises, has now been realised by the completion of Coronation Buildings adjoining the recently re-built Wellington Hotel.

The notable achievement stands to the credit of the well-known and old-established Merseyside firm of land and estate agents, Messrs. Boughey Bros., with offices in Liverpool and Wallasey, who acting on behalf of clients, purchased from the Wallasey Corporation the land on which the new and spacious buildings have been erected.

Subsequently, a private company was formed to develop a site which is one of the key positions of the shopping district of Wallasey, being situated in the center of the borough and abutting on to one of the main arterial roads upon which converge the principal bus routes not only inside but outside the borough boundaries, viz., Birkenhead, Moreton, Meols, Hoylake and West Kirby. Having due regard to the importance of the site, and the necessity for its development on lines consistent an eminent and experienced firm of architects was commissioned to plan and design the buildings, Messr. Norman Jones and Rigby, of Manchester and Southport. That Messrs. Boughey Bros.' ambition to see erected on the site business premises that will remain a landmark and a credit to the borough has been realised is the unanimous opinion of those competent to judge.

The bold and comprehensive scheme now completed by Messrs. Wallasey Contractors Ltd., makes provisions for a number of shops (some of which are already in occupation by firms of repute), with pleasing elevation and extensive floor space, having a depth of 84 feet. The importance of adequate lighting has not been overlooked, for although the buildings are on the sunny side of the road, spacious front windows and good windows at the rear of the premises, guarantee the maximum of daylight. First-class electric installations, embracing lantern lights, "turn night into day."

The windows to each shop have been so constructed that ample room is given for the display of goods - an essential feature.

The Government have realised the importance and central position of Coronation Buildings by leasing more than half of the upper floor to accommodate the entire staffs of the Income Tax, Customs and Excise, Old Age Pensions and Government Public Health departments.

Messrs. Boughey Bros. completed an enterprising scheme by purchasing two houses (to be demolished) in Wallasey Road on the corner of Coningsby Drive, on which site a large Insurance company intend erecting commodious premises.

A few shops and offices are still obtainable at Coronation Buildings, and early application should be made to Messrs. Boughey Bros., either at their Wallasey offices, 72 Wallasey Road, or at 67 Lord Street, Liverpool. Telephone, Wallasey 582, or Bank 4983.

Keizer & Co. Ltd.

The vitrolite glazing to facias, etc. for Coronation Buildings was carried out by Messrs. Keizer & Co. Ltd. Inquiries will receive prompt attention if addressed to 72 St. Anne Street, Liverpool, telephone North 344.

Messrs. John Gibbs & Son Ltd

The heating system for the Coronation Buildings was installed by Messrs. John Gibbs & Son Ltd., of 72 Duke Street, Liverpool, who were also responsible for the ventilation. Estimates free. Telephone Royal 2579.

Messrs. A.E.Chesters Ltd.

The comprehensive scheme of electrical installation at Coronation Buildings have been under the personal supervision of the well known firm Electrical Contractors, Messrs. A.E. Chesters Ltd., of Atherton Street, New Brighton.

Messrs. Chesters have carried out many large contracts in recent months and years, including the new Home for the Nurses of the Victoria Central Hospital, the Victoria Central Hospital extension and reconstruction, headquarters for Nursing Association, extension of South port Infirmary, New Brighton Swimming Pool and Boating Lake, New Brighton. They are also contractors to the War Office and the G.P.O.

All inquiries receive prompt attention. Phone Wallasey 656.

Messrs. Elliott, Confectioners

Messrs. Elliott's fine display of all kinds of cakes and confectionery is worthy of inspection at Coronation Buildings. A wide choice of numerous varieties of fancy cakes, sandwich spreads, tasty dishes of the highest quality and lowest price, are attractively displayed. "Rosmary's" famous savory biscuits are in stock, whilst wedding cakes are a specialty.

Residents and visitors will receive a cordial welcome by Elliott's at Coronation Buildings, where expert service will be placed at their disposal.

Messrs. Bakewell's

The well-known wholesale and retail tobacconists, Messrs. Bakewell, have a branch at Coronation Buildings, at which all smokers' requisites and every brand of tobacco, cigarettes and choice cigars is in stock. A fine variety of suitable birthday and Easter gifts are on view. An inspection is invited either at Coronation Buildings or at 154 Poulton Road. Telephone Wallasey 5620.

Coronation Pharmacy

The Coronation Pharmacy at Coronation Buildings, under the personal direction of Mr. H.T. Spence, M.P.S., dispensing and photographic chemist, has a complete stock of proprietary lines, perfumes, powders, cosmetics, toilet, surgical and holiday requisites. 1938 model cameras and all "Kodak" films, chemicals, etc., are available for inspection and a quick service developing and printing department is under the control of experienced hands.

National Health Dispensing is undertaken and the finest quality drugs only used for this and private dispensing.

Messrs. Ellison Bros.

Messrs. Ellison Bros. Ltd., of 15 Liscard Village, Wallasey, provided the Coronation Buildings with the sanitary fittings, including sinks, urinals, lavatory basins closets, flushing cisterns, etc.

Messrs. Ellison Bros are well-known in the borough as the leading merchants supplying plumbing goods, fireplaces, wallpaper and paints. At their warehouse in Liscard Village extensive stocks of all these materials are stored and displayed efficiently in their up-to-date showrooms. The Wallasey public are cordially invited to patronise Ellison Bros., as their prices are competitive in all departments, whilst their goods are the best obtainable.

Messrs. Wallasey Contractors Ltd.

The important building contract for the erection of Coronation Buildings was entrusted to Wallasey Contractors and Decorators Ltd. (better known as "Milestones"). That important work was carried out under the personal direction of Mr. J.A. Milestone, Senr., and was commenced in July 1936. The area, comprising 3,554 square yards, was prepared and the steel frame completed in eight weeks. Final completion was, of course, dependent upon lettings of shops and offices, and tenants' requirements.

Messrs. Hooton Brick Works Ltd.

Hooton bricks, manufactured by Messrs. Hooton Bricks Works Ltd., were utilised throughout the construction of the Coronation Buildings and the Wellington Hotel. Architects and building contractors are invited to secure quotations for Hooton Bricks which have been proved to be durable and of high quality by contractors in all parts of the country. All communication should be address to Hooton Brick Works Ltd., Hooton Road, Hooton, Wirral - Telephone 119 Willaston.

◆ ◆ ◆

SHIP WRECKS FERRY PIER

Liverpool Post

23rd May 1932

Egremont Pier and the 60-ton bridge to the steps were wrecked, on Saturday, by the 6,895-ton oil tanker *British Commander*. Nobody was injured, but damage estimated at £40,000 was done, and the ferry will be out of action for three or four months at least. It is only three years since a new bridge and stage were built, at a cost of £28,000.

The smash luckily occurred in mid-afternoon, between boats. The few people on the stage were thrown off their feet by the impact, but a ferryboat soon took them and the stagehands to safety. As even more thrilling escape was that of half a dozen people were walking along the pier towards the bridge a few moments before the tanker hit it. Had she struck the stage itself, some loss of life could scarcely have been avoided.

Anchor Cable Carried Away

The *British Commander*, with a crew of forty, left Cammell Laird's after repairs, about 12.30 on Saturday afternoon, and came to anchor. Shortly before three o'clock she was steaming down river on the ebb tide, and opposite Guinea Gap turned inshore to avoid an Irish steamer. There was a risk that the strong tide could carry her ashore, and the pilot ordered the dropping of the starboard anchor. This was done, but the whole of the cable, and the anchor carried away, and the tanker, now helpless against the tide, was carried against the floating bridge with great force.

Her bow grounded on the sand a few yards from the promenade, and her stern swung round and crashed into the pier. The bridge and half the pier collapsed with a roar, and all that now holds the stage is the mooring chains.

A crowd of several thousands gathered as vessels rushed up from all parts of the river. Seven tugs attached hawsers to the tanker's stern, but there was insufficient water to refloat her, and the attempt had to be postponed until about midnight.

Tanker Towed Off

Then the crowd which remained despite the rain saw the achievement of a difficult task. Two of the five attending tugs managed to attach hawsers, and the *British Commander* was towed off. The other tugs took hold, and the tanker was taken into the Alfred Dock, Birkenhead, and yesterday afternoon transferred to the West Float dry dock for repairs to her propeller and forward part. She is owned by the British Tankers' Company Ltd., of London.

Mrs. L. Walker, of the Promenade, Egremont, who was on the pier when the tanker struck it, said - "My mother, Mrs. White, and her companion Miss Laudie, who live at my address, had gone down to sit on the stage, and I was to follow them. When I set out along the pier I saw the huge form of the *British Commander* getting nearer and nearer as she came down with the ebb tide. I did not know whether to turn back or to go on. The ship approached within a few feet of the pier, and then seemed to stop, and I thought she had pulled up in time. At the same time the stern part of the ship seemed to swing slowly round and then stop, but a moment later it moved again, and with a noise like thunder crashed broadside on into the pier. I turned and ran back."

Bridge Crumpled Up

Mr. Kenneath Wood, also of Egremont Promenade, said: "I saw a man rush up the bridge, shouting a warning to a group of people who were going down for the next steamer. They all ran back, chased by the man, and it was the terror-stricken screams of the women that made me turn my glance to the river. The great tanker went straight into the bridge, which crumpled up like cardboard. Then, a tangled mass of wreckage fell before the advancing bows of the vessel and disappeared beneath the water."

Ferries Manager's Statement

Captain W.H. Fry, general manage of the Wallasey Ferries, who is in charge of the work, told the Daily Post that immediate steps were being taken to make safe the remaining structure. Another fifty feet of the pier are shaky.

"We shall take the bridge away, probably some time this week," he added, "and see whether it can be repaired or whether it will have to be scrapped. Repairs will occupy three or four months at the least. Much of the work will be tidal, the root of the damage being under water. I should say that about £40,000 worth of damage has been done, when you include the cost of clearing away the debris and the loss of traffic."

◆ ◆ ◆

WALLASEY BORN D-DAY GENERAL DIES

Wallasey NEWS

7th June 1969

General Sir Miles Dempsey who led the British Second Army in the invasion of Normandy and in North-West Europe, died yesterday at his home at Yattendon, Berkshire, on the 25th anniversary of D-Day. He was 72.

Sir Miles, who was born in New Brighton, Wallasey, was the son of the late Mr. A.F. Dempsey, a timber merchant. A former pupil of Elleray Park school, Wallasey and of Shrewsbury School, Sir Miles entered Sandhurst at the age of 17.

He became a 2nd Lieutenant in the Royal Berkshire Regiment in 1916, and served in the First World War from 1916-18. He was wounded, mentioned in despatches and received the Military Cross.

In World War Two he commanded the 13th Infantry Brigade at Dunkirk, the 13th Corps in the invasions of Sicily and Italy, after the invasion of Europe commanded the 14th Army in the re-occupation of Singapore and Malaya.

In 1945-46 he was C-in-C Allied Land Forces, South-East Asia, C-in-C Middle East Asia from 1946-47, and became ADC General to the King 1946-47.

He received his knighthood in 1944 from King George VI in the field.

◆ ◆ ◆

NEW FACTORY BRINGS THEM A NEW LIFE

Wallasey Chronicle

19th March 1949

Long-waited day for local disabled men and women came this week with the opening of the new "Remploy" factory in Poulton Road.

Newly-built, with a large airy work-rooms, comfortable benches, and a glass-sectioned sunshine roof, this special factory brings a new life, new hope and gladness, a new independence to men and women too seriously handicapped by war wounds or industrial accidents to be able to hold their own in the open market.

But through the doors of this cheerful robust industrial "sanctuary" they come to sheltered employment, a living wage, and self-respect.

Eventually 75 men and women will be sitting at these benches at their light industrial work. This week's first intake is 18 men and two women, mostly engaged in making mines' leather gloves and knee-pads under a National Coal Board contract.

"New Horizons"

"This place opens up new horizons for chaps like me," said 36-years-old ex-Merchant Navy engineer John Roberts, of

Kingsley Road, posted at a sewing machine instead of the huge diesel engines he once handled. And this is why.

John's old world closed on him on the night of February 3, 1942, when his cargo ship was torpedoed. Only engine-room survivor, he lay two days with a fractured right leg in the crew's leaking lifeboat as it drifted in the Atlantic. When his leg had to be amputated in a Newfoundland hospital, they also had to take off his other foot, because of frost-bite.

John had not done a day's work since then - until this week.

"It's just grand to be working again, and my wife - we have three kiddies - is delighted," he said. "I don't know what some of us could have done but for this factory."

For These, To The factory means new horizons also for chaps like -

Harry Tyrer, of Seabank Road, general clerk in the office, who lost his right arm going "over the top" way back at Ypres in the First World War.

Bill Lockley, of Kingsley Road, one-handed furnace man who slipped on to an electric saw when working on timber at the docks in 1938.

And for girls like -

Doreen Carson, 21-years-old shorthand typist, who cannot walk far because of dislocated hips, but finds that this factory two minutes from her home in Oxton Road is "just what the doctor ordered."

The works manager, Mr. Leslie Hughes - who is the only able-bodied man in the factory apart from a store-keeper who does the heavy weight-lifting - is also the workers' instructor in the art of glove-making and similar crafts, in which he is being temporarily helped by his wife.

◆ ◆ ◆

EIFFEL TOWER FOR NEW BRIGHTON

Liverpool Mercury

Monday, 10th February, 1896

Commencement Of Operations

There can be no doubt that the efforts being put forward by public bodies and private individuals to make New Brighton one of the most attractive seaside resorts in the north will meet with the approval, not only for visitors, but of the majority residents in the district. We announced in our columns a few weeks ago that a scheme had been decided upon for the establishment of a pleasure resort in New Brighton on lines somewhat similar to those at Olympia in London. That project has now assumed definite shape, and the site - the estate of the late Captain Molyneux on Rock Point - has been secured by a company (at the head of which is Mr. R.P. Houston, M.P.), who have paid a deposit of over £2000 to the trustees of the property. The grounds, as already indicated, are about 500 yards to the south of the pier, and are bounded on the east side by the river. The promenade, which is to be extended from the Magazines, Egremont, to New Brighton, will give convenient access to the grounds, whilst an upper entrance will be provided in Rowson Street. One of the principal features of the scheme will be the Eiffel Tower, such as was erected in Blackpool, and it will be interesting to the public to know that at the present times excavating operations are in progress in order to prepare the foundations of the tower. That the scheme is one of immense proportions will be readily realised when it is stated that it is the intention of the company to spend something like a quarter of a million of money in providing grounds, in which will be found attractions of every conceivable character. We understand that the company have also acquired the lease and interest of the Royal Ferry Hotel, close by the pier, with which establishment, we believe, Captain Walters has for some been connected. With a gentleman of enterprise like Mr. Houston at the head of affairs, it is expected that the scheme will be a great a success. There seems to be no reason to fear that the pleasure grounds will injure the Palace, for there will doubtless be generous support given to both places by the increased number of visitors who are sure to find their way to New Brighton. It should be added that the new company have spared no pains to secure every possible advantage in order to make the scheme as popular as possible. Indeed, it is stated that they recently approached the Wallasey District Council with a request that the present landing pier might be removed to a position directly opposite the grounds. This request they backed up with an offer to build the new pier if the council approved of the idea. That matter, however, we find, fall through, as the council could not see their way to interfere with the present position of the landing pier, which they pointed out was directly in a line with Victoria Road, the principal thoroughfare of the district

◆ ◆ ◆

FEARFUL EXPLOSION AND LOSS OF LIFE AT SEACOMBE

Liverpool Mercury

Saturday, 9th November, 1850

Between seven and eight o'clock on Wednesday evening last a dreadful explosion of naphtha, attended with fatal consequences, occurred in Mersey Street, Higher Seacombe, Cheshire. The house in which the melancholy occurrence took place is used as a Roman Catholic School and reading room in connection with St. Alban's Chapel, Liscard, and is under the superintendence of the Rev. Mr. Lennon.

It appears that on the evening in question, previous to the commencement of the duties of the school, Mr. Johnson, the schoolmaster, and six of the scholars, were in the front room, on the ground floor. The master was engaged in pouring some naphtha into a lamp from a tin can, containing about half a gallon; and a lad named John Crossie, about ten years of age, was holding a candle by his side. Never having before filled the lamp Mr. Johnson was ignorant of the quantity required, and before he was aware, the inflammable liquid ran over, and, coming in contact with the lighted candle, which was held by the boy Crossie, ignited. An instantaneous report, like that of a cannon, was heard, followed by a most tremendous crash, occasioned by the falling of the partition wall, about twelve feet long and nine feet high, which was forced with such violence against the opposite side of the lobby, that several deep indentations were made in the plaster work. In some places large portions of the wall removed, without being shattered, and forced against the wall forming the other side of the lobby. In the reading room, immediately above the scene of the explosion, were fourteen persons, one of whom was in the act of reading aloud an article from the Morning Chronicle. On hearing the report, and the noise which followed, they thought that the arches on which the houses were built, had given way, and a rush instantly took place to the door and window, through which a safe exit was made. Mathew Riley, who lived in the house, got out of the window, and the first person he saw was the lad Crossie, who was enveloped in flames, but his features could not be recognised. Riley immediately clung round the lad, and rolled with him on the floor until the flames were extinguished. The poor little fellow died between eight and nine o'clock on Thursday morning. Mr Johnson, and three lads are lying in a dangerous state, and little hopes are entertained of their ultimate recovery.

◆ ◆ ◆

THE QUEEN TOUCHED BY RINGING CHEERS

Wallasey NEWS

13th July 1957

Her Majesty the Queen and the Duke of Edinburgh told the Mayor (Alderman Harry Bedlington) that their visit to Wallasey on Thursday had been a most interesting experience. She was delighted with the welcome given to them by the 16,000 schoolchildren lining the route.

The Queen was particularly interested in the fact that the foundation stone of the Town Hall was laid by her grandfather, King George V, in 1914 and that he had performed the ceremony by remote control in Central Park.

Prince Philip's attention was attracted by the Stars and Stripes and the Union Jack hanging side-by-side at the top of the main staircase with a plaque commemorating the happy relationship between American servicemen stationed in Wallasey during the last war, and the people of the town.

In the Civic Hall, where the Queen was presented with a bouquet by 8 year old Ella Dingle, the thirty chosen people were presented to the Queen by the Mayor. Both the Queen and Prince Philip had something to say to those introduced to them.

Queen is greeted at Grove Road Station

As they were leaving the Town Hall, which was beautifully decorated with masses of flowers, the Queen expressed to the Mayor her appreciation of the floral display.

"Both Her Majesty and Prince Philip took a lively interest in everybody who was introduced to them and in everything they saw," the Mayor told a "News" reporter afterwards.

Just before the Royal train arrived at Grove Road station at 2.27 pm, where the Queen was welcomed by the Station Master, Mrs. E. Martin, and the Mayor, Mayoress (Mrs. Bedlington), Town Clerk (Mr. A.G. Harrison) and Chief Constable (Mr. John Ormerod) were presented by Lord Leverhulme (Lord Lieutenant of Cheshire), rain began to fall quite heavily. Despite the break in the weather, however, the five mile route was lined with people practically the whole way.

Town Hall Scene

Thousands made their vantage point in front of the Town Hall, in the entrance to which the Mayor presented the Borough Member (Mr. Ernest Marples, Postmaster General),

Mrs. Marples and Mrs. Harrison (wife of the Town Clerk). Before entering the building the Queen turned to wave to the crowd.

Nearly ten minutes later, the Royal couple appeared on the decorated balcony where they stayed for a moment to acknowledge with waves and smiles the warm welcome given to them by the people below.

There was renewed cheering when the Queen and Duke descended the Town Hall steps to re-enter the car. It drove slowly along the crowd-lined route to Duke Street Bridge and across the borough boundary, thus bringing to an end the first visit to Wallasey of a reigning Queen.

◆ ◆ ◆

NEW PROMENADE PIER AT NEW BRIGHTON

Liverpool Mercury

Tuesday, 11th June, 1867

New Brighton has been long noted as a favourite resort for visitors, who, in the summer months especially, crowd the sands in thousands, and enjoy themselves in a variety of ways. Beautifully situated at the mouth of the Mersey, the locality possess attractions of no ordinary character. The sloping shore, extending beyond the Red Noses, affords excellent facilities for bathing, and from the sandhills and elevated ground at the back magnificent views are obtained of the Cheshire and Lancashire coasts, as well as of the boundless expanse of sea in front. During the last quarter of a century the place had undergone a wonderful change for the better. Of late years a great improvement has been effected in the district by the Wallasey Local Board, and palatial residences and splendid hotels and lodging houses have sprung up in every direction. The former miserable landing place was a serious drawback to the prosperity of New Brighton. The local board were fully alive to the importance of the place, and with commendable spirit they applied to Parliament for powers to borrow money to enable them to erect a new landing stage. This power was obtained, and as a result New Brighton now posses a fine landing stage, connected with the shore by an iron pier about 730 feet in length. With good steamers, combined with punctuality in sailing, it may be expected that this charming watering place of the Mersey will attract yearly an increased number of visitors, as well as add greatly to its permanent residents.

The visitor to New Brighton will now find that another splendid improvement is in progress. This is a magnificent promenade pier which is in course of construction by the New Brighton Pier Company. It will be a similar structure to those at Margate, Blackpool, Brighton, Deal, and other places, all of which have proved highly successful. This new pier was commenced about six months ago, and already it is nearly half completed. It runs parallel with the ferry pier, on the north side, at a distance of 20 feet, and will be 550 feet long, and from 70 to 130 feet wide. It is a most substantial structures. built of iron columns and girders, the columns being sunk in the rocks. The new pier will be approached from the ferry pier by two entrances, each being 30 feet wide, one entrance being at the river end and the other at the shore end. The approach to the promenade pier will be by a flight of broad handsome steps.

At each side of these entrances there will be collectors' boxes for the taking of tolls. Opposite each entrance there will be a fine pavilion, constructed in the octagon form, with a clear space of 25 feet on all sides. Running at the back of the centre of the pier there will be a covered saloon, 130 feet in length, and the main portions of it 28 feet in width, extending to 34 feet in the centre. This magnificent apartment will be fitted with glass folding doors, and form a fine promenade in itself during unfavourable weather. It is also intended to make this saloon available for a variety of purposes, such as refreshment rooms, bazaars, flower shows, concerts, etc. Over the saloon there will be a promenade of the same dimensions, with a magnificent tower built in the Byzantine style of architecture, which will give the whole structure a handsome and striking appearance. At each end of the saloon there will be an elegant glass weather screen, intended for the protection of visitors while sitting in the open air. On the north side, and opposite the large saloon, the pier will widen into the form of a semi-circle or embayment, which will make the structure at this point 130 feet wide. The deck of the pier will be covered with a sort of concrete, to render it comfortable by walking in wet weather; and a line of comfortable seats, of handsome design, will extend round the entire structure, which will be 5 feet above the level of the ferry pier. From the deck of the new pier an uninterrupted view of the sea, the river, the shipping, and the busy and populous town on the other side will be obtained.

The work, as we have already stated, is of a most substantial character. The engineer is Mr. E. Birch, of London, who has successfully completed similar piers at other watering places; and the contractor is Mr. J.E. Dowson, also of London. If deemed desirable, one-half of the pier might be opened to the public in August next but the contractor is bound to complete the whole work by the end of the present year.

The New Brighton Pier Company deserve great credit for the spirit they have exhibited in proceeding with this undertaking in the face of much difficulty. This splendid promenade pier is sure to attract immense numbers of people to New Brighton, by which the ferry will reap a rich harvest. Under these circumstances it seems somewhat strange that but few residents of the locality have taken up shares in the undertaking, the greater portion of the capital being subscribed by Manchester gentlemen, who no doubt have looked upon the matter in a practical point of view, and calculated, from the success of such piers in other places, upon realising a handsome return for their outlay.

◆ ◆ ◆

FIGHT TO SAVE THE AVENUE

Liverpool Echo

12th August 1975

Liberal councillor Mrs. Kate Wood is fighting to prevent another of New Brighton's link with the past disappearing.

A group of sandstone buildings called The Avenue, which used to provide homes for lighthouse keepers 150 years ago, face demolition because of their poor condition.

A compulsory purchase order has been confirmed by the Department of Environment.

Mrs. Wood feels that recent reprieves granted to houses in nearby Egerton Street and Seymour Street should also include The Avenue.

"There has been too much demolition," she said. "With the shortage of housing, we don't need more vacant sites. The Government should offer more encouragement to keep old houses and have them upgraded rather than continually demolishing."

With intelligent planning, she said, the houses could blend in well with redevelopment plans for New Brighton.

Generations of New Brighton families have been brought up in The Avenue despite the absence of bathrooms and inside toilets.

The Avenue with Coucillor Kate Wood

Councillor Harry Deverill, Conservative Chairman of Wirral Housing and Environmental Services Committee, has visited the sandstone houses, but reserved his judgment until he gets expert advice.

Wirral's Deputy Director of Housing and Environmental Health, Mr. Ken Hodgson, said: "I don't really see that we can make a case for retaining anything within the existing programme.

"I can't see anything substantially different in respect of The Avenue than it was two years ago when the Department of the Environment confirmed the C.P.O.

"The houses can't be made fit for human habitation at reasonable cost. The only solution Is demolition and this has been confirmed by the Minister.

♦ ♦ ♦

THE LAST LINK

Wallasey News

12th April 1924

Gorsey Lane, Poulton, the last and main link of the series of roads connecting Birkenhead to New Brighton was publicly opened by the Mayoress of Wallasey (Mrs. A.H. Evans) and Lady Danson (wife of the Chairman of the Dock Board Finance Committee) on Wednesday afternoon.

The new road has been the subject of agitation on and off the Council for thirty years or more, and its completion, to which the unemployment problem and the grant from the Ministry of Transport were contributory factors, should be of considerable benefit to Wallasey, Birkenhead and the Mersey Docks and Harbour Board, and should serve to make for friendlier relationship between these authorities.

Nine hundred and twenty five yards long and 62 ft. wide, with 12 ft. wide footpaths, Gorsey Lane is the principal unit of a continuous north and south highway through the borough by way of Oxton Road, Woodstock Road and Belvidere Road to Grove Road. The total cost was £14,800, of which £6,042 was contributed by the Ministry of Transport, £1,600 by the frontages and the balance by the Council. One thousand eight hundred tons of special bituminous macadam, made at the Corporation works, were used in the construction of the road, and £4,000 was paid in wages to unskilled labourers recruited from the ranks of the unemployed, in addition to £750 paid to skilled Corporation workmen, Work commenced in January last year.

Gorsey Lane, viewing towards Poulton Road

A Happy Coincidence

The date of the official opening of the road was happily chosen, for in the evening the Mayor, on behalf of the Council and officials presented Mr. W.H. Travers, M.Inst., C.E., the ex-borough engineer and surveyor, was a handsome bureau on his retirement after thirty-one years' service with the Corporation. Mr. Travers not only designed the roadway, but was prominent in getting the scheme adopted by the Council; therefore, it was only fitting that the day of his retirement should be marked by the opening of a piece of work, which though, technically far from his most prominent effort, may have bigger results than anything else he has done.

Cutting The Tape

A tape had been drawn across the road and following an introductory speech by Alderman Eastwood, Mr. Travers presented the Mayoress of Wallasey with a pair of scissors with which to cut it. Before allowing her to do so, however, he demanded toll in accordance with the ancient Sheffield custom. The Mayoress seemed unprepared, but when

Councillor Reakes came to her aid with a farthing this was refused as "being unfair." A bright new halfpenny was procured and being duly paid, Mrs. Evans clipped the tape and declared the road opened. The Mayoress then led the crowd down the new road and walked the half-mile to the other end, where Lady Danson, who was accompanied by her husband, Sir Francis C. Danson, performed a similar ceremony.

❖ ❖ ❖

THE NEW DOCKS AT WALLASEY

Liverpool Mercury

Friday, 24th November, 1843

The sea wall will extend from Woodside Slip to Seacombe Slip, with a very slight inclination inwards to the entrance, and in a straight line from each slip respectively, the wall being nearly divided in two portions on each shore, and the longest on the Woodside shore. It has been ascertained that the foundations for the outer, and also for the dock walls, are, contrary to preconceived opinion, extremely favourable, and that not a pile will have to be driven. The only places which are soft to a considerable depth, are precisely those that are to be walled in, and very little excavation will be required. The outer harbour will have an open entrance of 302 feet in width; and the main dock will communicate with the harbour by double gates, or locks, extending westward into the pool, with a slight obtuse angle or elbow as far as the bridge at Poulton-cum-Seacombe. The outer harbour is intended to comprise of an area of 37 acres, and will have a depth at low water of spring tide of 12 feet. The inner dock, in its uninterrupted length from the outer harbour to the village of Poulton, will comprise a water surface, or float for vessels of all burthen's, of 30 acres, which added to the 37 acres in the half-tide basin, will give 67 acres of floating surface for shipping, or about 60 acres of accommodation more than all the Liverpool docks put together!

The gates to this immense dock will be made sufficiently wide for the largest steamers afloat, or likely to be constructed. The margin of the pool will be appropriated by the various owners of the property of the wharfs, slips, warehouses, and sheds. There will be shipwrights' yards and graving docks adjacent; and there will also be a tunnel made under the town of Birkenhead, from the tunnel at Monk's Ferry to the margin of the docks. The cost of the contemplated construction is stated to be about £300,000; and one main consideration with regard to the undertaking is, that it is contemplated it will be accomplished without resorting to taxation. The whole of the works are intended to be constructed by the Commissioners of Birkenhead with funds raised on the credit of the undertaking. Whatever rates are received beyond what is necessary to pay the interest of the loans, and whatever funds arise from property acquired and disposed of, will be applied in reducing the principal of the debt until the works shall have been relieved from all incumbrances. If the time should ever arrive, and such a time is confidently anticipated by our Cheshire neighbours, when the works shall become free of rates, the cheapness of the dock accommodation of Liverpool cannot fail materially to advance the interests of the port, perhaps to a much greater extent than we can now form an supposition approaching to accuracy.

◆ ◆ ◆

A SICKENING CRASH

Wallasey NEWS

13th September 1911

The athletic ground of the New Brighton Tower was, on Saturday afternoon, the scene of a serious accident in which a motorist ran into a crowd of spectators injuring himself and six others, one of them, a lady, being still in a critical condition. The feat which was being performed was a two miles motor team race between representatives of the Liverpool Mersey Motor Club and Birmingham, and the riders were W.E. Horsman, F.C. Jones, H. Birch, and T. Henshaw, representing Liverpool. And George W. Baker, George Hill, H.J. Wordgate and Vic Pratt, representing Birmingham. The accident happened in the first heat of the race, T. Henshaw, Liverpool, and Vic Pratt, Birmingham, being the riders. The first lap had been accomplished very smoothly. Toward the completion of the second lap the contestants were travelling at a terrific speed which was variously estimated at from forty to fifty miles an hour. Henshaw's machine was a 3½ h.p. Bradbury and it was upon rounding the western curve his machine who seen to swerve and then rush up the incline. The cycle struck the foot of a spectator, knocked into a wooden post, cut the rope and finally landed in a crowd of people. There was an immediate panic, men and women were knocked down and many women fainted. Still greater consternation was caused when the petrol in the tank of the motor burst into flames and there was the possibility of an explosion. A boy's clothing caught on fire, but this was quickly extinguished, whilst a number of men, realising the dreadful consequences of an explosion, rushed up to the blazing motor, and beat out the conflagration with their coats and jackets. At the time of the tragic occurrence Pratt, who was seated on a 3½ h.p. James, was rushing along at a headlong place in his endeavour to beat his opponent. His eyes were glued on the track, and his whole attention was occupied in watching his course. The rider was in absolute ignorance of the fate of Henshaw, and intense alarm was felt lest he should become involved in the accident. The presence of mind of the official starter, Mr. J. Cole, averted what might have been a terrible disaster. As the motorist was passing the eastern portion of the track, Mr. Cole fired his pistol, this being the usual custom at the conclusion of a motor race. At the same time he shouted a warning to the rider, who glanced up to ascertain the cause. He immediately took in what had happened, and clapped on his brakes, bringing his machine to a standstill before he reached the spot where the accident had happened, to the great relief of the spectators.

The whole affair had not lasted a few seconds, and as soon it had been realised what had happened the ambulance was telephoned for, while surgical appliances were obtained from the Tower. Drs. A.W. Riddell, Slater and A.W. Montgomery were quickly on the spot and rendered every assistance. In all there were seven people injured, but two only were seriously hurt, one of them being Miss Ethel Tennant, of 39. Percy Road, Bootle. She was found to be suffering from a severe wound to her head and a more complete examination revealed the fact that she had got concussion of the brain, and she still lies in a critical condition at the Liscard Central Hospital. The others who were admitted to the hospital were – Charles Haywood, 39 Percy Road, Bootle, cut head and sprained muscle of the arm; Peter Brown, 40. Midgehall Street, Liverpool, fractured leg; T. Henshaw, Victor Motor Cycle Works, Seacombe, compound fracture of the leg; Dudley Stewart, 29, Sandrock Road, New Brighton, injuries to ribs. Haywood had sufficiently recovered to admit of his removal from the hospital on Sunday, while we understand that with the exception of Miss Tennant all the patients are doing well.

The Probable Clause

The famous cycle track where the accident occurred has only been used for motor cycle racing during the last years, but there have only been a few accidents of a minor nature. The cause of the accident in this case is attributed by some to the fact that the saddle was not efficiently secured, and the other suggestion is that the motorist exhibited too great an anxiety respecting his opponent, and kept glancing over his shoulder. This latter explanation in the one which spectators seem to countenance the most.

Henshaw seemed to take his fate very philosophically. As soon as he regained consciousness he asked for a cigarette, which he calmly smoked while lying on the turf with his leg temporarily dressed. A word of praise should be given to the staff at the Victoria Central Hospital who promptly rose to the occasion and had everything ready to receive the injured. Drs. W. Crooke and J. Barry were in attendance and the patients received the best assistance.

◆ ◆ ◆

ESCAPE OF A LION : EXCITING SCENE

Liverpool Mercury

Saturday, 29th September, 1888

The visitors to Cross's Menagerie at the New Brighton Palace had certainly enough excitement for their money on Saturday night last. Early in the evening, while yet there were large numbers of excursionists about the place, Madame Talzero, an intrepid wild-beast tamer, proceeded to the cage, in which are some splendid African lions, in order to put them through their usual performance. There is invariably attached to the gateway of every den containing performing brutes a smaller cage. Into this the tamer first steps, and after closing the outer door, as a public safeguard, opens the entrance to the cage proper and walks in amongst the beasts. Through the negligence of one of the keepers the smaller cage was not in its place on Saturday, and Madame Talzero resolved to do without it. But scarcely had she opened the iron gate when a full-grown lion jumped over her head, and, almost before it could be realised, was amongst the people. Then the lazy suddenly became sprightly, and corpulent persons who for years had not congratulated themselves upon their agility now did wonders. A few of the fortunate ones managed to slip through the door leading into the Palace or out on to the 'ham and egg' promenade by the lower exit, whilst the remainder of the terror-stricken spectators crouched in promiscuous heaps in far off corners watching the movements of the king of the forest with a distinctively disagreeable fascination. But the noble beast, strange to say, was not eager to follow up his advantage, and appeared to be quite as much disconcerted at the sundry shrieks and howls of those who had paid for admission to see him as his before time admirers were to note his uncaged presence towering in their midst. At the sight of some keepers approaching the lion, which it seems is quite tame, ran into an unoccupied space, where it was detained for a few minutes until an empty cage was wheeled up to the spot, and into this it ran. Although it was announced that the lion was perfectly docile, some little time elapsed before the excitement subsided amongst those who had witnessed more than appeared in the programme.

◆ ◆ ◆

ANNE GLASSEY WORKSHOP CLOSES DOWN

Wallasey NEWS

2nd November 1974

Wallasey's Anne Glassey Workshop has closed. The building in Love Lane, which attracted the attention of doctors and welfare workers all over the world, is to be sold.

The workshop, founded 22 years ago, was the only voluntary unit of its kind in the county catering for sufferers from tuberculosis and other chest and heart diseases.

Dr. James Baxter, vice-president of Wallasey TB and Chest and Welfare Trust, told the NEWS this week that staffing problems and a big drop in the number of people needing rehabilitation had brought about the closure.

Dr. Baxter said the trust would now act as a charitable organisation to provide facilities for educational and occupational training. It also hoped to make grants in cases of need.

The workshop, which specialised in printing and woollen goods, was the means of returning more than 200 ex-patients to full-time employment during its 22 years existence.

It took its name from Anne Glassey, a former sister at Mill Lane Hospital, who founded the Wallasey TB Care and Welfare

Committee in 1944. Miss Glassey, who was awarded the MBE for her work, now lives in North Wales.

◆ ◆ ◆

EXTRAORDINARY ADVENTURE OF TOMMY BURNS: STRUGGLE WITH A SHARK AT NEW BRIGHTON

Cheshire Observer

Saturday, 9th August, 1890

An exciting and extraordinary scene was witnessed off the New Brighton shore on Thursday evening. Several hundred spectators had assembled at the pierhead and on the sands to see Tommy Burns, the champion bridge jumper and swimmer, leap into the river from the pier. This feat having been successfully accomplished, interest was centred in his aquatic feats. He had performed several movements, when he was observed to make a signal for help; and immediately afterwards great consternation was caused among the onlookers, who saw that he was holding deadly combat with a monster fish. A boat was immediately sent to his assistance; but in the meantime a desperate struggle was taking place. Burns showered vigorous blows upon the body of his assailant, and succeeded in keeping it at bay until the arrival of the boat. He was then handed a clasp knife, with which he quickly dispatched the dreaded creature by ripping it up. Burns, who was very much exhausted from his extraordinary adventure, was then brought to the shore, together with the fish; and he received quite an ovation from the anxious spectators. The fish was taken to the pier, where it was inspected with great interest by a large number of visitors. It is about 5 feet 4 inches in length, and has a formidable row of teeth. Professor Boston emphatically declares that it is a young shark, although many expressed the opinion that it was a dog fish. Burn's left arm is severely scared, the result of his desperate encounter; and he is to be congratulated upon overcoming so powerful an enemy with no worse injuries.

◆ ◆ ◆

NEWS IN SHORT

Shipwreck

London Morning Post
Wednesday, 8th November, 1820

On Wednesday night the brig *Mary and Betty*, of this port, Thomas Lambert, master, burden 180 tons, with a cargo of corn, pigs, and sheep, on her voyage to Liverpool, was wrecked on the Ultarf, near Mockbegger. We are extremely concerned to add, that, of the crew and seven passengers, only three were saved. The Captain is among the number of those who perished.

Cask Of Gold

Derby Mercury
Wednesday, 19th December, 1821

A cask of gold, in American, British and Portuguese coin, worth between eleven and twelve thousand pounds, was saved from the wreck of the American brig *Elizabeth* and placed in the custody of the Rector of Wallasey, by whom it has been given up to Mr.Hughes of Liverpool, agent to Messrs.Thomas Wilson & Co. of London, the owners thereof.

Punishment For Plundering Of Wrecks

Jacksons Oxford Journal
Saturday, 11th May, 1822

Thomas Moore, of Moreton, labourer, was convicted at the

Chester Assizes of stealing ropes from the wreck of the *Mary and Betty*, stranded on the Wallasey shore in October, 1820. and sentenced to death. It is hoped, that all those persons who have hitherto looked upon wrecking as a lawful trade, will learn from the sentence, that, by the law of the land, as well as the laws of humanity. It is considered a most atrocious crime. By the 26th of Geo.II. plundering a vessel in distress (whether wreck or no wreck) is felony without benefit of Clergy.

Fatal Accident

London Morning Post
Friday, 29th April, 1826

Friday, as Mrs Boode, of Mockbeggar Hall, was returning from Seacombe Ferry, the horse in her chise took fright, the vehicle was upset, and the Lady killed on the spot.

To The Public

Advertisement
Liverpool Mercury
Friday, 30th April, 1830

A boat will commence plying between Egremont Ferry and the Stair north side of the entrance into George's Basin, TO-MORROW (Saturday) the 1st of May. The owner of the Ferry authorises me to state that as soon as the *Hero* is completed she will also ply. When that takes place the terms for ferrying will be announced, and the Public may depend on the strictest attention to the regulations. At the commencement the boat will leave every hour, beginning at Eight in the morning, and running until dark in the evening.

Presentation Of Plate

Liverpool Mercury
Friday, 26th June, 1834

The inhabitants of the parish of Wallasey, in token of their respect and gratitude for the services of their churchwarden,

Mr. Henry Meadows, have subscribed a sum of money, which has been invested in plate, and was presented by a committee to him, at the Manor House, Poulton-cum-Seacombe, on Friday last. It consists of a handsome vase drinking cup and a coffee pot, on which are neatly engraved the following words : - "Presented by the parishioners of Wallasey, to Mr. Henry Meadows, in token of their respect for his firmness and perseverance in maintaining their right to manage their school estate, and for his upright independence as churchwarden for the year 1834.

Wallasey Inquests

North West Chronicle
Tuesday, 26th December, 1837

Inquest before F. Thomas, Esq., Coroner ~ At New Brighton, on the body of Joseph Arnett, who was drowned through the upsetting of a boat on the River Mersey. The deceased and seven others left Liverpool in a small gig for Liscard, and as they were going along, one of the party struck a light with a lucifer match, when the rest all rushed to him to light their pipes, and the boat immediately capsized and 3 of them drowned. At Wallasey, on the 12th, on the body of John Crellar, a boatman, cast on the shore of the Mersey. ~ On the 11th, on the body of Samuel Bennett, a child eight years, who was killed by a vicious bull at Wallasey. ~ Verdicts accordingly.

Malicious Shooting By A Boy

Liverpool Mercury
Tuesday, 25th January, 1848

The youth, Charles Miller, of Seacombe, who, three weeks ago, so wantonly fired a loaded pistol at a little boy, whereby he lost the use of one eye, and was otherwise injured, was brought up before the sitting, magistrates, Sir E. Cust and Henry Winch, Esq., at the Wallasey Court House. on Tuesday last, when he was sentenced to pay £2 5s. 0d., and in default, to be imprisoned fourteen days in Knutsford Gaol.

Local Board Of Health

Liverpool Mercury
Friday, 18th February, 1853

On Wednesday a bill was printed to establish local boards of health at the following places :- Wakefield, Elland, Wallasey, Dudley, Barnsley, Dorchester, Brighton, and Welshpool. The elections at those places are to take place on the 28th of April next.

Wallasey Local Board Of Health

Liverpool Mercury
Wednesday, 25th June, 1856

The return of the members of the new board, in the place of those gentlemen who retired by rotation, was made on Monday last. In the following two townships, in which there was no opposition, the members returned are - For Liscard : Messrs. W.H. Neville, H. Pooley, and T.B. Hughes. - Wallasey : Mr. W. Chambers. In Poulton-cum-Seacombe there was a contest, the candidates being Messr. J. Penny, J.Wilson, C.H. Hill, J. Byerley, and J. Singlehurst. The successful candidates were Mr. Penny, Mr. Wilson and Mr. Singlehurst.

Perpetual Curacies

North Wales Chronicle
Saturday, 2md August, 1856

Rev. R.D.Fowell, to the newly-consecrated Church of St. James, New Brighton, Wallasey, Cheshire.

Man Found Drowned

Liverpool Mercury
Friday, 12th October, 1866

A man named James Hodgkinson was found drowned in a pit at Sutton's Farm, Wallasey. It seems that the unfortunate man, who resided with his brother, at Heather Terrace, Claughton, was some time ago in an asylum. About two months since he was discharged as cured, but subsequently took to drink, and was attacked with delirium tremens. The medical man who attended him directed that his movements should be closely watched. He managed, however, to get out of the house on Tuesday morning, and made his way towards the Great Float, but was followed by his brother, who seized him as he was about to jump into the water near the Duke Street Bridge. He managed to extricate himself from his brother's grasp, and ran off and was lost sight of. Shortly afterwards his body was found in the pit, and, although restoratives were applied, life was found to be extinct.

The Census Returns

Liverpool Mercury
Saturday, 22nd July, 1871

Wallasey (including New Brighton) increased 4056, namely, from 10,273 to 14,779, the excess of births being 2016.

To The Editors Of The Liverpool Mercury.

Liverpool Mercury
Friday, 8th September, 1871

Gentlemen, - in reference to a police report in today's Mercury of a case of gross imposition on the part of donkey and horse drivers at New Brighton, will you permit me, as a resident of that district, to say a few words? The bad language these people use, their rapacity, and the quarrelsome deposition that characterises them, often bring them into strong collision with the excursionists, and scenes are enacted that more resemble the events at Donnybrook fair than those of a peaceful watering hole - save that there is no fighting, as at

Donnybrook, for "love and good humour", In some respect the horses and donkeys are an unmitigated nuisance. The great advantage of living in such a locality as Wallasey is that it has a splendid shore, where, under ordinary circumstances, families might really enjoy the healthy and bracing air for which it is famous. But the truth is, these donkeys and horses, goaded and tormented by their drivers, and doubly so by the majority of the persons who mount them, who know no more how ride on horseback than they know how box the compass, go rushing about the shore in the most reckless manner, so that persons walking have constantly to exercise all their skill to avoid being run over. As for ladies and children, they are excluded in this way from the enjoyment the sands would otherwise afford, and, of course, the locality suffers to a corresponding extent. Where proper order is kept, as at other watering places, I have nothing to say against the harmless trotter of donkeys; but the wild galloping among the people which is daily permitted at New Brighton is not creditable to the local authorities -
Yours etc.
C.
Sept.5, 1871.

Dead Woman Found

Lloyd's Weekly Newspaper
Saturday, 26th May, 1872

On Saturday the body of a woman, who is supposed to have met her death by unfair means, was found in a ditch between Leasowe and Moreton Station, Cheshire. An apron was twisted tightly round the neck. The deceased is supposed to have been a hawker.

Sale Of The Wallasey Concert Hall

Liverpool Mercury
Thursday, 22nd June 1876

This spacious building, which was erected by the Wallasey Social Club and Concert Hall Company, Limited, was offered by auction last evening by Mr. Thomas Whitehead, in pursuance of an order of the Chancery Division of the High Court of Justice. The building is situated in Manor Road, Liscard, and contains a large concert hall, billiard rooms, reading and dining rooms, luncheon bar, kitchens, and keeper's apartments, with extensive and well laid out grounds at the rear, the entire superficial area being about 6000 yards. We may state that the building, which cost about £7400, including furniture, billiard tables, etc., was opened on 1st January, 1875. For a few months the concern succeeded very well, and appeared to be highly appreciated by the residents of the district. Unfortunately, differences took place respecting the introduction of intoxicating liquors, some of the members being in favour of beer and other drinks being consumed on the premises, whilst other members were opposed to any violation of the articles of association, which prohibited the sale of drink. At meeting of the shareholders a resolution was carried in favour of introducing intoxicating drinks; but, upon the general body of shareholders being appealed to by the ballot, the resolution was not confirmed by the required majority. A question of law then arose upon the polling, litigation followed, and, as Mr. Ridhalgh, the builder of the hall, could not get the balance due him under his contract, he applied for an order to wind up the company. A Chancery order was accordingly granted, the result being that the concern was brought to the hammer last evening. The sale, which took place in the large concert hall in the building, attracted a considerable number of gentlemen, some of whom, it was said, represented those of the shareholders who wished intoxicating drinks to be sold on the premises, whilst others represented those who were in favour of the concern being conducted on teetotal principles. The building was offered with all the furniture, fittings, etc. The auctioneer having dilated at some length on the present and prospective value of the building and land attached, the bidding was proceeded with. The first bid was £3000, and to Mr. James Rogerson, of the Candia Works, who, we understand, acted on behalf of those of the shareholders favourable to the sale of intoxicating liquors on the premises.

The Wallasey Fire Brigade

Liverpool Mercury
Friday, 5th January, 1877

On Wednesday evening the Wallasey Commissioners' Fire Brigade met for the purpose of having their annual dinner. The men met at the Water Tower (Liscard), and, under the charge of Mr. Barrett, late superintendent West of England Fire's Brigade (who is their drill instructor), marched to the Queen's Arms Hotel, where a capital dinner was served up by Mr. John Alltree, the proprietor. The chair was occupied by Superintendent Leather, the vice chair by Sergeant Blakely. After the usual loyal toasts had been given, some excellent songs and recitations followed, and a very pleasant evening was spent. the visitors included Mr. Samuel Alltree, Mr. Blaylock, and Mr. Anthony Dunderdale, of Liverpool. The fire brigade are volunteers, and are a fine body of men.

Fire At Egremont

Liverpool Mercury
Friday, 5th March, 1880

At half-past five o'clock yesterday morning, a joiner's shed belonging to Messrs. Crawley and Davies, builders, Charlotte Street, Egremont. was found to be on fire. The Wallasey fire brigade and some constables were soon on the spot, and they extinguished the conflagration. The shed, which was constructed of wood, was destroyed, as were also some sets of tools. The damage, which was estimated at about £100, is covered by insurance.

Narrow Escape Of A Steamer And 200 Passengers

Leeds Mercury
Friday, 11th April, 1884

Last evening an alarming double collision occurred on the Mersey, whereby the lives of 200 passengers were placed in jeopardy. A Spanish steamer was proceeding up the Mersey, when she collided with the Wallasey ferry-boat *Water Lily*, lying at anchor off Egremont. The effect of this first collision was to snap her mooring chains, but no other damage was sustained. Then she collided with the steamer *Electric*, outward bound, with 200 passengers on board. Such was the force of the collision that the *Electric* had to be beached, her passengers being rescued.

No Road But For Lovers

Cheshire Observer
Saturday, 9th June, 1888

Some discussion took place with reference to the closing by the Wirral Railway Company of a footpath leading from Wallasey to Bidston, the subject being brought before the meeting by a letter received from the Wallasey Local Board requesting the waywardens to join them in resisting the action of the company.

The chairman asked if the footpath was one which was really needed and used, because there were some footpaths which were better lost then found.

Mr. Trelawny depreciated going to law about a mere footpath.

Mr. Parkinson said the road was of no use at all, and led anywhere.

Mr. Robinson did not think it was of much good, and did not believe it was much used; it was a good courting road, he believed, but that was all (Laughter).

The Clerk reminded the meeting that if once they lost the footpath it was gone for ever, and they did not know what it might be useful for in days to come.

Mr. J. Davies denied that it was a public footpath at all. The path had been allowed to be altered from time to time, and at present there was no settled footpath there at all.

The Board decided unanimously to take no action in the matter.

Seacombe -

The Melancholy Deaths

Cheshire Observer
Friday, 10th February, 1894

Mr. Henry Churton, county coroner, on the bodies of Hannah Adams and her six days old child. The deceased woman was the wife of Joseph Adams, a dock labourer, residing in Shakespeare Road, Seacombe, and since the Tuesday after her confinement, which took place a week on Sunday, she had not been, according to the evidence of her husband, in a perfect state of mind. The husband woke up about half-past eleven on Friday night and missed his wife and child from bed. He obtained the assistance of sound neighbours and the police, and a diligent search was made for the missing ones. The party continued their investigations all through the night, and at half-past seven on Saturday morning the husband saw his wife's body in a pit at the bottom of Geneva Road, Seacombe. He, with the aid of Constable Rowlands, recovered the body, and a couple of hours later Constable Sudlow, who was dragging in the same pit, also found the body of the infant. The jury, after a brief consultation, found that the mother destroyed the child's life by throwing it into the pit, and committed suicide herself while of temporarily unsound mind.

❖ ❖ ❖

BULLDOZERS SET TO LEVEL RESORT POOL

Wallasey NEWS

21st March 1990

One of Wirral's most famous landmarks – New Brighton's outdoor swimming pool – looks doomed.

Borough engineers have found serious structural damage following recent storms which battered the resort's unique art deco pool.

Merseyside Development Corporation have consulted with Wirral Council engineers and have found that extensive damage has been caused to both the structure and its foundation.

The investigation has also confirmed engineers' suspicious that the shallow foundations in sand and the scouring effect of the waves have weakened a much greater area.

This means that two large sections of the bath's perimeter wall have already had to be demolished in the interest of public safety.

MDC have reaffirmed their commitment to bathing facilities at New Brighton, and the possible development of a water theme leisure park on site. They estimate that the cost of restoring the baths would cost £5.8 million and neither the council nor MDC are convinced that the work is feasible.

Sally Davies, spokesman for the *Save New Brighton Baths*

Campaign, said that they accepted that much of the baths were beyond repair, but they still thought that the site could be used as an outdoor bathing facility.

She said: "There are a plethora of indoor swimming pools in Wirral. It is essential that we keep an outdoor facility.

"Although we accept there are structural problems with the existing building, we would like to see the pool site used for community activities, a gym club, luncheon club and community centre, for example.

"A community survey paid for by the MDC said there is a dearth of facilities for both senior citizens and the 13-17 age group. The pool site would be large enough to provide facilities for both.

"We are providing the MDC with ideas but we can't provide the money. That should be their job."

Council officers and MDC officials met last night to review the situation and an announcement is expected shortly.

End Of The Line For New Brighton Pool

Wallasey NEWS
24th March 1990

Merseyside Development Corporation has finally sealed the fate of the storm-battered New Brighton bathing pool – and demolition should be completed within a few weeks.

But Tony Potter, MDC director of development, declared last night: "We think the future for New Brighton is brighter than for more than 20 years. There has been a lot of talk and very little action – we are trying to reverse that."

After the MDC finally buried any prospects of saving the crumbling complex Mr Potter said: My board feels very strongly that while we don't want to do anything against what Wirral Council is saying, we can't afford to play semi-politics with public safety."

Wirral Labour group refuses to acknowledge that demolition is the only answer.

Members have produced their own plans to transform the complex into a major sports and leisure facility for Merseyside.

But Mr Potter insisted: "We have to demolish the building because it is unsafe."

And he pledged that MDC would use its best endeavours to try to get a public swimming facility in any redevelopment project at the site.

The MDC board also gave the go-ahead for a revamp of New Brighton marine lake which involves raising the height of the sea wall, increasing the depth of the lake and creating a small car park at its eastern end.

Jetskiers and sailboard enthusiast protested because it will mean a reduction in the size of the lake.

Mr Potter said :"The loss of the water area is only 10% and the sandy beach from the vicinity of the causeway."

Mr Potter did not rule out a marine lake project put forward by John Lamb, architect of the immensely successful beach nourishment scheme at New Brighton.

Mr Lamb's scheme envisages construction of a new causeway across eastern third of the lake, which would allow the creation of a curved sandy bay within the confines of the lake.

He claimed that the bay, sheltered from prevailing winds, would provide a suntrap, similar to marine lake beaches constructed in Holland.

He said: "The sand would help mask the harsh concrete lines of the marine lake and treble the amount of promenade/beach at the heart of the resort.

"I wouldn't rule out something like that being done in the long term. But we can't go in for the major surgery implied by this scheme until we have decided the development market for

P. DAVIES

New Brighton.

❖ ❖ ❖

FATHER GOES TO JAIL FOR HIS SON'S CRIME

Wallasey NEWS

15th February 1902

Before Messrs. W. Heap and J.C. Stead, at the Wallasey Police Court on Wednesday, Thomas Patrick White (13) Liscard, was charged on remand with having stolen 11½d. belonging to William Gordon Pemberton, at Liscard, on 14th January. His father was charged under the Youthful Offenders' Act. 1901, with having conduced to the commission of the offence by failing to exercise due care and control over his son. This was the first case under the new Act in the district.

On the date in question the lad was selling the "Echo" in Liscard, when prosecutor sent his little girl for one, telling her to take a half-penny from the shop till. He afterwards found she had taken a shilling.

Sergt. Swords said the lad admitted to him he had taken it, after having first denied it. He threw the coin on the grass when going into the police station.

The lad pleaded guilty.

Evidence that the older defendant neglected to look after his children was given by Supt. McDonald, Sergt. Swords and Inspector Kynaston (school attendance). The first-named said the lad had already been birched for housebreaking and convicted of theft. Another son was in a reformatory.

Defendant alleged that Mr. Kynaston had, in the course of a school attendance case, said he (defendant) did not pay for his lad being in the reformatory.

Mr. Kynaston indignantly denied having said anything of the kind.

Supt. McDonald also denied the allegation.

The book was then bought and it was shown that he had only paid 5s. for his son since last June. He had already been in jail for failing to pay.

A fine of 10s. or in default seven days was imposed for the theft, the penalty falling upon the father.

He asked for time in which to pay, but was refused.

His wife was in court, and when appealed to by her husband, flatly refused to pay the fine.

Defendant was also fined 5s. with the option of three days for having been drunk and disorderly in Liscard on Tuesday. He met a constable, and made allegations about Mr. Kynaston. Refusing to go home, he was locked up.

◆ ◆ ◆

CORONATION OF KING GEORGE VI

Wallasey Celebrates

Wallasey NEWS

1937

Why He Has Declined The Honour
10th April, 1937
Mayor G.L Reakes The Mayor of Wallasey (Councillor G.L. Reakes) yesterday (Friday) received an invitation to be present at Westminster Abbey on Coronation Day.

We are asked to state that whilst the Mayor deeply appreciates the honour he has respectfully declined the invitation as he is anxious to spend the whole Coronation week in the service of his Council colleagues and the people of Wallasey who have placed him in the position to receive it. The invitation was issued by the Earl Marshal (the Duke of Norfolk) at the command of the King.

The Mayoress (Mrs F.H Thornton) and the Deputy Mayor (Alderman F.H. Thornton) will, we understand, witness the Coronation procession from a Government stand in the vicinity of Palace Yard. In the Abbey will be the Lord Mayor of Liverpool (Alderman W. Denton), who is the brother to Mrs. Thornton, and the Lady Mayoress, who brother is Alderman Thornton.

Some Wallasey Arrangement

His Worship is anxious that the festivities should be worthy of the occasion and he is appealing to the public to assist the local authorities in making Wallasey's celebrations memorable.

At the last meeting of the Council, he urged everyone to do their utmost in the way of preparation and that all decorations to business and dwelling houses would be made ready in good time to obtain the right atmosphere.

The local arrangements include :-

A preliminary public service for all denominations in the Town Hall on Sunday evening, May 9th, beginning at 8-15. On the morning of Coronation Day, May 12th, there is to be a civic service in St. Hilary Parish Church, at 9.45. After the Mayoral party and representatives of organisation's taking part in the procession have entered the church, the remainder will proceed to the Central Park, via Broadway Avenue, Belvidere Road, Kingsway, Seaview Road and Liscard Road. At the park, the band of the Argyll and Sutherland Highlanders will play until 11 o'clock, when the broadcast service will begin.

The arrangements for the display of physical culture at New Brighton Bathing Pool on Monday, May 10th, have been approved. The children taking part are to be provided with the necessary and shoes, at an estimated cost of £250, and they are to be permitted to retain the articles afterwards.

The ferry steamers "Royal Iris" and "Royal Daffodil" will be decorated and illuminated, and also one of the Corporation motor buses.

Prizes

10 April, 1937

Prizes are offered by the Wallasey Corporation for the best decorated premises during Coronation Week for --

a) Dwelling houses with an assessment of £13 and under.

b) Dwelling houses with an assessment of over £13.

c) Business premises

Postcards should addressed to the Town Clerk, Town Hall, Wallasey, by competitors who desire to enter for the prizes offered.

The Local Programme

17 April, 1937

Following is the programme of local Coronation Celebrations as arranged to date. it is of course, subject to revision by the Reception Committee of the Council.

Events Throughout the Week

10 am to 9.30 pm - Relaying of special B.B.C programme in Central Park, Vale Park, Oakdale Recreation Ground, Marine Park and New Brighton Bathing Pool

3 pm and 7.30 pm - "Pierrot on Parade" on the Pier. 7.30 pm an illuminated and decorated motor vehicle will drive through the borough. Certain streets and buildings will be decorated and after sunset the ferryboats Royal Irish II and Royal Daffodil II will be illuminated.

Sunday, May 9

8.15 pm - Civic service at the Town. The Mayor, aldermen, councillors, magistrates and others will be present and the service will be conducted by the Revs. Canon A.S. Roscamp, H.P. Berkeley, W.J. Hartley, and A.C. Don, and will be addressed by the Revs. W.S. Coad and Hermes F. Johnson.

Monday, May 10

3 pm and 8 pm - Display at New Brighton Bathing Pool by school children. The band of the 1st. Batt. Argyll and Sutherland Highlanders will play selections of music.

7.45 pm - Frank A. Terry's Coronation Empire Broadcast

performance. Part proceeds to local hospitals.

Tuesday, May 11

3pm and 8 pm - Band of the 1st Batt. Argyll and Sutherland Highlanders (with pipers and dancers) at the Floral Pavilion. 3 pm - Presentation of souvenirs to school children, teas and entertainments in the various schools. 8pm - Wallasey Tradesmen's Club dance at the Town Hall. St. Alban's Church dance at the Grosvenor Assembly Rooms.

Coronation

8.45 am - Assembly for Civic Service at St. Hilary's Church, conducted by the Rector of Wallasey, the Rev. N.L. Betts, M.A. 9.45 am - The Mayor, aldermen, councillors and others will assemble at Manor Road Schools and proceed to church via Manor Road, Wallasey Road and Claremount Road. Mayoral party will enter church while remainder will proceed to Central Park and there disperse. The band of the 1sr Batt. of Argyll and Sutherland Highlanders will lead procession and will play selections up to 11 am.

10 am - New Brighton Bathing Pool will open for bathing for the summer season.

11 am to 3 pm - Broadcast of Coronation Service.

2 pm to sunset - Special celebration in Moreton area consisting of a fancy dress carnival, sports, races, dancing on the green, Punch and Judy show, minstrel show, football match, firework display and bonfire. The Shore Road Silver Prize Band will play at intervals.

8pm - The band of the 1st Batt. of Argyll and Sutherland Highlanders play at the Floral Pavilion. 8 pm to 2 am - Oldershaw Old Boys' Association Dance in the Town Hall with Roy Fox and His Band. Net proceeds in aid of the Victoria Central Hospital. At 5 pm and 9 pm - Special river trips from Seacombe and New Brighton.

Thursday, May 13

Mayoral reception and entertainment to old people at the Town Hall. 3 pm and 8 pm - Band of the 1st Batt. Argyll and Sutherland Highlanders (with pipers and dancers) at the Floral Pavilion.

Friday, May 14

2.30 pm to 5.30 pm - Mayoral reception and entertainment to old people at the Town Hall

3 pm and 8 pm - Band of the 1st Batt. Argyll and Sutherland Highlanders (with pipers and dancers) at the Floral Pavilion.

Saturday, May 15

3 pm - Band of the 1st Batt. Argyll and Sutherland Highlanders (with pipers and dancers) at the Floral Pavilion.

9.15 pm - Firework display from King's Parade, near New Brighton Bathing Pool. Frank A. Terry's special show at the Floral Pavilion.

Seacombe Sets An Example

Five shorts weeks ago a handful of residents of Byron Road, Seacombe, got together. They said to each other, "Now Coronation Day is going to be the greatest day of the year, especially for the children. Why not form a committee and arrange a day of festivities for the children? Let's show the people of Wallasey that Seacombe residents are not going to be lacking in patriotism." And in those five short weeks, the handful of patriotic men and women have laid out a programme and the children of Byron Road will have a party in the street on Coronation Day.

The Committee responsible for this good idea and who have put in such hard work during the past month include : Mrs A. Noteman (President), Mr. John Tobin (chairman), Mrs. W. Stacey (treasurer), Mr. Maxfield (secretary), Mrs. E. Price, Mrs. Wootton, Mr. E. Roberts, Mrs. B. Fuge, Mr. W. Fitzpatrick, Mr. H. Tilsley, and Mr. T. McKaigue.

The committee had raised money in many and varied ways

to provide this party for the children and to buy bunting to decorate the houses and several residents have helped greatly by gifts. Mr. R. Burns have been busy fashioning and painting shields which will be hung above the street. Shields have been made from cardboard procured from local shopkeepers.

Mr. John Tobin, chairman of the committee in an interview, with a "Chronicle" reporter yesterday, said: "it is very gratifying to see how well the committee have worked together. In five weeks an ambitious programme has been arranged and we are determined that the children will have a good time on Coronation Day. We are working under great difficulties owing to lack of funds but everything is going nicely now, and the children will get their party whatever happens."

Extensions of Drinking Hours

Wallasey magistrates yesterday granted applications by more than sixty local licensees for the extension of hours on Coronation Eve and Coronation Day. The extensions were from 10 to 11 pm., on May 11; and from 10.30 to 11 am., 2.30 to 3, 5 to 5.30 and 10 to 11 pm. on May 12.

Mr. J.M Rigby, who applied for most of the licensees, said familiar facilities had been granted in Liverpool.

An application by Mr. Dunn, on behalf of the proprietors of the Japanese Cafe, Tower Gardens, for extensions from 9 pm to 10 pm. on Thursday, Friday and Saturday in Coronation week, was also granted.

The Decorations

8 May, 1937

Work on the official decorations by the Corporation is now in full swing. It consists of the draping by means of flags, banners, pennants, shields and pylons, the lamp standards in certain sections of the promenade and streets, together with the most important of the public buildings.

As the cost of decorating the main roads and streets from end to end would be prohibitive and tend to localise any decorative scheme, the Reception Committee considered its advisable to distribute the decorations in such a manner that a large portion of the borough could be represented.

Decorations have been arranged at Moreton Cross roads, and practically the whole of Liscard and Wallasey Villages, also the junction of Borough Road, Wheatland Lane and Poulton Road, the promenade near New Brighton Ferry, Egremont Ferry and Seacombe Ferry Piers.

The motifs forming the decorations are arranged on each side of lamp standards and the effect produced by the varied colours of the real bunting flags and banners should be gay and effective.

At Seacombe Ferry approach, being the gateway to the borough from the river, four tall gilded pylons ornamented with flags and shields are erected.

The decorations to several of the buildings will be impressive, notably - the Town Hall, the police station in Manor Road, the electricity showrooms, also the frontage to Mill Lane Hospital and the adjacent Corporation's Works Depot.

The Marine Lake at New Brighton will be decorated with flags and streamers, and the illuminated launch will be a feature of the lake at night.

The New Brighton Pier and promenade will, of course, be a brilliant sight later in the evening with miles of fairy lights.

The whole of the street decorations have been designed by the borough engineer.

In The Streets

8 May, 1937

Acacia Grove

About six weeks ago, the residents of Acacia Grove, thought

they would like to give the children a Coronation open air party.

They formed a committee, viz :- Mesdames Conroy, Clutterbuck, Hind, Williams, Pryce (treasurer) and Mrs. Brown (secretary) with three male helpers, Messrs. H. Walker, A. Foster, and C. Davies. They collected weekly subscriptions from neighbours and held whilst drives in the secretary's house.

It is hoped to give a party to the children of New Street, Bridle Road, and Briardale Road and Acacia Grove.

Byron Road

The Capitol Dance Band will provide music. There will be races for the children, all of whom will receive Coronation cups and saucers and also handkerchiefs and toys - all presented by Mr. and Mrs. Stacey. Eighty children and adults will enjoy a street party. A Coronation cake has been presented by Mr. Price of Byron Road.

Shakespeare Road

Here, too, a band will attend, and there will be dancing from eight till midnight. Sixty children will have sports and a party in the street, while for the adults a party and entertainment has been arranged to be held under cover. The children will receive a medal as a souvenir. The street will be adorned with fairy lighting and floodlit at each end.

Lily Grove

The Mayor (Councillor G.L. Reakes) is to present prizes to the children who have succeeded in the sports. There will be community singing, a concert by local artistes and a conjuring exhibition by Professor A. Roberts. Jimmy Smith and his boys will provide music. Mr. A. Roberts, a newcomer to the grove, offered to take charge of the children's sports and will act as organiser and M.C. besides presenting the prizes.

Conway Street and St. Alban's Terrace

Final plans include a party for 150 children in the recreation ground behind the Electricity Showrooms and sports and races, on Coronation Day. If the weather should disappoint the party will be held in St. Thomas's Hall, Liscard. All the children will receive souvenirs. On Thursday a motor-coach trip for children and parents will run through the Mersey Tunnel and round Merseyside. The children will be taken free of charge.

Those who have taken a leading part in making and arranging decorations are Mesdames Corrigan, McCormick, Sprackling, Parry, Truman, Hooligan, Dwyer and Messrs J. McCormick, snr. J. McCormick jnr., J. Wilson, A. Wilson. T. Edwards, Truman, M. Wilcox and Palin.

Rossett Place

A party is to be given to fifty children in the street on Coronation Day, races will be run for prizes and each child will receive a souvenir cup and saucer. Later the adults will have a party provided out of funds and held in their houses. The street will be illuminated by electric lighting. The organisation of the events has been carried out by T. Preston (sec). and R. Preston (treasurer).

Greenfield Street

The neighbours have arranged to give a tea in the Wesley Hall, Liscard to two hundred children and adults. Children's races will be run in the street for prizes and each child will receive a souvenir. The chief decorative artist has been Mr. E. Sackey. Mrs. Robinson was treasurer.

Wallasey Schoolchildren In Inspiring Spectacle

Liverpool Echo
10 May, 1937

The spacious floor of the New Brighton bathing pool served this afternoon as the arena for a display of physical culture and country dances by 1,200 pupils of the Wallasey secondary and elementary schools.

This picturesque exhibition of what is being done to improve the health and fitness of the young folk of the town was witnessed by about 10,000 spectators, consisting chiefly of other school children and their parents.

To the accompaniment of the band of the 1st Battalion of the Argyll and Sutherland Highlanders, the entire body of performers took part in an opening march round in double file. When all were assembled in the baths arena, they joined lustily in the singing of the National Anthem.

Gymnastic children display at New Brighton Open Air Bathing Pool.

A kaleidoscopic effect was produced by the rainbow colours of the gymnastic costumes and sashes worn, and was enhanced by the dazzling whiteness of the specially-painted floor of the arena.

Country dances by a selection of the senior girls was followed by an amusing display by the junior boys of games and agility matwork. The junior girls then came into the picture with the Maypole and country dances, the senior boys following with games and tableaux.

After the singing "Land of Hope and Glory" by all present, the secondary boys and girls in turn gave an excellent exhibition of gymnastic exercises and the whole 1,200 performers then joined in a rhythmic evolution display.

The Mayor of Wallasey (Councillor G.L. Reakes) was present in his robes of office, accompanied by the Town Clerk, Mr. Emrys Evans, and members of the Council.

The whole programme is to be repeated this evening, when the general public will be admitted.

1,200 At Town Hall Service

Wallasey Chronicle
15 May, 1937

There was an attendance of twelve hundred at the civic service for prayer and consecration in preparation for the Coronation at the Town Hall on Sunday evening.

The Mayor (Councillor G.L. Reakes) attended in his robes and chain of office, and was accompanied by many members of the Town Council. Those present included representatives of all the religious denominations in the town, members of philanthropic and social organisation's, etc. The singing was most impressive, accompanied by the organ, presided over by Mr. Eric Barlow.

The Rev. W.S. Coad, rural dean and vicar of St. James Church, New Brighton, who delivered the first of two addresses, said that although the Coronation was accompanied by most impressive pageantry and by the sound of martial music, they ought not to be satisfied with that alone. There must be a quiet offering of the heart in absolute sincerity to the Throne of Grace.

In Westminster Abbey on Wednesday the King would be seen in quiet simplicity kneeling before the altar and receiving the Bread of Life, enabling him to do that for which he was destined. The rejoiced that their new King was a religious man who would uphold to the utmost of his power the moral standards of his God. They prayed that King George VI and Queen Elizabeth might be upheld by the Grace of God to be of benefit not only to our own beloved country but to the whole world.

It is wonderful to think of 400,000.000 loyal people with their eyes turned to Westminster. It was the love of God which kept the Empire together, and the Empire had been brought together by God for a purpose, some fulfillment of which they would see in the reign now beginning.

The Rev. Hermon F. Johnson (Poulton Road Methodist Church) said they were all convinced that their Majesties were entering upon a glorious reign, and that they would lead this great nation and commonwealth of nations to greater heights. By nature and grace they were equipped for their great task, and all their people wished them God-speed.

Just as the King and Queen consecrated themselves in the service of the country, the people in turn should dedicate themselves to the land they loved. Patriotism was not enough if they desired the maintenance and furtherance of all that was best in our national life, and there must be a dedication of ourselves to certain great causes - the causes of peace, freedom, justice and religion. It was religion and not Kings, statesmen, and soldiers that had made the England we knew. If they loved their country they must all get back to God and His holy ways.

An overflow service in the Brighton Street Methodist Church, attended by about 300, and at which the deputy-Mayor, Alderman F.H. Thornton, was present, was conducted by the Rev. J. Goldsborough (Claremount Road Methodist Church), and addresses were delivered by the Rev. W.J. Philpin

(All Saints' Church), and the Rev. Eric Lawson (Rake Lane Congregational Church).

Mayor Visits Schools

Wallasey Chronicle
15 May, 1937

The Mayor (Councillor G.L. Reakes) paid a visit to fifteen schools on Tuesday afternoon and made brief speeches to the scholars, who were assembled for the tea parties and presentations.

Accompanying the Mayor were the Chairman of the Education Committee (Alderman A.H. Evans, J.P.), and the Director of Education (Mr. F. Stephenson, M.A.)

The schools visited included St. Joseph's R.C (mixed), St. Alban's R.C (mixed), Vaughan Road Infants School, Central Girls, Riverside Junior Boys, Riverside Infants, Riverside Junior Girls, Somerville Juniors (mixed), Somerville Infants, Somerville Senior Girls, Manor Road Senior Boys, Egerton Grove Juniors (mixed), Egerton Infants, Church Street Junior Boys and Gorsedale Senior Boys.

When the Mayor reached Poulton Junior Boys the party had broken up, the length of the programme of visits being responsible for the late arrival. The Mayor, however, decided to visit Poulton schools at an early date, and also other schools in the borough which could not be included in Tuesday's tour.

"I will never forget seeing so many happy children. We owe a great debt to the teaching staff for the way they make the children happy. The decorations were delightful, "" stated the Mayor to a "News" reporter at the conclusion of the tour.

At Gorsedale Road Schools, Seacombe, commemorative oak, ash, birch, and elm trees were planted by the captains of the school "houses" so designated, and each of the four boys were presented with a new Coronation florin.

The Civic Procession
Wallasey Chronicle
15 May, 1937

Wallasey civic procession from Manor Road Schools to the ancient parish church of St. Hilary, where the service was held, made stately spectacle for large crowds lining the main parts of the route.

The procession was composed of the following :- Mounted Police, band of the 1st Battalion and Argyll and Sutherland Highlanders, Royal Naval Volunteer Reserve (Mersey Division), 178th Battery of the Lancs. and Ches. Heavy Brigade, R.A (T.A.), 4/5th (E. of C.) Battalion The Cheshire Regiment, Lancs and Ches. Anti-Aircraft Cadet Battery, police, firemen, Men's V.A.D., British Red Cross Society, Women's V.A.D., St. John's Ambulance Association, Wallasey detachment, ferrymen, motor-bus men, postmen, boys of the Sea Training Homes, Boys Scouts and Wolf Clubs, Boys Brigade, Girl Guides, representatives of local organisations and institutions, co-opted members of committee of the Town Council, principal officials of the Corporation, Justices of the Peace, councillors, alderman, ex-Mayors, Mayor's Chaplain, Mayor's Sergeant and Mace-bearer, the Mayor, Deputy Town Clerk, ex-Mayoresses.

The following members of the Council attended the service :- Alderman Atkin, Airey, Brick, Charlesworth, Dale, Evans, Flanagan, Milward, Thomas, Thornton, Councillors Apperley, Ashton, Baker, W.D. Burrows, Bellis, Blackshaw, Crichton, Dingle, Gill, Griffiths, Hannaford, Hall, Hardy, Masefield, Pennington, Rees Williams, Swain, Todd, Wensley, Wilson, Young.

The Rev. S.G. Barton conducted the service. Representing the Free Churches were the Revs. R.F. Chisholm, E.J. Law son and J. Goldboroughs. The lessons were read by the Rev. E.J. Lawson.

Children's Treat At New Brighton

Wallasey Chronicle
15 May, 1937

Two hundred children were entertained to a treat at the Embassy Rooms through the generosity of a large number of people who had supported the effort promoted by the New Brighton Children's Outing Association and organised by Mrs. G. Balshaw. The committee consisted of Mrs. E. Crellin (chairman), Mr. G. Balshaw (hon. secretary), Mr. and Mrs. Payne, Mr. and Mrs. Hughes, Mrs. Lewis, Mr. McGovern, Mr. Duncan, Mrs. Willis, Mr. and Mrs. Merill and Mr. G. Willis hon. sec. Association). The children thoroughly enjoyed their repast and on returning home were each given a bar of Coronation rock, an orange and a new penny.

They were delighted with the entertainment provided by Miss. B. Balshaw's clever Coronation troupe of dancers consisting of Betty Roberts, Peral Balshaw, Patty Walsh, Margery Smith, June Ridgeway, Maureen Flinn, and the turns given by Dorothy Drew (tap dancer) and the Two Babettes (June Ridgeway and Margaret Lutus).

During the evening the Mayor and Mayoress visited the children and expressed to Mrs. Balshaw their admiration of what had been done for the enjoyment of the little guests. Last Christmas the organisation gave a treat to 200 children at the Tivoli. An outing for 300 children to Magull has been fixed for September.

Scenes In The Streets

Wallasey Chronicle
15 May. 1937

Buchanan Road

Buchanan Road children had a splendid tea party in the street. Jelly creams, fruit salad, cakes, ices, and those delicacies that children love were enjoyed and tea was followed by races, games and other sports organised by Mrs. S.E. Hyde and Mrs. Crane. Mrs. Hyde iced a huge seven pound weight Coronation cake and we are sure that there is very little left.

Byron Road

Captain Stacey and his good wife were busy all day in Byron Road. They helped at the tea and games and Captain Stacey presented each child with a Coronation cup and saucer. Mrs. Stacey, not to be outdone, placed a little handkerchief in each cup.

The Capitol Cafe dance band played in the street until early morning and visitors and residents alike enjoyed the day's celebrations. Mr. John Tobin supervised and carried out his unenvious job extremely well. Byron Road was, by the way, the first street visited by the Mayoral party. A huge Coronation cake presented by Mr. and Mrs. Price of Byron Street, was cut by Mr. F.H. Thornton (acting Mayoress).

Shakespeare Road

The children of Shakespeare Road, assisted by several grown-up children, got through three gallons of ice cream, seventeen dozen fancy cakes, ten dozen bottles of mineral water and tea and sandwiches, fruit and cream.

Mr Hewitt, of Hewitt and Booth, the proprietors of the pipe cleaner factory in Shakespeare Road, donated £3 to the fund and Mrs. Hewitt performed the cake cutting ceremony. The committee engaged a band but the band did not arrive, but an impromptu but quite efficient band kept on until the wee small hours.

The high winds and the deluge of rain wrecked the decorations on Tuesday night but not to be outdone, the men went at it again on Wednesday morning for the third time since Saturday and the street was as good as ever when the Mayor arrived.

Mr. Lew Jones acted as M.C. for the dancing, while Mr. S. Thomas was at the piano.

Abbotsford Street

Abbotsford Street, off Church Road, Seacombe, was a village on its own. Residents had roped off both ends of the road and each was picketed.

The Mayor did not open the proceedings, cut any tapes or cakes, make any speeches, because the committee had forgotten to extend an invitation.

Just the same, the residents had a good tea, the children especially, and races, sports and dancing was carried on during the afternoon and evening.

The adult race was won by Mrs. L. Gartland, Mrs. Cheetham and Mrs. Thompson.

Nearly every resident of the street entered for some race or other and the winners included Messrs. J. McDermot, J. Martin, Joseph Gartland, S. Williams, W. Gartland, Miss E. Molyneux, Mrs. R. Critchon, Miss. P Gartland, Miss. G. Williams, Miss. W. Littler, Miss. M. Crabtree, Mr. H.W. Littler, Mr. H. Wainwright, Miss. R. Bee, Miss N. Taylor and Master B. Thompson.

Lilly Grove

The celebrations in Lily Grove opened with singing and dancing in the streets, Jim Smith's band providing the music. At. 3.30pm nearly 90 children were lined up and headed by the band they marched up to the Social Club, St. Paul's Road, for tea. Ninety young children cheered the Mayor when he arrived and Mr. T. Foy responded to the Mayor's remarks.

The afternoon sports were preceded by an entertainment by Professor Smith, a local conjuror, but the best disappearing act had already taken place -- at the tea table. Miss Betty Smith sang and gave a clever display of tap-dancing followed by three other versatile performers, Miss Lily Morgan, Miss Norah Stott and Miss Buckley.

Mr. George Williamson, always a favourite at parties in the district delighted the children with songs at the piano, while Mr. R. Littler and Mr. Prosser concluded the programme.

Mr. Roberts of Lily Grove, was a capable M.C. and he was assisted by a band of willing neighbours. Dancing to the wireless went on until one am.

The children of this street were fortunate in having as patrons, the Birkenhead Brewery Co., who sent a gift of sweets. Mrs. Newcombe of the "York" Hotel who supplied ices and the Wirral Mineral Water Co., who donated minerals for the children.

The prize-winners in the races were as follows :- Girls : Joan Pugh, Kathleen Cavanagh, Mildred Goulden, Grace Pugh and Vera Green. Boys : Richard Doyle, George Whitby, Robert Delap, Alan Holland and Arthur Smith. Tiny tot's race : Charlie Minner. Ladies : Kathleen Ashurst.

Hawthorne Grove

There was a good crowd of residents assembled round the tables in Hawthorne Grove and the Mayor and Mayoress were well cheered. It did not take long for the children to start their tea. The adults had tea afterwards and the children played games.

Granville Terrace

There were very happy celebrations in Granville Terrace on Coronation Day culminating in a jolly tea for the children complete with balloons and favour's and all that goes to delight the kiddies' hearts.

Rossett Place

In Rossett Place and adjacent streets, the fun was just as good and in the former a really fine piece of work was displayed, a model of the Queen Mary executed to scale by Mr. Edwin Williams of Rossett Place and brilliantly lighted after sundown. Moseley Avenue, too, was beautifully decorated with loyal greetings and dancing was indulged in till quite a late hour.

Another cul-de-sac in the neighbourhood which had been very attractive was Pear Tree Grove.

Primrose Grove

Ten-years-old Eileen McFarlane of Primrose Grove, Seacombe was crowned Coronation Queen on Wednesday just before a party was given to nearly 50 children. The Mayor opened the proceedings and the fun was carried on after tea when the children were presented with trumpets and Mr. W. Sedgwick improvised a band. Mrs. Leay, Mrs. Taylor and Mrs. Lightfoot were in charge of the arrangements.

Palatine Road

The residents of Palatine Road and Woodview Avenue only decided 10 days ago to hold a children's party in the street, but, chiefly due to the fine work of Mrs. L. Williams, Mrs. M. Wynn, Mrs. Amery, Mrs. M. Moore and Mrs. Smithers nearly 60 children had a really happy time. Councillor G. Russell and the Mayor had lent a hand towards financing the party, but owing to an oversight the Mayor had not been asked to attend the celebrations. Not to be outdone, however, little Miss Annie Wynn, ran down to Lily Grove for the Mayor and brought him back, hand-in-hand.

Most of the residents of this road heard the broadcast service from London in the street as a radio set was brought out into the street.

Palermo Street

Four-years-old 'Pops' Johnston is a proud Queen to-day. She was crowned Coronation Queen by the Mayor and she presided at a party with 100 of her friends. Mrs. Openshaw, and Mrs. Weir arranged the party and Mr. McWilliam organised race and dancing in the street afterwards.

Parry Street

The residents of Parry Street decided a fortnight ago to hold a party for the children but in those two weeks they collected over £5. Out of the fiver 60 children had a party, received a Coronation cup, saucer and plate, sweets and fruit. How the residents of Parry Street managed to do that on £5 no one will ever know, but they did it and what's more, they had races afterwards and presented prizes.

Oakdale Avenue

Eighteen pounds of slab cake, 112 fancy cakes, 100 oranges, 4 lbs. of sweets, 1½ gallons of ice cream, tea, bread and butter and fruit vanished suddenly when 80 children of Oakdale Ave. sat down to a tea-party in the street organised by Mrs. Henderson, Mrs. Read, Mrs. McGraw, Mrs. Walker, Mrs. Mazier and Mrs. Marlowe. The children waited for some time for the Mayor to arrive but he didn't so they attacked the 18lbs, of slab cake, 112 fancy cakes, 100 oranges, 4 lbs. of sweets. 1½ gallons of ice-cream, tea and bread and butter!

Hawthorndale Road

Mrs. I. Davies and Mrs. Bates were responsible for 50 children having a party in the decorated street. The Mayoress (Mrs. F.H. Thornton) cut the Coronation cake (and took a portion with her) and Ald. Dr. Dale and Councillor Bellis also attended.

There was dancing and jollification in this street to music from the radio-gram

Cherrybank Road

One resident of Cherrybank Road dragged a piano out into the street so that young people could dance in the evening. The gaily-decorated street presented a pretty scene when, after 50 children had enjoyed their tea-party the mayoress cut the cakes. There were two Coronation cakes presented by friends and workers who arranged the tea included Mrs. T. Griffiths, Mrs. G. Roberts, Mrs. H. Cornah, Mrs. J. Atherton, Mrs. Kelly and Mrs. Gregory.

Larch Road

Mr. J. Gratton designed a clever trellis-work archway across Larch Road, and the men of the street erected it. It looked very charming and a coloured ribbon was stretched across the entrance waiting for Alderman Dr. Dale and Councillor Bellis to cut the ribbon and declare the party open. When they did cut the ribbon, the little girls, dressed in dresses made of Union Jacks and the little boys in sailor suits cheered and cheered. Each youngster received a Coronation cup and saucer and after the tea the following children sang and danced : Peggy Herion, Lily Walker, Cecilia Bickerton and Joan Herion, Mr. Jack Gratton and Mr. and Mrs. Walker also entertained the children.

Mrs. S. Langton, Mrs. E. Scrugham, Mrs. E. Herion, Mrs. W. Crompton, Mrs. G. Povell and Mrs. J. Clarke were the committee in charge of affairs.

Short Street

When the Mayor party arrived at Short Street off Ashville Road, Seacombe four years old Maureen Pope presented Mrs. F.H. Thornton with a tri-coloured sheaf of followers and 5 years old Arthur Neville with a cigarette case. The Mayor and Mayoress were genuinely surprised at this charming gesture and they suitably replied.

A band attended in the afternoon after tea was over and Mr. J. Ashley took all the children for a drive in his car. Mr. and Mrs. W. Halton, Mr. J. Edwards and Mrs. D. Neville were in charge of the celebrations.

On Thursday, Mr. W. Hindley gave the children of Short Street another party in honour of Dennis Brown, who was celebrating his sixth birthday. Sheila White and her brother Joe entertained the party in the afternoon with a display of step-dancing.

Middle Road

The Mayor was quite delighted at his present from Short Street which is next to Middle Street, so when Mr. H. McTeer invited him into his house to drink to the children's health, the Mayor pocketed one of the Coronation mugs (after draining it) as a memento. Mr. Lyndsay Clegg (Deputy Town Clerk) followed the Mayor's example.

Guildford Street

Close on 200 children from Guildford Street, Union Street, Gresford Place, Water Street and Darlington Street was assembled in Guildford Street on Wednesday afternoon when Ald. and Mrs. D.P. Charlesworth arrived to formally open the festivities. The Alderman and his wife were cheered to the echo and they both accepted the invitation to "stay for tea". Ald. Charlesworth had presented the children with a huge coronation cake and Mrs. Charlesworth cut it. She was deeply touched when the oldest resident of the street, Mrs. Gerard, who has lived in Guildford Street for over 41 years presented her with a bouquet of red and white and blue flowers.

The Mayoral party arrived later in the afternoon after the children had been presented with a Coronation cup each, Mr. F. Pumford and Mr. Bradshaw arranged races and games after tea and Miss. Joyce Jenkins and a friend, both from the "Chrysanthemums" danced for the children in the street. The dancing and the festivities were carried on until 10.30 pm with the aid of a piano.

Mrs. J. Locke, of Guildford Street, although she had been bed-ridden for some time with rheumatism, was the leader of the committee, which included Mrs. C. Clarke, Miss. A. Winrow, Miss. N. Winrow, Mrs. Jenkins, Mrs. F. Pumford, Mrs. Lloyd, Mrs. James and Mrs. Lynch. The committee, who worked very hard were ably assisted by nearly 30 neighbours who had tea in the street later in the afternoon.

Greenfield Street

The centre of attraction in Liscard on Coronation Day was undoubtedly in Greenfield Street, Rossett Place, St. Alban's

Road and Conway Street.

Sixty-three children marched to the Wesley Hall for tea and afterwards the Mayoral party visited the street and admired the now famous portrait of their Majesties done in oils by 17 years old Edward Sackey, of Greenfield Street. The street was gaily decorated and was admired by hundreds of passer-bys.

St.Alban's Road decorations

The committee who worked so hard included Mr. G. Blakemore (chairman), Mr. F. Oakwell (vice-chairman), Mr. and Mrs. W. Robinson, Mr. A. Ward, Mr. and Mrs. C. Thornton, Mr. and Mrs. J. Upton, Mrs. Christy, Mr. and Mrs. Littler, Mrs. Hatton, Mrs. Fogg, Mrs. Sackey, Mrs. E. Blakemore, Mrs. Oakwell, Mrs. Parker and Mr. W. Robinson.

Conway Street

Everything went off as arranged by the Conway Street and St. Albans Terrace committee on Wednesday and on Thursday evening. Eighty children and 50 adults went on a charabanc trip round Wallasey, Birkenhead and Liverpool via the Mersey Tunnel. Pitt Street evoked much admiration and the party was conducted around by the residents. Each child was presented with a bottle of lemonade, an orange and biscuits.

Councillor and Mrs. Hannaford, who formally opened Wednesday's celebration had tea with the party and later the Mayoral party paid a visit.

Coronation Film

Full Crowing Ceremony Pictures at G.B. Cinemas
15 May, 1937

The Gaumont Palace, the Trocadero, and the Marina are showing a great film at the crowing ceremony in Westminster Abbey, on Monday and throughout next week. Every detail of those historic moments is clearly revealed and the sound effects give to the picturisation a reality at which the watcher must glow with wonder and pride. No one, especially no child, should fail to see this picture -- the first of the sort ever made.

◆ ◆ ◆

A NEW PARK FOR WALLASEY

Local Government Board Inquiry

Liverpool Mercury

Wednesday, 8th January, 1890

At the Public Offices, Egremont, yesterday, Major-General C.Phipps Carey, R.E., held an inquiry on behalf of the Local Government Board into the application of the Wallasey Local Board to borrow £25,000 for the purchase of land to be used as a public, and £350 for works of sewerage. Besides a very large attendance of the public, the following members of the Wallasey Local Board were also present :- Messrs T. Dean, G.H. Peers, R. McGeoch, J. Davies and W. Evans. Mr. Danger (solicitor to the local board) supported the application on behalf of the local board, and Mr. A.T. Wright appeared on behalf of owners of land and for the New Brighton Ratepayers' Association, opposing the application.

Mr. Danger said that the estate which the board wished to convert into a public park consisted of 50 acres, upon which the Liscard Hall, with washhouses, cottages, stables, and vineries, with two entrance lodges, stood. About 22 acres was arable and meadow land, and it had a long frontage along the Liscard Road and on the north end of the Mill Lane. On the west side, and behind the Liscard Hall, there existed what was now termed the recreation ground, which was presented to the parish by a gentleman, well known in the district about four or five years ago. These grounds were, however, not freely used, in consequence of the difficulty of access. The proposed park could be purchased for £23,000, at the rate £460 per acre. The contract had been entered into, subject to the Local Government Board, giving their sanction to the borrowing of £25,000 for the purchase and other expenses. The board had taken the feeling of the ratepayers on this matter by means of a vote in answer to the question which was addressed by circular to every ratepayer, "Are you in favour or not of the acquisition by the Wallasey Local Board of the Liscard Hall estate for the recreation and games". The result of this inquiry was 2799 votes in favour of the proposed scheme and 575 against.

Mr. Vickess (clerk to the board) having explained the financial position of the board, Mr. Heap (chairman of the board) said that he considered the board should acquire the park, as its financial position quite justified the expenditure necessary to do so. (Hear, hear).

Major Chambres, Messrs. James Smith, Henry Wall, F.Johnson, W.G.Holland, G.H.Peers. R.McGeoch all spoke in favour of the scheme, and remarked on the advantage which the poor of the district would derive from the park, and the benefit the inhabitants generally would receive from it.

Mr.G.H.Ball opposed the application. In doing so he said that the scheme itself of constructing a park was most desirable for public health and improvements if all kinds were, no doubt, of great advantage to the district; but what they had to consider was whether they could afford to expend on this park. So far as the scheme itself was concerned, it was feasible and reasonable if they would limit the park to something like 23 acres; but 50 acres made it too large to sustain. (Cries of "no, no"). He referred to the park at Stanley, which he said, was over 100 acres in extent; but a portion was sold off for building purposes. so that it was limited to an acre of something like 90 acres. To maintain that 90 acres an expenditure of something like £1100 or £1200 per annum was necessary, and yet the park was in a deplorable condition (A voice : "More shame to the Liverpool Corporation"). It had been stated that the annual charge for the purpose of the proposed park would not exceed 1⅞d. in the pound, but that was the cost of the land only, and nothing whatever was charged for maintenance. The £2000 which had recently been borrowed was calculated to provide something like £100 a year towards the expenses of maintaining the park. As to the canvass among the ratepayers, no reliance whatever could be placed upon it. A large proportion of the persons who had signed were not ratepayers, and the ratepayers themselves had been derived as to the actual cost. It was not true that the whole of the opposition had come from New Brighton - it had come from Wallasey. (A voice : "It has come from yourself alone." Laughter).

Mr.W.Colbourne also opposed the movement, remarking that the park would not be an advantage to the whole of the district (Hear, hear).

The Rev. J.H.D.Cochran, on behalf of the working people, strongly advocated the utility of the proposed park. He had worked in a crowded parish of Liverpool, but in no part of Liverpool were the poor people so densely crowded together as in the village of Liscard. He thought, like the rich, the poor people should have a garden and recreation ground wherein they could enjoy their leisure, and to be any use that park or garden must be within half a mile of the people. (Hear, hear).

Mr. M.T.Graveson maintained that a park would develop the property in the neighbourhood. If the land fell into the hands of the builders, as most assuredly it would do, there would be a large wilderness of streets and the rural character of the district would be completely changed, and the property which would be built on the site would almost ruin the good property in the neighbourhood. He contended that the park would prove one of the greatest blessings to the district. (Hear, hear).

Mr. J.M. Hawkins spoke of the depreciation in the value of property as having now stopped, and that the board had acquired the park at a reasonable rate when the value of property was greatly depreciated. Mr. Ball did not represent the feeling of the board - (Hear, hear) - and he doubted whether any scheme had come before the Local Government Board with a greater preponderance in its favour, both in the board and amongst the outside ratepayers. (Hear, hear). He referred to the great increase in the ferry receipts - over £4000. This would entirely cover the cost without an increase in the rates, and in a few years they would have cleared off a debt for which 6d. in the pound was now being paid by the ratepayers. The policy of the board was to acquire the park when it could be acquired, but to leave the laying out until the time when more funds were available. The proposal of the board was not to spend a large amount in maintenance, but to acquire the park and leave any larger expenditure in laying it out until a further period. (Hear, hear).

Mr. Brooks, a ratepayer in Liscard, said that out of 1600 people he had visited between Seacombe and New Brighton, only 25 were directly in opposition to the proposal.

Mr. Peers also supported the scheme.

Mr. Wright then called a number of ratepayers and property owners, who gave their views in opposition to the scheme. The feeling expressed by these witnesses was that the park was totally unnecessary for the welfare of the neighbourhood, and that the financial condition of the board was not such as to justify so large an expenditure simply for the purpose of amusement and recreation. Some of them were in favour of a modified scheme.

At the conclusion of the evidence Mr. Wright, in reviewing the various arguments addressed in opposition, remarked that the board was in debt to such an extent that they ought not to be allowed to increase it. Already it amounted to about £16 per head of the population as compared with £6 in Liverpool. The site was not central for the whole district, although it was central for Seacombe and Liscard, but these townships were not alone going to pay for the park.

Mr. Danger having addressed the meeting, the commissioner signified his intention of reporting the results of the inquiry to the Local Government Board.

◆ ◆ ◆

A BURGLAR AND HIS YACHT

The Penny Illustrated Paper and Illustrated Times

Saturday, 28th May, 1887

The Cheshire Police were on Monday engaged investigating the antecedents of a man who gives the name of William Moody, and who was arrested on Saturday, charged with burglariously entering the premises of Mr. Peter Davies, known as the "Pioneer" Stores, [Brighton Street] Seacombe. Mrs. Davies saw the man enter her bed-room, and screamed out, awakening her husband, who leaped out of bed and seized the burglar. An investigation revealed that the prisoner had poisoned the watch-dog and secured some valuable property, including £30 actually taken from Mr. Davies pockets. He was furnished with a complete set of housebreaking implements.

Now comes the remarkable part of the story. The police, continuing their investigation, discovered the prisoner was occupying a luxuriantly-fitted yacht now at anchor at Tranmere. There valued property, including dressing-cases, jewellery, and articles of virtue, which it is believed are proceeds of previous burglarious raids. One curious find was a South Eastern Railway Company's dividend for £41, payable to Joseph Beaumont Stockwell. The prisoner, it appears, bought the yacht from a Cheshire gentleman a short time back for a considerable sum of money.

GETTING IN AT THE WINDOW | DESPERATE STRUGGLE WITH A YACHTING BURGLAR AT SEACOMBE. | THE POLICE TAKE POSSESSION OF THE PRISONER'S YACHT

The purchase of the yacht was an adroit move by which he calculated confidently on eluding the police, for when the chase became inconveniently close it was easy to avoid it by retiring to the snug berth which he had thoughtfully provided for himself in the vessel, and then, lifting the anchor, proceeding to sea.

The fellow, who is of slender build and dressed in the garb of a sailor, has been remanded formally by the Cheshire magistrates until Friday.

◆ ◆ ◆

BROKEN BOLTS CAUSE WALLASEY BUS TRAGEDY

Wallasey NEWS

22nd August, 1931

Mrs. WHITMAN.

A tragic story of how the breaking of two bolts caused a woman to fall from the inside of a Wallasey Corporation motor bus on to the revolving shaft by which she was killed, was told at an inquest conducted by Mr. J.C. Bate, with a jury, at the Police Court, Manor Road yesterday (Friday).

The accident occurred in King Street on Tuesday shortly after five o'clock, the victim being Mrs. Elizabeth Cecilia Whitman (39), of 15, Seabank Road, Wallasey, who was returning from a shopping expedition in Liverpool with her husband, Edgar Francis Whitman, chief operator at the Lyceum Cinema.

Mrs. Whitman's clothes were torn from by the revolving shaft, and she received terrible injuries. The many passengers in the bus were greatly shocked, one woman fainted, and Mr. Whitman was almost overcome.

At the inquest, Mr. H.B.M. Pidgeon and Mr. Wilson Kenyon, the Deputy Town Clerk, appeared on behalf of the Corporation; Mr. J.D. Eaton Smith, of Huddersfield, represented Karriers Motors Ltd., and the relatives were represented by Mr. J.A.L. Humphreys.

The Coroner explained to the jury that Mr. and Mrs. Whitman had been to Liverpool and were returning on the motor bus from Seacombe Ferry when the accident happened. When the woman was picked up it was found that her injuries were so bad that she was dead. The cause of the accident was that something went wrong with the under portion of the bus. Two of the bolts connecting the universal joint broke and an eccentric action was set up. It was for the jury to say how the accident happened. There were one or more explanations. Three possible causes were mechanical defect in construction, want of proper inspection and overhaul, or unskillful or improper driving.

Husband's Story

Evidence of identification was given by Edgar Francis Whitman, the deceased's husband, who said he was a cinematograph operator. On Tuesday he and his wife returned to Seacombe on the ten minutes to five boat from Liverpool, and boarded a Corporation motor bus at Seacombe Ferry, intending to get off at the bottom of Trafalgar Road. They took the two seats on the right hand side of the bus immediately behind the driver.

"Nothing unusual happened until nearly at the stopping place," he said. "As the bus was pulling up I got off my seat and walked towards the exit, expecting my wife to follow me. I got just on to the platform when I heard a noise. I turned round and saw a hole in the floor and I saw through it a wheel turning round. Then I looked to see if my wife was there, but she was not, and I looked down the road and saw her shoe. Then I saw her lying on the roadway."

Jury Inspect The Bus

The jury then went to the Tramway sheds to inspect the bus, the shaft with the clothing wound round it being exhibited in the Coroner's Court.

Arnold Jasper Sumner, Mount Pleasant Road, Wallasey, a passenger on the bus, said it was a little after five o'clock when the accident happened. The bus was approaching the stop at the Lyceum Cinema when he saw some persons get up to alight. They were passing along the gangway towards the back of the bus, when his attention was attracted by a bump and a scream. He was standing on the platform at the time. He looked inside the bus and saw a woman disappearing through the floor. From what he could see the driver applied his brakes immediately he heard there was something wrong. The bus had stopped, he looked to the back of the bus and saw a woman lying on the roadway between the tramlines with her feet towards the bus and her head towards Seacombe Ferry. Apparently she was dead.

Norah Bellas, of Zig Zag Road, Wallasey, another passenger sitting on the left side of the lower deck, said she heard a dreadful noise and then saw a lady drop down a hole in the floor.

In reply to the Coroner, she said she had heard a very similar noise on a previous occasion, but the conductor had told her not to be alarmed as it was only an "overrun."

Technical Evidence

Technical evidence was given by Mr. Albert Baxendale, the Rolling Stock Works Superintendent of the Wallasey Tramways Department, who said the bus in which the accident happened was a Karrier, and had been in service since the beginning of 1928. It had been periodically inspected, the last inspection being on August 10th. The bus was overhauled in April, 1929. The portion of the machinery under the bus was taken down, and as he was not satisfied with the studs (round the brake drum) which were slightly worn and the threads slightly damaged in taking them out of the brake drum, he had them replaced. These studs were fixed into the brake drum and riveted over after being screwed up. There was no "play" whatever in the stud fitting into the drum. He had seen the bolts that gave way. They were two of the bolts fixed in the drum and had broken away immediately behind the shoulder. One portion of the breakage on both sides was smooth and the actual breakage was in the centre.

Coroner: Could I suggest to you that the portion that was smooth had been previously cracked? – No, sir.

The crack does not bear the appearance of a sudden and complete crack of the bolt? – No.

In witness's opinion the bolts were strong to stand the strain, judging from the tests they had had.

Coroner: Can you suggest how it was they gave way? – I am very sorry, I cannot give any theory as to why.

In answer to the Coroner, witness added that it was an instruction to drivers to de-clutch before applying the brakes. It would be putting an extra strain on this portion of the car if those instructions were not carried out.

The bus was overhauled in April, was inspected on August 10th, and was then turned out sound as regards this portion.

In answer to Mr. Humphreys, witness said that the previous bolts were replaced at the April overhaul. They connected very heavy working parts, but he considered that the bolts were strong enough to take the drive. The previous bolts had been in a little more than eight months, and had gone for ten thousand miles.

In reply to Mr. Pidgeon, witness said he had nothing to do with the design of the shaft; it was the design of the shaft; it was the design of the makers, and new parts were secured from them. An examination took place every month, and between every forty to fifty thousand miles the buses were completely dismantled.

Drivers were instructed to report any peculiar or unusual noise immediately. If it was a loud noise they were to stop the bus and report immediately on the nearest telephone, and not to drive the bus away until it was inspected. There was also an instruction to report any defect, however slight. Any defect found by inspection was repaired, and in addition the whole of that part of the bus had to be inspected. Afterwards the fitter tested the bus himself, and if it was satisfactory to him it was handed over to the foreman, who took the vehicle on the road. If passed by him it was booked out for service.

No Objection By Drivers

In reply to the foreman of the jury, witness stated that there had been no complaint about that bus from the drivers.

Witness also replied to the Coroner that he did not think the bus had been improperly driven.

Ernest John Boundy, of Lycett Road, Wallasey, the conductor of the bus, said there was nothing prior to the accident that was unusual. He was just going up for the stop at the Lyceum, where he heard a bang and saw the deceased woman behind the bus.

P.C. George Herbert Benfield spoke of removing the deceased from the roadway, twenty yards behind the bus, to the Victoria Central Hospital. Nearly all her clothing had been torn from her body, and there were severe injuries to the head as well as other parts of the body.

Inspector W. Nicholson, of the Fire Brigade section of the Wallasey Police, described his examination of the bus. He found the trap door of the bus immediately above the coupling shaft wedged between the floor and the underside of the seat, apparently having been forced upwards. The coupling shaft was hanging by one stud, the other two having broken away. The effect on the shaft revolving with only one stud holding would be to increase the radius, and the footboard would be knocked up. The trap door knocked up was 24 ins. by 18 ins. There was very little room between the shaft and the side for a body to go through. Both bolts were broken at the shoulder. He could give no reason why they had snapped, as they were comparatively new bolts. Theoretically, they may be big enough, but it appeared to him that they were a little on the small side. They had not served the purpose for which they were made. For ordinary driving they would be all right, but they had apparently not been able to stand the heavy strain placed on them at times.

In his opinion it was a sheer break at the time of the accident, and not an old crack.

The driver of the bus, Seldon Phelp Smith, Moseley Avenue, Wallasey, said he had driven the bus many times before. They did not always drive the same bus. He did not remember sending in any report regarding this particular bus. He took it over at 3.40 pm on this day, and there was nothing unusual in the driving of the bus. At the time of the accident he was pulling up at the top of Trafalgar Road. The usual thing was to take his foot off the accelerator and let the bus run in gear until she had slowed down, then slip the clutch and apply the brake. On this occasion he had taken his foot off the accelerator, and the bus was slowing down when he heard the noise. The bus was in top gear when the woman fell. He did not know what the noise was, so he slipped his clutch and applied his brake.

Norman Edward Ward, engineer, of Oldhall Street, Liverpool, expressed the opinion that there was a fault in the metal of the bolts, and he believed that the breaking was due to crystallisation of part of the metal.

In reply to Mr. Pidgeon, he said the smooth part of the bolt showed perfectly sound metal but the rough part was crystalline and in his opinion a fault in the metal. No external examination could show that crystallisation. It was latest, but could not be seen.

The Coroner: The bolt would be apparently sound when put in? – Yes.

It had stood the strain of work for some three or four months? – Yes

Normally, the greatest strain put on this would be at starting up. When the omnibus is running there would be little strain on it? – That is so.

Coroner: And that is when it broke? – I understand it broke when the omnibus was only running the engine.

It broke when the driver's foot had been taken off the accelerator and the omnibus was running with two brakes. In those circumstances there would be a slight reverse strain. How is it that you expect this bolt, otherwise sound, to give way when there is only a small strain on it? – Owing to the crystallised state the margin of safety in the bolt is reduced by a half. A bolt such as this might give at any time.

You would not expect it to break when the strain is taken off? – You cannot theorise, but, naturally, one would expect it to give way from the strain.

Is this crystallisation an increasing condition? – Not necessarily.

The bolt was just as sound the moment before it broke as it was when it was put in? – Yes, it is quite possible that this was the last straw. The last starting up probably sheared one of these bolts, and when the omnibus came up to the final stopping place this particular stud was just hanging on until it got that slight reverse strain which sheared the other bolt as well.

You attribute the breakage to the crystallisation of the bolts? –

Yes.

The Coroner, reviewing the evidence, remarked that there was evidence that the bus was being driven in an ordinary and usual manner at the time of the accident, while there was no evidence of the lack of inspection. It was difficult to understand the bolts giving way at the time they did when there would be on starting. It had been suggested, however, that one of the bolts may have given way when the omnibus started from the previous stopping place, and the other subsequently gave way with the slight reverse strain on stopping.

It is not for the jury to say how the makers should construct their vehicles, he added, but if they felt the accident was due to lack of strength in the bolts they should say so.

After an absence of twenty minutes, the jury returned a verdict that the deceased woman was killed by falling through the trap door opening on the floor of a motor bus and being crushed by the revolving coupling shaft, this being in consequence of the bolts of the coupling shaft breaking off, and that it was due to an accidental cause.

Steel Supports Suggested

The jury added that there had been no neglect in the maintenance of the bus, but they would suggest that steel supports should be used under the trap door instead of wood in future.

Mr. Kenyon, in extending the sympathy of the Wallasey Corporation to Mr. Whitman and his daughter, said the Mayor of Wallasey and the chairman of the Tramway Committee desired to be personally associated with that expression.

"With regard to the jury's rider," said Mr. Kenyon, "the Wallasey Corporation have already taken steps to secure something in the nature of stronger resistance underneath the floors of the omnibuses, subject to the Ministry of Transport's approval.

P. DAVIES

The Internment

The funeral of Mrs. Whitman will take place today (Saturday), leaving St. Columba's, Egremont, at 11 am.

❖ ❖ ❖

THE "NOAH'S ARK" REFRESHMENT ROOMS

Liverpool Mercury

Thursday, 11th April, 1895

Willaim Hayes, 35 Pleasant Street, Liscard, was summoned [before Wallasey Police Court] for permitting a nuisance to exist at "Noah's Ark" refreshment rooms on the New Brighton shore. Mr. Pugh appeared for the Wallasey District Council, and Mr. McConchie defended. A number of witnesses were called by Mr. Pugh to show that a very foul smell proceeded from the interior of the "Ark", a vessel which had been stranded on the beach, and which is used as a refreshment room. In addition to the smells from the interior of the vessel there were also bad odours arising from the pools surrounding it. -- Mr. McConchie, for the defence, called witnesses, who stated that the smells from the vessel were no worse than those which arose from the decayed shell fish, &c., on other parts of the shore. He contended that the "Ark" was not "premises" under the Act, and did not come under the section. -- The Chairman said the bench had decided that the "Ark" was used as refreshment premises, and were also a nuisance. He thought the owner and the district council might come to terms. -- Mr. Danger : (law clerk to the council) said the defendant or his predecessors had brought the "Ark" there and ought to take it away. The negotiations to take it away had not been successful because the sum asked (£50) was considered too high. -- Mr. McConchie said that if the place was "premises" it was curious that the council had never rated them; and Mr Pugh in reply, pointed out that the council had control over the foreshore. -- Ultimately the Bench made an order that the "Ark" be removed within a period of two months.

The "Noah's Ark" Nuisance

**Liverpool Mercury
Thursday, 4th July, 1895**

William Hayes, 35 Pleasant Street, Liscard, was summoned [before Wallasey Police Court] for neglecting to carry out the order of the magistrates to remove the hulk called the Noah's Ark, lying on the shore at New Brighton. Mr. Bascombe, nuisance inspector, said nothing had been done since the case was last before the bench, except that a piece of the stern had been removed. The nuisance was now almost as bad as when the case was first brought up in April. Mr. W. Danger, clerk to the district council, said that a fortnight ago the bench imposed a nominal continuous penalty. The defendant said he had offered the wreck to the district council, and he could do no more. He had no means of removing it. Mr. Danger said the council would be willing to take the wreck and get rid of it, but for there being several owners. A little gunpowder would blow it up. The Chairman said the bench were proceeding by stages, and would continue to do so. Defendant would be fined 5s. per day for the 14 days covered by the summons, and 8s. 6d. costs -- £3. 18s. 6d. in all.

❖ ❖ ❖

WALLASEY A MECCA BATHERS

Wallasey NEWS

9th June 1934

On Wednesday next, Lord Leverhulme opens the New Brighton Open Air Bath – an aquatic arena of 4½ acres – Wallasey, with its Derby Pool and Guinea Gap Baths, will become a veritable Mecca for bathers. The event will prove one of great importance to the borough and definitely place Wallasey on the map as one of the leading health and pleasure resorts of the country.

New Brighton Bathing Pool

Occupying a position to the west of the Marine Lake and immediately opposite Marine Park, the new open air bathing pool has been designed to face due south so that maximum sunshine and shelter will be obtained.

The pool has been constructed of mass concrete with the floor reinforced with steel mesh and expansion joints have been provided of asphalt in the floor and walls. During construction the diving area was left in after concreting. The side walls for about half the length were supported on reinforced concrete piles, 14 in. 14 in. at 12 ft. 6 in. centres.

The area of the pool is approximately 6,500 square yards, the extreme length 330 feet, and the maximum width 225 feet.

Construction of the bathing pool

The special championship area on the south side is 165 ft. long (32 laps to one mile) by 60 ft. wide and the central portion of the pool for general swimming is 330 ft. (16 laps to one mile) by 60 ft.

On the north side is the shallower area, 330 ft. long by a maximum width of 105 ft.

The maximum depth is 15 ft., in the diving area, and the depth at the north side of the shallow area is nil, so that bathers can walk down an artificial sloping beach into the water.

The average depth over the central area is about 5 ft.

The pool contains 1 3/8 million gallons of pure sea water which will be constantly changed, purified, filtered, and chemically treated at the rate of over 172,000 gallons per hour.

As a regular supply of water is available from the Marine Lake, which acts as a huge storage and settlement tank, it is possible (if necessary for cleansing and scrubbing down purposes) to empty the pool at night and refill ready for the following morning.

Filtration And Turnover

As regards filtration and turnover – Three open rigid gravity filters have been constructed, each 20 ft. long by 14 ft. wide with non-corrosive fittings, valves, outlet control, etc., and filled with Leighton Buzzard sand 3 ft. deep.

The total filter area equals 861 square feet and the rate of filtration is 200 gallons per square foot hour the turnover period about eight hours at 172.000 gallons per hour.

The plant includes the usual up-to-date chemical tanks, aerator, ammoniator, chlorinator, air compressor and electric motor for aeration, ditto for agitating filter bed and duplicate 30 b.h.p. centrifugal pumps and electric motors for pumping water from the lake or pool to the filters or from the pool to the lake.

From the filters the pure sea water gravitates to the pool through an ornamental cascade fitted with an electric booster pump and jets under separate valve control. Six other pure water inlets are arranged round the pool all controlled by valves.

Under-water lighting is provided for by twelve special electric lamps fixed in a duct at the deep end of the pool and above water flood lights have also been arranged.

General Description Of Bath Buildings

The shape of the pool, together with certain site restrictions and method of administration, have more of less determined the general lay-out of the buildings in connection with the scheme.

In order to follow the general lay-out it is essential to appreciate the proposed method of administration as this has been an important factor in the general design.

Bathing and sun bathing have increased in popularity in recent years to such proportions that special hygienic methods and systems of control are imperative in order to safeguard the health of the vast numbers of the public interested in the pasttimes.

The sole public access to the bath is the way of the main entrance block on the south side of the bath.

This block consists of administrative offices, comprising manager's office, general office, central pay boxes and turnstiles, mess rooms for male and female attendants, male and female competitors' dressing boxes flanked on each side by three lock-up shops, the total over-all length of the block, including shops, being over 238 ft.

The committee room leads to a large balcony overlooking the deep diving and competition section of the bath.

The public will pay for admission at the main entrance turnstiles and if wishing to bathe will proceed round the promenade (which is elevated approximately 9 ft. 6 in. above the water level) to the entrances of either the ladies' or gentlemen's dressing boxes, where turnstiles will again have to be negotiated and the difference paid for bathing, towels, costumes, etc.

Bathers will be given tickets which must be presented at the towel issuing office; tickets will be stamped and returned together with wrist bands numbered to correspond with the lockers occupying the centre of the corridor.

Having secured towels and bathing costumes, bathers enter the main apartment housing the dressing boxes and lockers, which is a comparatively lofty structure (12 ft. 6 in. high) arranged so as to derive the maximum sunlight. "Glasscrete" panels are inserted in the roof and large horizontal steel windows in the walls give efficient lighting and ventilation.

Bathers will then undress in the dressing boxes and after donning their costumes will place their clothes in the numbered lockers corresponding with the numbered wrist bands issued to them, and after securely locking the doors will then proceed down the staircase to the basement, which is arranged slightly above the bath surround level.

Special foot sprays and showers are provided in the basement, whilst the floor of the exit to bath is so arranged that each bather must perforce pass through an ankle-deep water splash before entering the bath.

Every precaution has been taken to prevent pollution of the bath water by the introduction of a post and rope barrier round the bath surround from which non-bathers will be rigidly excluded.

Conveniences are centrally arranged for the use of bathers.

The dressing boxes are constructed of timber framework, having asbestos sheet divisions with flush panelled doors.

The scheme provides for 108 dressing boxes for ladies and 820 lockers; 148 dressing boxes for gentlemen and 1,084 lockers, and accommodation for 10,000 spectators.

The café and kitchen occupy a central position between the ladies' and gentlemen's dressing boxes.

A first aid department is provided to deal with any casualties which may occur either on the baths premises, Marine Lake or adjacent seashore.

Two wards are provided, each large enough for two beds for male and female patients, also a bathroom and drying chamber for drying people's clothing after accidental immersion, etc.

Two large blocks of conveniences are provided on the bath premises for the use of spectators.

The ladies' block is provided with a mother's room where babies and young children can be attended to, also a parcels office where luggage or light articles can be left in the care of the attendant.

The bath surrounds, spectators' tiers, and promenades are constructed in reinforced concrete, the surrounds being finished with a non-slipping indented surface and the promenades with coloured cement and green granite.

An ornamental fountain cascade forms a central feature in front of the café. At the bath surround level the fountain will be formed in concrete lined with coloured concrete and faience work.

The approximate cost of the work is £89,137.

Mr. L. St. G. Wilkinson, M.Sc., M.Inst, C.E., was responsible for the design of the pool and we are indebted to him for the forgoing notes.

◆ ◆ ◆

THE DESTRUCTION OF NEW BRIGHTON COLLEGE

Liverpool Mercury

Wednesday, 29th October, 1862

We are now enabled to lay before our readers full particulars of the disastrous fire at New Brighton College on Monday night, the announcement of which appeared in yesterday's *Mercury*. The premises, consisting of a capacious house, with stabling, and the necessary out-buildings, were situated midway between Egremont Ferry and New Brighton, and were well known to all frequenters pf the Cheshire shore. At the time of the outbreak of the fire there were in the house besides the family of Dr. Poggi, the principal, Miss Jones, the family governess; Messrs. Cooper and Pawson, the resident masters, Mr. Pollesfen. a gentleman commercially connected with Liverpool, but residing with Dr. Poggi; 24 resident pupils, and several servants. About seven o'clock the attention of one of the female domestics was attracted to the upper part of the building by a strong smell as of fire, and on proceeding to the corridor leading to the attics and to one or two lumber rooms she found it densely filled with smoke which strengthened her suspicion that something was wrong. She instantly informed one of the pupils, and they were proceeding in company to alarm Dr. Poggi, when on the stairs they met Miss Jones, the governess, with one of the younger members of the family, whom she was escorting to bed, and informed her of what they had seen. With great prudence they sent for the doctor, who was seated with Mrs. Poggi in the sitting room (that lady only being confined only a fortnight) and stated that he was wanted; immediately he was acquainted with the facts he rushed upstairs and found the flames pouring from one of the attics and a lumber room opposite, so completely severing all communication with the other rooms on the corridor that any attempt to recover the property which they contained would have been alike futile and dangerous. On the stairs Dr. Poggi met five working men whose attention on the outside had been arrested by the bright light in the upper stories of the house, and by the volumes of smoke which poured from the windows, and who had rushed in to render what assistance they could.

It was, however, quickly discovered that the fire had obtained too strong of the promises to be easily reduced, and attention was consequently turned first to safety of the inmates and then to the recovery of such property as was within reach. The doctor conveyed the news to the inmates, and speedily every member of the family, including Mrs. Poggi and her infant, was placed beyond the reach of harm, and the pupils were scattered. The painful position in which Mrs. Poggi was placed might under such circumstances have occasioned the most serious consequence, but Charles Holland, Esq., a magistrate and a near neighbour, with a sympathy which reflects upon him the highest credit, took Mrs. Poggi and her eight children, with the governess and nurse, to his residence, which they still make their home. Long before this time, crowds of persons, attracted by the flames, had assembled on the spot, and there, arranged and superintended by Mr. Holland, proceeded to remove from the lower part of the premises all the furniture contained in the morning rooms, nursery, library, and dining room. Of course in the excitement and the haste much of the valuable property was damaged and rendered comparatively worthless. The rooms mentioned were, however, cleared, and amongst the property saved is the valuable library of books.

This done, an effort was made to save the property from the next floor, but with the exceptions of a few articles from the bedrooms it was found impossible to rescue any of the valuable property on that floor. The flames had previously burst through the roof, and the weight of the burning joists and timbers falling above the heads of the men engaged on the second floor rendered further efforts extremely dangerous, and they were therefore most reluctantly compelled to abandon the task. The property rescued from the burning pile was removed to the Fort, where it was left in safe custody, but it formed an insignificant portion of the furniture of so large a house, and will be of little value.

At an early period an engine from Birkenhead arrived on the spot, and began to throw a limited quantity of water on the fire, the supply being exceedingly short; but from the first it was felt that all hope beyond that of saving the mere walls was visionary and groundless. It continued, however, to play until three o'clock yesterday morning, when the fire was sufficiently subdued to enable the firemen to return to their homes. The fire burnt with great fury during the early part of the evening, the flames being distinctively visible from the landing stages; indeed, it was at first thought that some vessel lying in the river had ignited, and one of the steam tugs put off to render assistance. but came back when the nature of the conflagration was ascertained. The fire continued to burn throughout the night, and was raging in the cellars even yesterday afternoon, but no further damage was apprehended. Nothing remains but the bare walls of the building, which are in a very dangerous state, if we except the back kitchen and stable, which was preserved from destruction by the efforts of the firemen, who obtained a supply of water from the premises of Mr. J.B. Hughes, a short distance from the spot.

The house, which belongs to a Mr. Kenyon, living near Warrington, is insured, and Dr. Poggi's lost is fully covered by insurance in the Royal Office. The furniture of all the bedrooms, the linen, the wearing apparel of Dr. Poggi and all his family, together with every article which the maters. governess, and 24 pupils possessed, have been destroyed, not one of them having saved even a change of clothing. In addition to this loss, Dr. Poggi only two months since expended £75 in painting and repairing the house so as to render it a more comfortable home for the gentlemen committed to his case. A body of the Cheshire county police from Wallasey, under the charge of Inspector Rowbottom and Sergeant Hindley, were present, and rendered valuable and efficient service, and the greatest praise also is due to the labouring men and sailors, who vied with each other in striving to save from the devouring element as much as possible of the valuable property. To Mr. Holland the reverend gentleman feels laid under great obligation, for the prompt and gentle-manly offer of his residence as a home for himself and family; nor are his friends less cheerfully accorded to Mrs. Murdock, of Manor House, and to J.B. Hughes. Esq., who jointly undertook the charge of the pupils.

The origin of the fire has not been positively ascertained, but there is every reason to think it was occasioned by an explosion of gas in one of the upper rooms. Dr. Poggi having only a few moments before the alarm was given been somewhat startled by the diminution of light in the sitting room; that supposition is also strengthened by the strong smell of gas which pervaded the house when Dr. Poggi first ascended the stairs; but how it became ignited will probably ever remain a mystery. The fire was still smouldering in the cellars of the house yesterday afternoon, but no further mischief was apprehended.

♦ ♦ ♦

A MAN AND HIS WIFE DROWNED

Leeds Mercury

Saturday, 5th July, 1862

On Tuesday night last, a melancholy occurrence took place at Wallasey, which has produced a very painful feeling throughout that parish. A man named Thomas Howard, who was employed as a journeyman painter by Mr. Grinnell, of New Brighton, was drinking at a late hour in a beerhouse kept by a person named Copeland, at Little Brighton. At eleven o'clock, his wife Hannah Howard, who was accompanied by his brother, a lad about fourteen years of age, called for him at the beerhouse, and, it is said, remonstrated with him for getting tipsy and stopping away from his own house and family. The husband became angry and excited, and gave his wife a slap with his open hand on the face. Soon afterwards, however, they left the beerhouse, apparently on friendly terms, and, accompanied by the boy, proceeded along the high road in the direction of their residence, in Green Lane, Wallasey Village. Midway between Little Brighton and Wallasey Village there is a pit known by the name of the "Captain's Pit", from the circumstance of a captain having been drowned in it some years ago. This pit, which in some parts is of considerable depth, is partially open to the high road, and is used for horses and cattle to drink from. On reaching this spot, the intoxicated husband suddenly stopped, pulled off his coat, and rushed into the pit. The wife, alarmed for her husband's safety, followed into the water and seized him round the waist, at the same making an effort to get him out. The boy stood at the edge of the pit, and could render no assistance. The unfortunate woman screamed, and they both were seen by the lad to fall. Their feet had evidently stuck fast in the mud, which, it is said, is unusually deep in this particular pit, and, not being able to raise themselves, both husband and wife were drowned. The youth immediately gave an alarm, and in a few minutes after the sad occurrence, a man named John Booth, who also had been drinking at Copeland's beerhouse at Little Brighton, came up, but he could not muster sufficient resolution to venture into the pit to rescue the unfortunate couple. Other persons were soon on the spot, and drags having been obtained, the bodies were taken out of the water. After being immersed about half an hour, it is scarcely necessary to say that life in each was quite extinct. The bodies were removed by the police to the residence of the deceased. One child is left to mourn the fate of its parents, and it is stated that the mother was pregnant. It is supposed that Howard rushed into the pit for the purpose of frightening his wife, and not with intention of committing suicide.

◆ ◆ ◆

'THE LIGHTHOUSE' HAS FASCINATING NAUTICAL THEME

Wallasey NEWS

18th June, 1966

Birkenhead Brewery Company's new public house, 'The Lighthouse', in Wallasey Village, has been built to replace the 'Lighthouse Inn' which stood on a part of the new site.

It is generally believed that the "Lighthouse Inn" was named after the New Brighton Lighthouse, which was built between 1827 and 1830, as a Shore Light in the shipping approach to Liverpool, using the Crosby Channel.

The Leasowe Lighthouse, built in 1763, displayed four lights to guide the ships coming into Hoyle Lake. The new Lighthouse has been designed to include references to the history of Wallasey and its connections with shipping.

The public bar is called "Red Noses Bar", after the rock formation on the shore which contained caves, believed to have run from the shore to the infamous "Mother Redcaps", the haunt of smugglers and wreckers.

All the features of a traditional bar are incorporated in the "Red Nose Bar", including ample counter space and fixed seating.

Darts Recess

Saddle tan leather upholsters the seats and backs, and several domino tables have been provided, together with a self-contained darts recess, which is lined on the playing end with cork tiles. The room has a split level ceiling.

All the wall surfaces are finished with timber veneered boarding in Chateau oak and birch, except the wall above the fixed seating at the end of the bar. This is used as a display panel mirrored window glass panels from the old Lighthouse.

The flooring is of rubber tiles with large tiles of light and dark tan, patterned with smaller squares of red tiles.

Oak frames the counter and backfitting of the service area and the counter front has glazed panels of material with a nautical theme on oak panels. The counter top is of red plastic, complete with arm rest.

"Mother Redcap's" is the front lounge and has been designed as a focus for the history of Wallasey. The room combines traditional features of beans, a stone fireplace and moulded panelling with a lowered ceiling, contemporary light fittings and vertical panelling.

Painted Mural

Both the panelling and fitments are made of teak, contrasting with copper and the orange shade of the carpet, chairs and stools.

Over the window section of this room is a lowered ceiling, finished with a acoustic tiles and copper facing. The ceiling over the backfitting is used to illuminate this display and a painted mural which depicts the semi-humorous aspect of the Leasowe Light.

Ships of alternate polished copper and teak dorm the counter front, and photographs and paintings of old Wallasey are displayed on the panelled walls.

Several of these photographs are unidentified and customers are asked to provide the answer to the questions; "Who and Where in Wallasey?"

French windows lead from the rear lounge (Trinity House) to a verandah and small garden. In this room, copies of the original drawings from Eddystone Lighthouse, Smalls Rock Lighthouse, Needles and Bishops Rock, together with photographs of new and traditional lighthouses can be seen.

In "Trinity House"

Natural rosewood is used for the panelling in this room, which is either full height or panelling with white painted surfaces to ceiling level.

The ceiling is at two levels, the lower level being finished with acoustic tiles and copper facing, and the higher level framed with beams, giving diamond-shaped panels finished in blue material, creating a lantern light impression.

The service area had a backfitting with silvered display glass featuring boats and water, whilst the counter front has display panels of lighthouses and shields.

The room is fully carpeted, with red-hide covered seats and tables with natural rosewood tops.

Beer Cellar

A feature of "Mother Redcap's" and "Trinity House" is that customers may be invited by the management to view the beer cellar by way of a secret passage and staircase, thus gaining a certificate as a qualified inspector and taster of the brew from "The Lighthouse".

The beer cellar is temperature controlled and the beer is served by metered measure dispensers.

During the summer months, customers can take of the fine weather by going through the French windows to the verandah. This leads to a small garden which has a rock pool and a small stream. A special garden service is available for customers who go on to the verandah.

The new premises have been designed with a central service to all rooms and they also have an off-sales shop. Incorporated in the central service is a preparation area for snacks, which is fully tiled and provided with stainless steel and plastic covered worktops.

Mechanical ventilation is provided to all parts and oil-fired central heating to the ground and first floor.

Manager's Flat

On the first floor is the manager's flat, which provides comfortable and attractive accommodation, consisting of four bedrooms, lounge, kitchen, bathroom and office.

The architects responsible for this building are the Architect's Department of the Birkenhead Brewery Company Ltd. – chief architect, Jonathan D. Bingham – who are also responsible for all the internal and external furniture and fitments.

❖ ❖ ❖

CORONATION OF QUEEN ELIZABETH II

It Was A Great Day For The Children

Wallasey News

6th June 1953

Coronation Day was party day for thousands of children in all parts of the Borough and, despite threatening rain and a cold wind, tables and chairs were brought into many of the streets, and jellies, lemonade, cakes and trifles disappeared with alarming rapidity.

Other streets, playing safe with the weather, booked church halls and schoolrooms for their parties and practically every school and hall in the borough echoed to the sound of children's excited and happy voices.

The Major and Mayoress (Ald. and J.P. Ashton) visited as many parties as possible and a number of local councillors called in to see the children having a good time at other celebrations.

Over fifty children who attended the Edith Road party will be able to boast in later years that the traffic was stopped for them on Coronation Day because as their Coronation Queen, fourteen years old Nora Sadler went in procession with ten attendants to Riverside School, police held back passing cars to let them go by.

Children of Edith Road were mostly in fancy dress and when it came to choosing whose was the best, nine years old Maureen

Sadler, carried off first prize as a soldier of the Queen. At Riverside School the children, with 14 old age pensioners, settled down to tea and afterwards Coronation cups and saucers and other souvenirs were given out.

Celebrations in Charlotte Street

The crowning of the Queen was carried out by Cllr. B. Brooker, who was accompanied by Mrs. Brooker, and the organisation was done by Mrs. S. Thompson, Mrs. Hughes, Mrs. J. Lockley, Mrs. Blackmore and Miss. E. Yates with a band of helpers.

After the party Edith Road didn't forget friends in hospital and sometime this week Mrs Annie Seary, who was 86 on Coronation Day, received in St. Catherine's Hospital, a large basket of fruit and the bouquet which had been carried by the Coronation Queen.

Children living in the first 25 houses of Gorsedale Road saw their magnificent cake, which was in the form of a crown, long before the time came for eating.

The cake stood with coloured lights shining down over it in the window of number twenty-one for quite a while before the party. Decorated with yellow icing studded with silver, green and red, the cake was made by Mrs. S. Barrow, of Eton Road. In front stood a model of Queen Elizabeth.

But the twenty-five children soon made short of the cake in the infants' hall of Gorsedale Road on Tuesday even though they had just eaten ice cream, cakes, jelly and so on. After games and dancing they went home hugging a toy, a mug and 6d. each. Their party was organised by Mr. J. McEvoy and Mrs. F. Jamieson with helpers.

The middle section of Gorsedale Road held their party in St. Peter's Hall and just before ten o'clock things were still going with a swing - so much so that when technicians recording a Coronation events called in to get a few impressions they were treated to a lusty rendering of In a Golden Coach. Games were held during the evening with prizes for the winners and when music was needed, blind pianist, Mr. William Gowling, who was present with a number of blind friends from Cumberland, Stockport, Bootle and Speke, obliged.

Heading the eager band of organiser's and helpers were Mrs. C. Lewis, Mrs. J. Wright, Mrs. Burleigh and Mrs. Hamilton.

Forty children at the Rossett Place party in Derby Hall will be seeing themselves on a screen at the home of Mrs. E.M. Patterson shortly, for Mrs. Patterson's son-in-law was busy throughout Coronation Day with his cine cinema. During the day prizes won in the games and races were presented by Mr. G.L. Reakes, who also distributed Coronation souvenirs, cups and saucers.

Credit for the Rossett Place party organisation goes to Mrs. E.M. Patterson and a committee of helpers.

Next door in Greenfield Street celebrations went on until 2.30 on Wednesday morning and with music blazing from a radiogram over a hundred men and women danced and sung the night away.

Earlier they had entertained 84 children and seen Cllr. A. Noel Owens crown eleven years old Irene Davies, whose birthday falls in April on the same day as the Queen's, Coronation Queen. Then she, with her two attendants, Pauline Molley and Gillian Upton, and page Robert Parry, went with all the children to Marymount Convent.

It was a red carpet day for Greenfield Street, literally as well as metaphorically, and throughout the celebrations a long carpet stretched over the specially built stage and down the entire road. And to remember this special day each child was presented with an attractive certificate indicating that they had attended the party.

Donkey's Paid A Visit

There were also some unusual visitors to the Greenfield Street party - four donkeys turned up to help the children enjoy themselves!

It was not only the children who made the most of the arrival of the animals either, and their party presence helped to make the party, organised by Mrs. M. Robinson, Mrs. E. Upton, Miss. M. Ward, Mrs. M. Upton, Mrs. E. Sackey, Mrs. C. Thornton and all the neighbours, go with a swing.

The same donkeys also called in to see 125 children enjoying themselves in Silverlea Avenue. There the children had been celebrating right through the day from ten o'clock when they went in two double decker buses for a tour round Wallasey and Birkenhead.

After races in Belvidere Field these children had come back to Silverlea Avenue where a ten pound Coronation cake decorated in red, white and blue, and topped with a marzipan crown, awaited them.

Souvenirs were distributed not only to all the children, but to the old people in the Avenue, too. And at the end of the day roles were reversed, the children presenting gifts to the organiser's, Mrs. J. Ellis and Mrs. N. Taylor.

In Ashville Road, Seacombe, 53 children had tea, games, community singing and dancing, and after a bus tour to see the decorations of Moreton, Birkenhead and Wallasey, and at the end of it all received a Coronation mug and Princess Anne saving stamps. All the neighbours helped for the party headed by Mrs. A. Williams, Mrs. N. Murray, and Mrs. J. Tucker.

Massey Park Party

Ninety-five children of Massey Park competed in twenty-one sporting events on Oldershaw School field on Coronation Day, and after such strenuous exercise were more than ready for their large tea. One hundred and twenty-six oranges which two of the organiser's, Mr. and Mrs. H.S. Ashworth, won in a competition, were distributed and each child received 5/- piece and a Coronation handkerchief. After tea came a puppet show at the Roycroft Hall and then the excited children returned to Massey Park where the triangular green in the centre was floodlit showing up a large model of a crown made by Mrs. Ashworth.

During the day the Mayor called in with the Town Clerk, Mr. A. G. Harrison, and Cllr. J.R. Lindsay, who with Cllr. S.F. Chalk, had given the Massey Park neighbours a lot of help with their party.

Chairman of the organising committee was Mr. J. Deanne, treasurer, Mr. F. Jefferies and Mr. and Mrs. Ashworth were vice-chairman and secretary, respectively.

A pageant, which went back to the first Queen Elizabeth, was put on by the children of Prescot Street, New Brighton, when their Coronation Queen, nine years' old Barbara Lythgoe was crowned, and after this spectacle a fireworks display, lasting nearly an hour, was held.

In between the two events came, of course, a bumper tea at which the centre piece was a two feet square Coronation cake decorated with a miniature golden coach drawn by two horses.

Liscard Road (town centre) view of celebrations. View towards junction with Wallasey Road and Seaview Road

To finish of their Coronation day what could be better than the old favourites - chips and pop? Certainly the 30 children of Prescot Street thoroughly enjoyed their supper treat and went off very happy with the party arrangements made by Mr. and Mrs. Sixsmith, Mr. W. Church, Mr. Robinson and Mrs. Earl.

Coronation Day coincided with the birthday of Mrs. F. Watson, one of the organisers of the Melbourne Street and district party, and after all the ice cream and cakes had been eaten and all the lemonade drunk, the children presented Mrs. Watson with flowers and a pair of nylons.

This party, for nearly a hundred children, took place at the Ennerdale Church Hall where races were run and souvenirs given out.

Upper Brighton Parties

Despite the fact that she is over sixty years of age, and, as well as looking after her own house, still goes to work, Mrs. E. Pemberton organised a party for eight-four children of Sutton

Road on Tuesday.

The party held at the Field Road Mission was attended by the Mayor, Ald. and Mrs. R.Y. Knagg, Cllr. and Mrs. T. Mann. Cllr. and Mrs. Morris, and Cllr. and Mrs. B. Stroude.

Cakes, lemonade, and all the other delicacies that made a special tea were there in galore but even so, there is enough money left over to take the children for an outing to Bell Vue when the weather gets warmer.

Children of Sutton Road were to have been joined by some children from the Albion Street home but, because of illness, the kiddies were unable to leave the house. However, they did not miss their food for their share was sent with souvenir mugs filled with sweets, by the Sutton Road residents.

Parcels of food were sent to the home by the Sandridge Road party organisers who were also to have entertained some of the children.

Sandridge Road held their party in the Field Road Mission, and they too were joined by the Mayor and the four Councillors who visited the Sutton Road kiddies.

During the afternoon there was plenty of singing with the accompaniment of an accordion, and when it was over the children went home carrying Coronation mugs printed with the name of their road. Old people in the road were given an ashtray and the men got special presentations of chocolates. Women without children were not forgotten either and to them went a lapel brooch of the Queen.

Sandridge Road party arrangements were carried out by Mrs. E. Lowndes, Mrs. J. Shirley and Mrs. A. Towers.

A colourful scene greeted the eye of the Tick Tock Cafe, New Brighton, on Tuesday, when 80 children of Grosvenor Drive, and Seymour Street East and West, were given their Coronation party.

Following the serving of tea, gifts of Coronation mugs, ball pens, sweets, chocolates and biscuits brought the party to a climax, and later music and games with mothers joining in, brought the party to a close.

Among the band of willing workers were Mrs. Marsden and Miss. Pollock and Miss. Balshaw, who decorated the room and the tables.

Nearly 140 children were entertained in the Gresford Place area, Egremont. Each child was given a Coronation cup filled with sweets, and the party ended with a bus tour of Wirral.

The Mayor paid a visit in the afternoon to Limekiln Lane, Poulton, where sixty-four children and twenty old age pensioners saw a variety show and had a street tea. The children were taken on a bus tour, and received presents.

Children of Walmsley Street and Greenwood Lane put on a special show at their Coronation party, which was attended by Cllr. and Mrs. H. Ellison, Cllr. A.E. Warriner and Cllr. W. Farrell.

With twelve scenes and a cast of 24 children, the show contained four complete changes of costume.

The party was held in the Presbyterian Hall, Manor Road, and after the tea, each child was given a Coronation glass filled with sweets and fruit.

Organising was carried out by Mrs. Parry, Mrs. Wheeler, Mrs. Montgomery, Mrs. Bowden, Mrs. Crosden and Mrs Chittick, and the costumes were made by Mrs. Parry, Mrs. D. Parry and Mrs. Little.

Wednesday was Egerton Street's day for celebrating, There were ice creams, sweets, cakes and a host of good things to eat and later each child was given a Coronation mug to take home. Their happy day ended with a tour by bus of Liverpool and Birkenhead decorations.

But the next day Egerton Street remembered In procession they walked down to the nEw Brighton war memorial to lay a wreath at the foot of the column.

Next Monday their week of special events comes to an end with a trip to the Floral Pavilion. The organisation was carried out by Mrs. P. Henri, Mrs. E. Williams, Mrs. M. Cross. Mrs. J. Gilmore and Mrs. E. Banks.

Giant Cavalcade And Torchlight Procession

End To Eventful Coronation Week

6th June 1953

All the romance of the old days when Morris dancing troupes and processions led by glittering hands or horse drawn chariots were seen on English, will be revived in Wallasey today.

> **WALLASEY CORONATION CELEBRATIONS**
>
> EX-SERVICEMEN'S
>
> # TORCHLIGHT PROCESSION
>
> SUNDAY, 7th JUNE, 1953
>
> Assembly 9-30 p.m.   Leave 10-15 p.m. for
> Tower Promenade, New Brighton.   Central Park.
>
> **TORCH - BEARER'S CARD**
>
> SEE OVER FOR DETAILS.

A giant procession of Morris dancers, decorated vehicles, and four bands, will be led by a horse drawn chariot through the town from Seacombe to New Brighton Tower Grounds, where colourful displays and numerous competitions will, if the weather is fine, be watched by thousands.

Marshalled by the Chief Constable, Mr. John Ormerod, the procession will leave St. Paul's Road, Seacombe, at 1.30 p.m. and will march through Liscard Road, Liscard Village, Rake Lane, Rowson Street, St. James Road, Atherton Street, Wellington Road, New Brighton Promenade, Egerton Street and Molyneux Drive.

Gates will be opened at the Tower at 2 p.m. and until the procession arrives at about three the crowd will be entertained by the Wallasey branch of the Women's League of Health and Beauty.

The afternoon's programme includes Morris dancing and entertainment by special troupes, jazz band contests for prize money totaling over £100, jumping displays by show ponies and intermingling amongst the crowd will be the Carnival mystery man, who when challenged correctly will present a £1 note to the challenger.

Prizes will be presented by the Mayoress (Mrs. J.P. Ashton), who will be present with the Mayor (Ald.J.P. Ashton) and other alderman and councillors.

To-morrow evening ex-servicemen will march in the light of 400 torches which they will carry from the Tower Promenade at 10.15 p.m. through Victoria Road, Rowson Street, Seabank Road, King Street and Church Street to Central Park.

In the park the parade will be viewed by the Mayor and other officials from an illuminated rostrum.

The parade will be led by the 1st Battalion The King's Regt. and spectators in the park will be invited to join in the singing of hymns by the light of torches.

Opening Ceremony

This will be the finale to a week crowded with events - a week which began last Saturday when the Mayor, officially opening the week's celebrations, dispatched Elizabethan dressed couriers on horseback carrying the national flag to Moreton.

Several hundred watched this ceremony which took place outside a floodlit Town Hall and heard reports on the progress of the two riders as they neared Moreton Cross.

At the Cross, garlanded and decorated for the occasion, the residents assembled to welcome the Mayor and Town Clerk at 11.30 p.m. and after the Town Clerk had read the loyal proclamation representatives of the British Legion hoisted the flag.

The Mayor's civic service and the Town's Coronation service were incorporated at St. Hilary's Church on Sunday morning.

Before the service a civic procession headed by Foden's Motor Works Band left Manor Road school and marched via Manor Road, Liscard Village, Wallasey Road and Claremount Road to the Church.

After the service, during which a sermon was preached by the Mayor's chaplain, the Rev. R.F. Johnson, the procession returned to Manor Road by the same route.

Although the weather marred Coronation festivities during the rest of the week it could not damp the ardour of the people.

Despite all too frequent heavy and prolonged downfalls of rain there were dry interludes which enabled most of the street parties and open air events to run according to schedule, though the drill display in which 1,400 children took part had to be held on Thursday instead of Wednesday. Items at the display included national dancing, gymnastics, free standing movements, and skipping demonstrations

The children's touring show "Coronation Capers" met with great success during the week and presents its final performances today at 4 p.m. and 6 p.m in Belvidere Field.

Other events which have been held included a Coronation motor car and motor cycle rally on King's Parade on Saturday and Sunday, two massed concerts by 500 children conducted by Mr. Albert Price, Wallasey's music organiser, and many dances and fairs in all parts of the borough.

Oldershaw school playing field was taken over by members of the Wallasey unit of the Women's Junior Air Corps last Saturday for a Coronation garden fete during which 14 years old Barbara Hodkinson was crowned Rose Queen.

The crowing ceremony was performed by Mrs. E. Jefferies, wife of Lieut. Jefferies, of the Sea Cadets, and many those present were Ald. J.H. Wensley, who opened the fete, and Mrs. Wensley, who was presented with a spray by Sgt. Audrey Johnson.

After the crowning a colourful display of dancing was given by dancers carrying hoops decorated with roses, and then the three hundred who attended, visited the various stalls on the field.

Prizewinning Streets And Houses

6th June 1953

So high was the standard of street, house and business premises decorations in Wallasey that the judges, led by the Mayor (Ald. J.P. Ashton) have decided to give additional consolation prizes.

Winners are :-

Best decorated streets -- £5 each to Felicity Grove, Greenfield Street and Middle Road. £2/2/- each to Lily Grove, Beaconsfield Street, Brooke Street, and Rossett Place.

Best decorated house (rateable value under £13) -- £5 to Mrs, Bristol, 7 Fairfax Road.

Best decorated house (rated over £13) -- £10 to Mr. Cousins, 58 Littledale Road; £5 to Mr. G.A. Payne, 11 Marsden Road; £1 each to Mr. P. Winstanley, 29 Manor Road, Mrs. Johnstone, 46 Trafalgar Road, Mr. Prenton, 201 Seaview Road, Mrs. Shirley, 17 Sandridge Road.

Best decorated business premises -- £10 to W. Dutton, The

Tuck Shop, 413 Poulton Road, £2/2/- each to Mr. J. Cairns (Community Club, St. Paul's Road), Mrs. Elliot (Needle Art King Street), Messrs Coker's, 67 Seaview Road, and Messrs. H.M. Ellison, Liscard Village.

Scouts' Big Bonfire

6th June 1953

The huge signal bonfire on the Breck, built by the Boy Scouts from materials supplied by the Corporation, was set alight at 10 0'Clock on Coronation night by the Mayor (Ald. J.P.Ashton). Soon Wallasey's blazing welcome to the Queen shone over Wirral.

Despite the heavy and steady downfall of rain, a crowd of several hundred watched this ceremony and then joined in community singing as the bonfire burned itself smaller and smaller.

Fireworks were let off in the background by family parties eager to contribute to the festivities and play their part in the welcome to the Queen.

Under bad weather conditions over the weekend Scouts from 3rd (Emmanuel) and other groups spent the period in camp on the Breck, and under the leadership of Mr. Bohs build the bonfire.

The Scouts' press correspondent, Mr. Robert J.Bell, writes expressing the Scouts' thanks to the Borough Surveyor and Engineer (Mr. H. Crowther) and his staffs for their help and to the police and fire services for their duties on the Breck on Tuesday night.

Carnival Parade Seen

By Large Crowds
13th June 1953

Something of the old time carnival gaiety returned to Wallasey on Saturday when in pleasant weather the Coronation parade from Seacombe to New Brighton enlivened the crowd-lined streets. The turn-out was highly creditable to the organisers, particularly when it is borne in mind that similar processions in Liverpool and Birkenhead drew many individual entres for fancy dress.

The procession, headed by the Barton Hall Works Band and a contingent from Wilkie's Circus, left St. Paul's Road, Seacombe, marshalled under the direction of the Chief Constable, Mr. John Ormerod, O.B.E., and proceeded to the Tower Grounds.

Prior to the arrival of the procession there was a display by members of the Wallasey branch of the Women's League of Health & Beauty. On reaching the Tower Grounds the parade was reviewed by the Mayor and Mayoress of Wallasey (Ald. J.P. Ashton and Mrs. Ashton). Watched by a crowd of about 5,000 people, it provided a striking spectacle and the Mayor made the remark that it was the finest carnival parade seen in Wallasey for many years.

During the afternoon there were Morris dancing contests, entertaining troupes contests and a display of jumping by ponies which was greatly enjoyed. The ponies were ridden by Misses Irene O'Brien. Pauline Jessop, and Betty Hale, of the British Show Ponies Society, who came specially from West Derby to give the display.

Results : Open Morris dancing : 1. Greenfield Stars, Flint; 2. Imperial Troupe. Bootle; 3. (equal), Grosvenor Troupe, Haydock and Harlequins Troupe, Little Sutton.

Entertaining Troupes : 1. Wallasey Kilties; 2. Pegrams Crazy Gang, Liverpool; 3. Maree Kay School, Wallasey.

Jazz Band : Walk over, Gwersyllt United Star Jazz Band.

Decorated trade vehicles : Birkenhead Co-operative Society, Ltd.

Comedy vehicle : New Brighton Rugby Football Club.

Most spectacular vehicle : National Hospital Service Reserve.

Decorated cycle : Marylyn Brown, Wallasey.

Members of the Committee, which had been engaged on organising the parade since last October, are Messrs. C.E. Protector (chairman), Jackson Earle (vice-chairman), Jack Taylor (hon. secretary), Jack Taylor (hon. secretary), C.A. Huntington (hon. treasurer), A.W. Micklewright (hon. publicity officer), Cllrs. Stanley R. Baker. J. Lindsay and T. Mann, Mesdames Olive lloyd, Messrs. H.G. Beattie, A. Clement, F.R. Ferns, H.C. Gurney, F.W. Harrison, F.C. Jenkinson and F. Jones.

The success of the parade has encouraged the committee to entertain the idea of making it an annual event, the organisers feeling confident from the experience gained that they can put on an even better show.

One of the most admired of the dancing troupes was the Gunners' Troupe from Llandudno, sponsored by the Royal Artillery Association, Llandudno. They were dressed in the uniform of the Royal Horse Artillery and presented a colourful scene.

Torchlight Procession

The Coronation celebrations ended on Sunday night with an ex-Service men's torchlight procession in which members of the following organisations took part -- British Legion, R.A. Association, R.N. Old Comrades Association, R.A.F.A., Mersey Far Easters P.O.W. Association, 6th Cheshire (Wallasey) Home Guard. The stewards were members of the local branch of Toc H. British Legion took part.

Headed by the band of the 1st Battalion of the King's Regiment, the procession marched from New Brighton promenade via Victoria Road, Rowson Street, King Street and Church Street to Central Park, where they were received by a civic party including the Mayor and Mayoress (Ald. and Mrs. J.P. Ashton).

Wallasey's Motor Bus Department's illuminated historic tableau was in the procession.

◆ ◆ ◆

NEWS IN SHORT 2

Lifeboats

The Lancaster Gazette
Saturday, 20th October, 1821

Several lifeboats, of very large dimensions, and constructed on different principles, are, we understand, now building at Liverpool, to be stationed on the adjacent coast. One of them, we have heard, will be stationed at Wallasey.

Melancholy Accident

Liverpool Mercury
Friday, 15th October, 1824

On Tuesday evening last, Mr. Hampson, of Wallasey, while proceeding down the steps at the south end of the Prince's Dock pier to the steamboat, either in consequence of a broken step, or under the influence of a fit, fell down the precipitous flight of steps, and was so much injured by the fall, that, though attended by several of the most eminent professional men, he expired yesterday morning. The accident affords an additional proof of the absolute necessity of some amendment in the structure of the several landing places on our piers, on which subject we have so frequently urged what we conceive to be the wish of the public.

Steam Boat Incident

Liverpool Mercury
Friday, 11th March, 1825

On Monday morning the steam boat Alice, property of

Mr.Parry, of Seacombe Ferry, took fire by some accident, whilst at anchor off that place. As soon as the fire was discovered the men endeavoured to extinguish the flames; but, finding their efforts unavailing, they determined to scuttle the vessel, as the only chance of saving her from total destruction. She was immediately scuttled, and sank opposite the hotel. As she lay on the edge of the bank, the ebb tide (which was remarkably strong) forced her over into the deep water, where she now lies, and is likely to prove a complete wreck. The Alice was one of the finest steam boats on the river, and sailed very fast. Mr.Parry, we understand, was only half insured : his loss by the accident will, therefore, we regret to state, be very great.

The Star Chamber

The York Herald
Saturday, 27th August, 1836

The materials forming the interior of the old Star Chamber in the ancient Palace of Westminster were at the recent sale purchased by the proprietor of the Leasowe Hotel, on the Cheshire coast, where, having been arranged into an apartment, it forms no inconsiderable object of attraction to antiquarian visitors.

New Independent Chapel

Liverpool Mercury
Friday, 9th September, 1842

Yesterday week a chapel, in connection with the congregational Independents, was opened at Liscard, near New Brighton [Rake Lane]. The morning service was conducted by the Rev. Dr. Raffles, of this town; he took his text from the words of the eleventh psalm, "The Lord is in his holy temple". The evening service was conducted by the Rev. Caleb Morris of London, assisted by the Rev. Messrs. Sleigh. Appleford, Pridie, and Tallstall. The chapel has been built, and provided with an organ, at the sole expense of J.A. Marsden, Esq., and by him presented as a free gift to the above body of Dissenters. The building combines the simple beauty of the Lancet Gothic, or Tudor style of architecture, with suitability for the present as well as prospective wants of an increasing congregation. The site is well chosen for effect, as it stands on high ground, and forms a prominent object from the river, and, though now rather away from the more populous part of Seacombe, yet, being near to such a favourable resort as New Brighton, a very few years will, most likely, find it surrounded by a dense and wealthy neighbourhood. When completed, it will give upwards of 800 sittings; but at present the upper part is only finished on a level with the galleries, to accommodate about 500 people. There is more than usual interest connected with it, as the spirited donor has procured and fitted it up with the pulpit and some of the oak pews of the chapel which was occupied by the Rev. Dr. Isaac Watts, in St. Mary Axe. London, and the marble monument commemorative of that eminent divine he has had, in fine taste, placed in the vestibule of the choir.

Accidental Death

Liverpool Mercury
Friday, 26th March, 1847

On Saturday week, a young lad named Gordon, son of Mr. Gordon, butcher, New Brighton Cheshire, was accidentally burnt to death. He went to a piggery near his father's house, and while playing with some Lucifer matches, a quantity of shavings lying near were ignited. The flames communicated to his clothes, and the result was, that before any assistance arrived, he was so much burnt that he died shortly afterwards.

Inquest Of A Supposed Follower Of William III

London Daily News

Thursday, 20th January, 1848

On Sunday last a man named Appleton perceived a human skull embedded in the clay near the shore of the Mersey, between Seacombe and Liscard; on further examination he found it was a part of a skeleton, which he conveyed to the Seacombe Hotel. It was inspected by different medical gentlemen, and information having been given to the coroner, an inquest was held on Monday. The skeleton was produced in a hamper. The thigh bones were each about 1 feet 8 inches in length, indicating that the deceased must have been a tall person. The upper and lower arm bones were in proportion. The vertebrae of the spinal column were produced, but loose. The skull was nearly perfect in form. The bones generally were quite blackened. The teeth were perfect, of a good colour, and firm in the sockets, showing that the deceased at the time of his death was, in all probability, in the prime of manhood. There was no appearance of flesh adhering to these remains. The body had been apparently buried in north and south position. Amongst the bones found near the skull was a queue, or pig tail, very neatly plaited, and tied with black silk ribbon. The hair was black and long. Close to the skeleton were found, and also produced, portions of wearing apparel, apparently front facings of upper garments or coats, rounded, in the old country style, from the lappel to the bottom of the skirt, and each perforated with numerous well-worked button-holes. There might be about twenty button-holes in each. No buttons or buckles were, however, found, so far as we can learn; otherwise a date possibly have been arrived at. Some coins were, about a year ago, found near the spot. There were guineas of the reign of Charles II, and nineteen of them were acknowledged to be found. Some of them were sold at 38s. each. Some few ancient copper coins have also been picked up in the same locality. Various are the conjectures amongst the gossips in the neighbourhood as to the identity or quality of the deceased - some conceiving that he was one of the nobles in the retinue of William III., when on his passage to Ireland, just before the battle of the Boyne; and it will be remembered that William embarked at "the Leasowes". near Hoylake. Some of the retainers, it would appear, landed upon and embarked from various points in the Wirral Peninsula. The King himself, it is recorded, slept at Wallasey, about 2½ miles distant, on the eve of his departure. This, however, as well as other speculations as to the body, rests upon grounds too vague and uncertain to be seriously tenable. The jury, at the inquest, returned the only verdict at which they could arrive under the circumstances - to the effect, that the remains were those of a man unknown, but how he came to his death there was no evidence to show.

Advertisement

The Blackburn Standard
Wednesday, 22th June, 1859

Valuable Hotels & Dwelling Houses

To Be Sold By Auction

By Messrs. Walker & Ackerley

On Wednesday, the 6th Day of July, at One o'clock, at the Clarendon Rooms, South John Street, Liverpool, in the following or such other Lots as may be agreed upon at the time of sale, and subject to such conditions of sale as shall be then produced, by order of the Trustees of the Will of James Atherton, Esq. :--

LOT 1. -- TWO semi-detached DWELLING-HOUSES, in Montpelier Crescent, in the occupation of Joseph Shee and Richard Guinnell, at rents amounting together to £140.

2. – TWO semi-detached DWELLING-HOUSES, in Montpelier Crescent, in the occupation of John Dredge, at the rent of £120.

3. – TWO semi-detached DWELLING-HOUSES, in Montpelier Crescent, one in the occupation of E. Erickson, at the rent

of £60, and the other House (being partly supplied with Furniture by the owners) in the occupation of J.Oldham, at the rent of £120.

4. – TWO semi-detached DWELLING-HOUSES, in the occupation of J. Morgan, at the rent of £120.

All the above Dwelling Houses are commodious, and have been fine Sea Views.

5. – The valuable HOTEL, called the 'ALBION HOTEL', in or near Montpelier Crescent, with the billiard room adjoining, in the occupation of Mr. C.S. Fielding, at the rent of £100.

6. – The valuable HOTEL called the 'New Brighton Hotel' in the main road leading to the Ferry, in the occupation of Thomas Longden, at the rent of £130.

The whole of the above Lots are Freehold of Inheritance.

For further particulars apply to Mr. Henry Cole, surveyor, 34, Castle Street; and Messrs. Carson, Ellis & Field, Solicitors, 3, Fenwick Street, Liverpool.

The New Brighton Artillery Volunteers

Liverpool Mercury
Monday, 27th August, 1860

The 4th Cheshire (New Brighton) artillery volunteers commenced firing practice on Saturday afternoon last, at the Rock Perch Battery, and the 5th Cheshire (Birkenhead) artillery corps, under the command of Captain Laird, attended by invitation to witness the firing of their comrades in arms, by whom they were afterwards hospitality entertained. Five rounds of blank cartridges were fired, namely, two rounds with intervals of three-quarters of a minute, one with intervals of ten seconds, one with intervals of eight seconds, and one with intervals of about two seconds, and the manner in which the guns were handled called forth the admiration of the regular artillerymen in charge of the fort. The spectators included a large number of ladies and gentlemen living at New Brighton and in the neighbourhood, for whose gratification the band of the 5th performed several pieces of music during the evening.

Central Relief Society For Wallasey

Liverpool Mercury
Tuesday, 12th October, 1869

Last evening a meeting was held in the Assembly Room, at the Egremont Hotel, for the purpose of Wallasey. Mr T. Bouch occupied the chair, and amongst those present were Major Chambres, the Rev. W.C. Greene, Messrs. H. Pooley, C. Holland, W.S. Caine, Harold Littledale, H. Wall, &c. -- The Chairman, in opening the proceedings, stated that he had been a member of the Central Relief Society in Liverpool since its commencement. That society had risen to such dimensions that last year they had raised £9200 in donations and subscriptions, and about £900 from the sale of soup and bread, making altogether a sum of £10,100, which was a very fair sample of what societies of that kind could do. He described the mode of relief as being very simple, and said that in Liverpool the operations of the society had the effect of considerably diminishing mendacity. He urged that the clergy of all denominations in the parish should assist a society of this sort, and held that it would be wise and to the advantage of the institution that they should all act with unanimity.

Inquest At New Brighton

Liverpool Mercury
20th November 1870

An inquest was held yesterday at New Brighton, by Mr.Churton, coroner, on the body of John Green, aged 50, keeper of the Rock lighthouse, New Brighton. It appeared that the unfortunate man, about ten o'clock on Monday night last ascended the ladder for the purpose of examining the light. About ten minutes afterwards he was found lying insensible on the balcony by his assistant. He was at once conveyed to his home at New Brighton, and Dr. Mushet was called in, but he died on the following day. A verdict of "Accidental death" was returned.

New Brighton -- Skeleton Found

Liverpool Mercury
Tuesday, 19th September, 1876

TO CORRESPONDENTS.

"On Tuesday last the workers engaged excavating for the foundation of the New Brighton Aquarium found the skeleton of a human body, which they placed in a shed on the ground. The remains were found about three feet below the flooring of one of the houses that originally stood there, known by the name of the "Devil's Nest", and which were pulled down two years ago. Up to this day (Monday) the skeleton still remains in the shed, and, though known to the police, no action has been taken; and my object in writing you is in hope that an inquiry might be held, and so put an end to the indifferent rumour now in circulation, for about 18 years ago a builder from Seacombe, after leaving here for his home, was never afterwards seen."
Watch.
New Brighton

Selling Drink On Unlicensed Premises

Liverpool Mercury
Thursday, 7th November, 1878

At the Liscard Petty Sessions, yesterday, before Messrs. W. Chambres, I. Penny, G.B. Kerferd, L. Mann, and W.T. Jacob. Mr. Frank Redfern Hindle, landlord of the Griffin

Inn, Victoria Road, Seacombe, appeared on an adjourned summons charging him with selling intoxicating liquors on an unlicensed portion of his premises. It appeared that the defendant had enlarged his place of business by the addition of adjoining property. At the annual licensing session the magistrates refused to include under the license the enlarged portion of the premises. On the 12th ultimo Inspector Lawton purchased some whiskey in the unlicensed part of the building, and as this was considered an infringement of the act of Parliament, the defendant was summoned. Mr. Bremner, who was for the defence, contended that the law had not been broken so long as there was continuity of premises, with no change in the occupation. The magistrates held that the defendant had committed an offence against his license, and inflicted a penalty of £5 and costs. John Upton, of the Travellers' Rest beerhouse, Wallasey Village, was also fined £5 and costs for a similar offence on the same day, he having sold to the police a half pint of beer on a new portion of his premises. In both cases Mr. Bremner gave notice of appeal.

Seacombe Licensing Applications

Liverpool Mercury
Friday, 24th August, 1888

John Hughes, beerseller, Seacombe, applied for a full license to the Wallasey Castle Hotel, Seacombe, Mr. F. Smith supported the application, and Mr. R.B. Moore opposed on behalf of the Welsh Presbyterian Church, Liscard Road, and others. Mr. Smith stated that the applicants present held a wine and beer licence at the Five Bars Rest beerhouse, which was near the premises in respect of which he applied. The hotel would be particularly adapted to accommodate master of vessels, who constantly had a difficulty of finding good accommodation of this kind. At the time the application was made there were only 295 houses in the district, and there were now 1370 new houses erected, so that now there 1660 houses, for the comfort and supply of which there were only two licensed houses. -- This application, which was opposed by Mr. Moore on behalf of the Welsh Presbyterian Church in the neighbourhood, was refused.

James Hobell, applied for a full license of the Brighton Hotel, situate at the junction of Brighton Street and Buchanan Road, Seacombe. Mr. R.B Moore appeared for the applicant, and Mr. Peddar opposed on behalf of some of the ratepayers. The Rev. R. Peart, minister of the Seacombe Wesleyan Chapel, objected to the license being granted, as it would be an objection both to the congregation of the chapel ann the Sunday Schools.. It was contended that, in consequence of the rising population and the distance from any other public houses, the hotel had now become a necessity. A large number of the residents in the neighbourhood had signed a memorial in favour of the licence being granted. The application was granted by the bench.

Alice Morris, of the Royal Oak Hotel, Seacombe, applied for a full license. Mr. R.B. Moore supported the application, which was refused.

William Ashbourne, of the Bird In Hand beerhouse, applied for a full license. Mr Stewart appeared for the applicant. The application was refused.

Mr. Albert Graham, of the Brighton Hotel beerhouse, applied for a spirit license. Mr. A. F. Moore appeared in support of the application, which was refused.

Suicide Of A Wallasey Lady

Liverpool Mercury
Wednesday, 22nd January, 1890

A painful sensation has been created in the neighbourhood of Wallasey by the untimely death of Mrs. Brewin, the wife of Mr. Joseph Brewin, of the Mosslands, Wallasey. The circumstances of her demise - which occurred on Saturday - are sad, and, out of respect to the feelings of her friends, they were not allowed to transpire until the coroner's inquiry, which was held yesterday at the residence of the deceased lady, before Mr. H. Chuton. From the evidence adduced, it appeared that Mrs. Brewin - who was 59 years of age - had suffered for many years from disordered liver. As a result she was subject at times to fits of depression, during which she was not altogether compos mentis. On Friday and Saturday last she had one of these attacks. When breakfast was taken to her bedroom on the morning of the latter day the attendant thought she detected the odour of phosphorus. Suspicion was aroused, and a search was made, but nothing was discovered. Dr. Craigmile was sent for, as Mrs. Brewin seemed to be somewhat worse, but he did not attribute her increased illness to anything unusual. Mrs. Brewin, however, gradually sank, apparently suffering little pain, and died about midnight on Saturday. After her death a closer search was made, and at the back of one the drawers of the dressing table of the dressing table in the deceased's bedroom was found a sixpenny jar of phosphorous, a poisonous concoction, employed usually as a rat destroyer. The jar was nearly empty, and at the bottom was a crust of bread which had the appearance of having been used for the purpose of extracting the paste. How the poison got into the house no one could say, and it was concluded that deceased herself must have obtained it. That she died from the effects of taking it was the conclusion arrived at medically, from examination made after her death. At the conclusion of the evidence the jury returned a verdict of "Committed suicide while temporarily insane." In the district of Wallasey Mrs. Brewin was known as a generous and kind-hearted lady. Much regret is felt at her death and great sympathy is expressed for her family, who have been long resident in the neighbourhood. The funeral, we understand, will take place tomorrow (Thursday) at Wallasey Church.

The Health Of Wallasey

Liverpool Mercury
Monday, 18th May, 1891

The Medical Officer of Health of Wallasey (Dr. Craigmile) has just issued his report for 1890 regarding that district. He states that the mortality statistics for the year were extremely satisfactory up to the time the severe cold set in November, when the death-rate rose rapidly. The estimated population at the end of 1890 is put down at 35,190, not including a floating population in that portion of the docks and river belonging to the Wallasey district of 400. The increase in the number of inhabited houses for the year was 336, as compared with 231 in the previous year. In 1890 the number of deaths was 550, or 30 more than in 1889, thus giving a death-rate of 16.17% per annum as against 16% in the previous year. For England and Wales the death-rate was 19.2%. The urban death-rate was 20.1%, and in the rural districts 17.5%, so that the Wallasey death-rate is 4% below the average urban rate and 1.4% below the rural rate, while it is 3.1% below the English rate. Birkenhead has for 1890 a death-rate of 19.70%, and Liverpool 23.3%. The number of drowning cases for the past year was only 9, all those non-residents except one. Excluding these, the death rate is 15.94%. Of the deaths, 269 were males and 290 females. The number of births was 953, compared with 957 in 1889, a decrease of 4. This gives the birth rate 28.02%, as against 29.44% in 1899. The national increase in the population, i.e., the excess of births over deaths, is therefore 403, as against 437 in the proceeding year. The birth rate for England and Wales in 1890 was 29.7%, against 30.5% in 1889, so that our birth rate was 1.7% below the general English rate. The English birth rate had steadily declined since 1876, when it was 36.3% per 1000. Of the births, 493 were males and 460 females. The report contains facts specifying the locality and number of diseases of various kinds. It appears that no cases of smallpox, typhus, relapsing fever, or cholera were notified. The hospital for infectious diseases in Mill Lane has done good service, 20 cases having been treated during the year. Dr. Craigmile concludes by drawing attention to the acquisition of a park on the Littledale estate, which it is expected will prove of the utmost benefit to the health of the district, and referring to the likelihood of a magnificent promenade, extending between Seacombe and New Brighton eventually.

Tragedy At New Brighton

**Liverpool Mercury
Saturday, 2nd July, 1892**

Great sensation was caused at New Brighton on Thursday by the discovery on the beach of the bodies of a woman and child, lying about high water mark. The discovery was made by two working men named Young and Bennett, who in passing along the shore at about six o'clock in the morning saw the remains at a spot beyond the Red Noses and to the north of the vessel known as "Noah's Ark". They were lying on a grey striped macintosh. The woman appeared to be about twenty-eight years of age, and the child, a boy about twelve months old, was lying across her breast. The woman was well clad in a maroon coloured dress, blue bodice. two flannel singlets, new chemise marked W. (or M.) Robinson, and black stockings. She had a morocco purse, which contained a return ticket from Liverpool to Southport, issued on Saturday last, a pawnticket for three rings issued on Wednesday by Mr. Mason, Liverpool, who lent 3s. upon the articles. On the woman's body was found a letter scribbled in pencil on a rough sheet of paper. It ran :- "This is mother and son. Home and friends all gone; nothing to live for. We have friends at this address, Greenhithe, Huddersfield. Whoever finds us let them know. Robinson." The bodies were conveyed to the deadhouse at the Magazines, awaiting identification. The infant, from the way in which it was lying when discovered, must have been actually drawing from its mother's breast at the time of death. The unfortunate woman is entirely unknown either in New Brighton or the neighbourhood. There is little doubt that the deceased crossed over from Liverpool to New Brighton some time during Wednesday. The police have communicated with the authorities at Huddersfield, with a view of finding either relatives or friends; also with the Coroner (Mr. H. Churton), who held the inquest yesterday (Friday).

Sacrilege
Cheshire Observer
Saturday, 10th December, 1892

When St. Paul's Church, Seacombe, was opened for public service on Sunday morning it was discovered that the sacred edifice had been entered some time during the previous evening, and a considerable amount of damage had been done to the fittings and drapery. Entrance had been gained by the door being unlocked, but considering that the only thing taken was a small brass cross it is not believed that robbery was the object of the act. A curtain near the altar had been damaged as if cut by a knife. A window was also broken and a gas bracket torn from the wall.

Poulton Clearance Order
Will Affect 118 Families
Wirral NEWS
19th January 1963

Another clearance scheme involving over 100 houses occupied by 118 families in Poulton was approved by the Wallasey Council on Thursday. The clearance area – No. 110. Clayton Lane, Clearance Order, 1963 – affects the following properties:-

Even numbers 2/44 inclusive, Rankin Street; odd numbers 3/15 inclusive and even numbers 2/22, Clayton Lane; even numbers 2/18 inclusive and odd numbers 1/17 inclusive,

Juliet Street; even numbers 2/20 inclusive and odd numbers 1/21 inclusive Portia Street; even numbers 2/24 inclusive and odd number 1/5 inclusive, Rosalind Street; even numbers 2/14 inclusive and odd numbers 1/9 inclusive Romeo Street; odd numbers 65/69 inclusive and 73/85 inclusive, Limekiln Lane, and the stables at the rear of No. 3 Romeo Street.

The Council approved the making of the Compulsory Purchase Order which will be submitted to the Minister of Housing and Local Government for confirmation.

The Council's decision follows a representation made to the General Health Committee by the Medical Officer of Health and the Chief Public Health Inspector requesting that the area be compulsory acquired for housing purposes on the grounds that the dwelling houses in the area are unfit for human habitation or are by reason of their bad arrangement of the streets dangerous or injurious to the health of the inhabitants of the area. The most satisfactory method of dealing with the conditions was the demolition of all the buildings in the area defined on a map in such manner as to exclude from that area any building which was not fit for human habitation or dangerous or injurious to health.

The Council is satisfied that where suitable accommodation available for the persons who will be displaced by the clearance does not already exist the Council can provide or secure the provision of such accommodation in advance of the displacements which will from time to time become necessary as the demolition of buildings proceeds.

End Of The Ferries Pier

Wallasey NEWS
13th October, 1973

In a series of ear-shattering bangs and great clouds of smoke a piece of New Brighton history is disappearing. The pier which led to the ferryboats is being demolished.

The last of the landing stage was blown up this week. Now the concrete sections of the pier are being dismantled.

The work is likely to take until the end of the year. Those old builders built well and the structure is a tough one.

The New Brighton Ferry service closed over a year ago, despite protests and petitions to keep it going as a summer time attraction. Its boats carried millions of passengers and brought trippers to New Brighton in great droves.

◆ ◆ ◆

ONE-WAY PRECINCT 'GREAT SUCCESS WITH SHOPPERS

Wallasey NEWS

13th June 1980

The new £327,000 one-way system is a great success with leading traders in Liscard.

They are "extremely happy" with the improvement, Mr. Ken Savage, chairman of the Liscard Traders' Association, said this week.

Mr. N. Wood, manager of Marks and Spencer, backed up Mr. Savage's comment. "I think the one-way system is excellent and can only benefit the traders and public. We have seen an improvement in our sales since it was opened. It is definitely money well spent."

With the one-way system came the pedestrianisation of Liscard Way.

Shoppers can relax without the added worry of dashing across the roads and avoiding traffic.

"Pedestrianisation relieves the tension of shopping," said Mr. R. Oswald, manager of Woolworths. "Mothers do not have to worry as much about their children running into the road while they are shopping. I think this idea is good for the community. There are no hassles at all from the traffic.

There is also less risk of accidents.

Mr. George Edwards, road safety officer, said: "When people get used to the system, it can only benefit them. As to accidents, I think the rate will drop because there were no longer frustrated drivers trying to go through the centre of town on busy shopping days."

Wirral Borough Council has realised its plan to make Liscard a pleasant, traffic free area.

Mr. D. Bott, assistant director of engineering, said; "We are trying for as much additional off street car parking facilities as possible. Thus can only enhance the attraction for shoppers".

◆ ◆ ◆

JOBS GO AS CO-OP PULLS OUT OF LISCARD

Wallasey NEWS

1st May 1976

The Co-Operative store in Liscard is to close. Most of the 39 staff will lose their jobs.

The main reason for the closure, according to regional general manager Mr. Sidney Stott, is that "Liscard has shown in the past 13 years that it cannot support a department store."

He told the NEWS: "I think it is very regrettable that the Liscard store should have to close, but, unfortunately, we find it necessary to protect the total interest of our 2,000 employees, our 550 pensioners and our many investors."

The Co-operative Retail Society Limited, which took over th Birkenhead and District Co-operative Society in June last year, is now concentrating on the development of the Grange Road, Birkenhead, and Woodchurch stores.

Mr. Stott continued: "In all these circumstances we have made a very close assessment of existing shopping facilities. We have taken into account how well they have been used,. and the new facilities being provided in Wirral, for example the huge new Birkenhead shopping centre and also the present economic climate which is affecting all retailers."

Other Jobs

Although no actual date has yet been fixed for the closure. Mr. Stott is hoping that many of the staff will be able to find alternative jobs in the meantime. Only an "extreme few" will be transfered to other stores.

Mr. Stott went on: "We are investing considerable sums of money in retailers in the Wirral. We are the biggest retailers in the peninsula, and the biggest retailers of many individual groups such as groceries, milk, clothing and furniture. We also have easily the biggest funeral department in the Wirral.

"In other words, there is no question of anything other than the normal process of business change, in this case being accelerated by inflation of expenses and the general economic climate."

Advertising manager Mr. Brian Miller pointed out that many of the employers at Liscard were "near retirement age anyway."

The employees at Liscard had been informed of the decision, almost as soon as it had been made, he said.

Chairman of Liscard Traders Association, Mr. Ken Savage, said the most of the local traders he had spoken to about it did not see it affecting their business adversely.

Inflation

Mrs. Lynda Chalker, Wallasey's M.P, told the NEWS: "I'm stumped. I have been in and out of the Co-op over the years, and I know they have been in difficulties, but it is exceedingly hard on the people involved. This sort of shock is the result of the long continued mammoth level of inflation. We must see what can be done for those people being made redundant. It is so tragic."

Conservative leader of the council, Coun. Malcolm Thornton, commented. "This is particularly worrying because of the very high level of unemployment we have got on Merseyside."

❖ ❖ ❖

ON THE WALL OF THRILLS AT NEW BRIGHTON

Wallasey News

21st June 1930

Few motor cycling stunts, even dirt track racing, has aroused more interest than the exploits of those American daredevils who are on the Promenade, New Brighton, at the moment, under the title of the "Wizards of the Wall." It has been called the thrill of the ager. But of what age, for it is not so recent an innovation as many people think.

Actually it began nearly twenty years, ago, when someone who saw the possibilities of the sport set to work to develop it. In 1909 an American saucer track racer, named Sam Anderson, accidentally covered several laps of the perpendicular safety fence on the rim of the little track, whilst cutting in on a rival. Sam had no intention of doing it; he just couldn't help himself, and when he came out of hospital he tried it again as an experiment. So, in time, by way of very steep angle "dromes" the perpendicular wall evolved to its present form with its accompanying thrills and dangers.

There are many facts about wall-riding which few people who have seen it, realise, and in a chat with the riders and manager of the "Wizards" I learnt something of the danger and the secrets of the game.

In the first place it takes about 12 to 18 months to learn to ride the wall. The potential rider is first given a thorough training on the pillion of one of the machines until he has overcome the giddiness and blindness which temporarily assails him. As a matter of fact, this is never really eliminated, for riders of many years' experience are often afflicted with a passing fit of giddiness and blindness.

The pupil also have to learn how to overcome the terrific pressure of centrifugal force, which, in the early stages forces him down over the handlebars, and has been known to press a man down on to the front wheel. No one would realise the truth or possibility of this unless, as I have, they have experienced it. But it's true.

In time, the pupil takes a machine by himself on to the steep angled starting track, and so by stages to actually riding the wall itself. And then he can try out a few tricks, such as standing on footrests, sitting on the handlebars, sitting cross-legged on the machine, and other diverting stunts.

Out of one hundred potential riders very few, about two or three survive the initial stages, physical or technical reasons account for most of them, although the physical qualifications are the most important, for without the ability to stand the strain, no one could hope to become an accomplished wall-rider.

The risks of the game are enormous. A seized motor, a broken wheel spindle, or a chain coming off; all have done so, to the riders. Tyre bursts are the most common events, and nearly every rider on the wall to-day. I was told, has at some time or other, crashed through this form of failure. The pressure on the tyres is so great that they are apt to expand and fly off the rims!

In the event of an ordinary cut out, through oiled plugs, choked jets or magneto failure, it is usually possible to coast down. As a matter of fact, Suicide Curley Cody, one of the Wizards, uses his back brake to slow down when coming off the wall!

Incidentally, contrary to the advertisements, the highest maximum speed attainable on the wall, according to the riders, is round about 60 or 65, and above that, is suicidal. The lowest speed at which a machine will hold the wall is thirty-five, although when a pillion passenger is taken a higher speed is needed to take off on to the wall.

The machines are stripped Indian Scouts, standard except for the rigid forks and springless saddles. Curiously enough, the riders can only use their own machines, so sensitive are they to the touch and feel of their mounts.

Visitors to the Wall will see a robust maiden, of 15 years of age. The aspirant is "Dare-devil Winnie Scatter," who is acclaimed as the youngest girl in the world who accomplished the feat of riding the vertical wall. Yes, Winnie is certainly a Wizard on the Wall. She and Curley have looked so long into the eyes of death that they have started him out of countenance.

◆ ◆ ◆

TRAGEDY AT NEW BRIGHTON

Nottinghamshire Guardian

Friday, 1st December, 1876

On Sunday morning the inhabitants of the village of Upper Brighton were alarmed by the report that one of their residents, a young man named William Fullarton, had attempted to murder his wife, and then had disappeared, and was supposed to have committed suicide by drowning himself in the sea, near the Red Noses, at New Brighton. Fullarton had for some time been a clerk, but had lost his situation through dissipated habits, and has been out of employment for some weeks. He is twenty-two years of age, and has resided in Upper Brighton village with his wife for several months. About six o'clock on Sunday morning he got out of bed, and his wife heard him walking about the room in an excited state. It was quite dark at the time, and she could not see what he was doing, but in a few minutes she was suddenly aroused by feeling something sharp drawn across her throat. She did not feel any wound at the moment, but immediately got up and struck a light. As soon as she did so she saw her husband standing near the bed with an open razor in his hand, and then discovered that he was bleeding at the throat from a wound which, from the fact that the razor he had in his hand was covered with blood, he had evidently inflicted himself. In her alarm she shouted for assistance, upon which her husband threw down the razor, and saying to her "Good-bye, Annie, you won't be seeing me again," rushed out of the house, and made his way to the sea shore. The police station is not far from the house, and Sergeant Shore being informed of the circumstances, went at once to the place and found Mrs. Fullarton in the greatest distress, and the neighbourhood in a state of alarm and excitement. The wound in the man's throat must have bled considerably, for the officer was able to trace the marks of blood from the room, downstairs to the front door, out of the house, and thence down to the shore. On proceeding thither the officer discovered a pair of boots lying near the high-water mark, where they had apparently been thrown by the tide. The boots were identified as belonging to Fullarton, and this fact, together with his parting exclamation, gave grounds for the surmise that he had drowned himself. Every search was made, but for a considerable time without avail. Fortunately, the efforts of the police proved successful about noon, when the unhappy man was found lying in Molyneux's Woods, about a hundred yards from the beach, nearly starved to death. If his searches had not discovered him when they did, in a very short time the tragedy which his two attempts on his life by the razor and drowning had failed to effect, would have been completed by his exhaustion and exposure to the weather. Restoratives were applied, and the unfortunate young man was conveyed to the bridewell at Liscard, where he will be brought up before the magistrates.

◆ ◆ ◆

THE GREAT PUSH

Wallasey Chronicle

July 1916

Wallasey's Heavy Toll
Many Local Men Killed And Wounded

As was only expected, the great push by the British in France has entailed a heavy list of casualties, and unhappily numerous Wallasey men figure amongst the killed and wounded.

While Gallantly Leading Platoon

The death is announced of Second-Lieutenant Frank Paterson, of the King's Own Scottish Borderers. Lieut. Paterson resided at 9 Zigzag Road, Liscard. He was twenty-nine years of age, and had been engaged as a ledger clerk in the Borough Treasurer's department of the Wallasey Corporation for thirteen years.

When war broke out he had been for seven years in the Liverpool Scottish, and immediately entered upon his duties as sergeant, receiving his commission in the Borderers in June of last year. After serving in Egypt, he was sent to France, and Colonel A.J. Walsh, in communicating the sad intelligence of his death, writes that he was killed in action on the morning of the July 1st whilst gallantly leading his platoon to the attack, and on behalf of all ranks of the Borders he conveys their deepest sympathy and condolence.

Lieutenant Paterson was an old boy of Liscard High School, and played for the Old Boys' team in cricket and football, and he had won two cups in connection with the Liverpool Scottish – one for shooting and the other for a marathon race. He was a member of St. Mary's Church, and acted for some time as the local secretary of the National Service League.

He was deeply loved by a large circle of friends in Liscard, who regard his loss as a very personal matter.

Grammar School Champion Killed

Official intimation has been received of the death of Lieutenant Ralph V. Merry, King's Liverpool Regiment. Lieut. Merry was twenty-two years of age, and the second son, of Mr. A. Merry, 0f 63, Manor Road, Liscard. On the outbreak of war he joined the Liverpool "Pals," and later received his commission in the same battalion. He was an old boy of the Wallasey Grammar School, and will long be remembered for his athletic feats in the connection. He won the school championship for two years in succession (1910-11), and had many medals, for swimming, running, and the high jump, besides representing the school in the football and cricket teams. He had travelled about a good deal in connection with mine engineering, but immediately prior to the outbreak of war he was engaged in the Liverpool office of a London firm of metal merchants. His elder brother holds a commission in the 6th King's Liverpool at the present time.

Harrowby Footballer Killed

All interested in local football will deeply regret to hear that George McGuinness, the popular Harrowby forward, who belonged to the Liverpool "Pals," has laid down his life in his country's cause. He was a schoolmaster in Liverpool, and resided at Falkland Road, Egremont. His brother, James McGuinness, who is also a well-known Harrowby, was recently wounded, and is now in hospital at Bath.

Three Wallasey Brothers
Two Out Of Action

Another Wallasey man to participate in the great "push" was Sergeant Thomas Herbert Barton (Liverpool "Pals"), of 11 Perrin Road, who is at present lying in Mill Road Hospital, Liverpool, suffering from shell shock. Sergeant Barton, who was in the second line at the time of the advance, and also received wounds in the arm and leg, declares that the British steel helmets were instrumental in preserving many valuable lives. The sergeant is well-known in Wallasey Village and prior to enlistment was employed by the Mersey Docks and Harbour Board, He had completed five years' service with the Territorials before broke out.

A brother, Corporal John Frederick Barton, has also been "in the thick of it," though happily he has come through the ordeal unscathed. Another brother, Private Albert Ernest Barton, also of the Liverpool "Pals," is unfortunately suffering from spotted fever, and has been in Netley Hospital for 19 weeks. Regrettable to relate, the young man has had a relapse, and much anxiety is felt by his parents.

"Don't Worry"

An example of the stoical fortitude which the British "Tommy" invariably shows in the face of adversity will assuredly be found in the case of Lance-Corporal Charles Edward Jagger, of the 18th King's Liverpool Regiment (2nd Liverpool "Pals"). At present lying in a French hospital, this unfortunate young man sustained a bullet injury to the wrist which has necessitated the amputation of the left hand. In spite of his misfortune, however, Lance-Corporal Jagger is wonderfully optimistic, as will be seen from the following letter which he has written to his parents at Church House (Egremont Presbyterian), Seabank Road.

"You will doubtless have received by now the field postcard sent by the chaplain stating that I am wounded. However, it is nothing to worry about. The bullet got me in the left wrist, and my hand has had to come off. Am very comfortable in hospital;

nothing to do but be there and eat three meals a day. Have not had much pain so far.

Don't worry: there are many worse cases than mine."

The field postcard referred to has not yet arrived. In a latter epistle the wounded soldier says he is on ordinary diet and getting along well. Every kindness is extended to him by the chaplain, the Rev. S. Hamill Wilkinson, who is, by a singular coincidence, personally acquainted with several Liscard ministers.

Seriously Injured

A field postcard also announces that Private. G.H. Woodhead, of 5 Ripon Road, Wallasey, has been wounded. This soldier is another "Pal," being attached to the 18th Battalion King's (Liverpool) Regiment. The injuries are said to be fairly serious.

Old Wallaseyan Falls

Another old Wallaseyan to lose his life is Rifleman Hugh Murdock, of the King's Liverpool Regiment, whose parents reside at 19, Rudgrave Square, Egremont, although he himself had been living in Liverpool latterly. Mr. Murdock has received a letter from his son's friend, Walter S. Baker, who says that Rifleman Murdock was killed at 8 am on July 1st during an attack on the German lines, and buried at 7 pm, the same day in a little cemetery in the village where they are billeted, just three miles behind the firing line.

The brave soldier was twenty-eight years of age and the son of Mr. Hugh Murdock, of H.M. Customs and Excise, Liverpool. He had only been married just over two years, and leaves a widow and one young child. He joined the Army in September, 1914, and was sent out to the front in the following September, and had five days leave only this last Christmas. He was engaged in Messrs. Singlehurst's shipping office, Liverpool, prior to enlistment.

Twice Wounded

Mr. Tunstall, 15 Kenwyn Road, Liscard, has received intimation that her son, Private George Tunstall, of 19th King's Liverpool Regiment (Pals"), is at present lying in a French hospital, and will probably be removed to England very shortly. The informant does not disclose the nature of the injuries.

Private Tunstall, who is 20 years of age, was formerly employed in the purchase department of the Canadian Pacific Railway, Liverpool, and enlisted at the outbreak of hostilities. This is the second occasion on which he has been wounded, as during the earlier portion of the year he was buried beneath the debris in the collapse of a dug-out along with a former member of the Chronicle staff, who has since been killed.

In the Queen Mary's Military Hospital, at Whalley, near Blackburn, Lce.-Corpl. F Bedson, Wallasey "Pals," 1 Balmoral Road, New Brighton, is lying seriously wounded. He was a ferry employee, and a member of the New Brighton Lifeboat crew. There are fourteen New Brighton lifeboatmen serving in the Navy and Army, and Lance-Corpl Bedson is the first to be seriously wounded.

Egremont "Pal" Killed

Another "Pal" who has fallen in the country's cause is Stanley, the only son of Mr and Mrs F. Booth, of 22 Glenalmond Road, Egremont. He was 19 years of age, and was killed in action on July 1st.

An All-Round Athlete

The death is announced of Lance-Corporal Leonard Herbert Pringle (23), of the 19th King's Liverpool Regiment, who was killed in action on July 1st. Death, which came instantaneously, was caused by the explosion of a shell, and at the time deceased was attached to a trench mortar battery. Several sorrowing chums carried out the burial service the same day, and a cross was placed on the grave before leaving.

Deceased, who resided with his parents at 29 Brougham

Road, Seacombe, was a familiar figure in Liverpool commercial circles, having served his time with Messrs. Larrinaga and Co. His education was received at Sefton School. A good all-round athlete, Lance-Corporal Pringle had carried off quite a number of medals for skill in football, cricket, and swimming. The possessor of a voice of excellent timbre, he was a prominent member of the choir at Ullet Road Unitarian Church. He enlisted at the commencement of the war, and had been out in France since November last.

Warren Drive Bereavement

Mr and Mrs J.H. Woods, of the Croft, Warren Drive, New Brighton, have received notification of the death of their second son, Private Albert Rothwell Woods, Liverpool "Pals," who was killed in action on July 1st; and, according to the informant, an officer of the battalion, death came instantaneously. Private Woods, who was only eighteen years of age, had been in the Army some fifteen months, and prior to enlistment was an employee of Messrs. Ralli Brothers, Liverpool. An ardent motor-cyclist and a keen sportsman. He was formerly a playing member of the Aughton Hockey Club.

Singularly enough, deceased's eldest brother, W.F. Woods, was slightly wounded in the shoulder on the same day, and is at present lying in Alder Hey Hospital, West Derby. Please to relate, however, the wounded soldier is making satisfactory progress towards recovery.

Heroism Of The Cheshires

The heroic part the Cheshire are playing in the great British offensive, which is now making such brilliant progress in France, is graphically described in the following despatch from the front by Mr. W. Beach Thomas, which appeared in the Daily Mail of Saturday last:- "To the east of the Albert Bapaume road some troops, principally recruited in Cheshire and Lancashire, were given an objective some 800 yards to their front; and while consolidating this patrols were to be sent to a yet further point. This manoeuvre went according to the book except in one detail. Everyone went too far, just as the padre of Souchez went too far, because the object of their walk was unrecognisable or had ceased to exist. There was no trench where a trench ought to be, had been, was till yesterday. As an infantryman said, "That is the worst of our artillery. They destroy your landmarks."

Whatever reason – mistake, or keenness – the fact was that at dawn several platoons found themselves in a short piece of trench running like a half-crossed "t" across the chief communication trench. They were absurdly in advance, "in the air," with the enemy on both sides of them, but they decided that it was a great place to see from. So they manned this cross of the "t" with guns and machine guns.

The enemy, of course, discovered them and telephoned to the artillery, who made good shooting. But in spite of losses, they stood it, perhaps because they knew that the real visible enemy would follow the shells, and it was so. Before the day was old, little groups of Germans were seen gathering in a dozen places in front and on the flanks. On these they had their revenge, but the little party was whittled down to nothing in a trench both blocked and opened out by shell fire.

At last an officer and six men found themselves alone in the extreme edge of the trench. All they could do was to cut and run across the open by the shortest possible paths to the communication trench. Two of them, an officer and a sergeant, got safely through, formed a defence post as far up as possible in the communication trench, and prevented any further progress of the enemy. Last night the whole place was absorbed in cur, advance.

New Brighton Private's Experiences

Private Francis Woods, 4th Company of the King's Liverpool Regiment, of 25 Warren Drive, New Brighton, who is among the wounded, relates some interesting facts about the work of the Liverpool "Pals" in the great offensive.

"Our work" he says, "was to follow up the other companies and to clear out the trenches. We bombed and searched dug-outs, cleared the trenches of prisoners and dead, and held on. The prisoners seemed rather pleased than otherwise to fall into our hands, as for eight days they hardly any food to eat, and that the shelling by the British had been terrific. They were in a fearfully unkempt condition, with days of growth on their faces, and some of them looked to be quite fifty-nine years of age. In fact, one man was fifty-nine. This prisoner said the war would last some time yet, as the Germans have got plenty of men."

Sorely Stricken Street

Although it contains rather than thirty houses, Tower Street, Liscard, has made a name for itself, not only as regards the patriotism of its inhabitants but for the heavy toll under which it has laid by the war. Its latest bereavements concern Private R. Rogers, of the Cheshires, and Lance-Corporal Henry Price, of the Welsh Fusiliers, both of whom were killed on the recent "push."

Private Frank Robertson, R.F.A., who has had the great distinction of gaining the French Medaille Militaire, which practically ranks equal with the English V.C., has been wounded, and is now in hospital in Glasgow. Lance-Corporal Mercer. R.E., has been seriously wounded, but is now reported to be going on well in a base hospital in France. Other Tower Street residents who have lost their lives during the war are Private Owen Parry, Canadians; W. Tipping, who was killed by an explosion on H.M.S. La Marguerites; Private Crawley, Cheshires. Private R. Simmer, of the Cheshires, has been missing for the last twelve months. Corporal H. Light, Loyal North Lancashires, who has been at the front since the outbreak of hostilities, has been twice wounded and once gassed, and Lance Corporal J. Therwell, of the Cheshires, has also been wounded.

Poignant War Tragedy

Seacombe Brothers Killed

A poignant tragedy of the war will be found in the deaths of two brothers who were killed in action on the same day, July 1st. They are Sergeant Harold S. Price (33) and Private Oswald W. Price (31) of 24, Harcourt Avenue, Seacombe. In the case of the sergeant who belonged to the Liverpool "Pals," official notification was received from the War Office, but the news of Oswald's death was received from a sergeant in the Royal Inniskilling Fusiliers, to which regiment deceased was attached. Oswald Price was a Regular, and his time would have expired in September next. Both were members of the Seacombe Presbyterian Church, Brougham Road.

❖ ❖ ❖

BATTLE OF THE BRICKWORKS

Liverpool Mercury

7th December 1877

Wallasey Local Board Meeting
Works And Health Committee

The committee had been in communication with the Wallasey Brick and Land Company with reference to the closing of the footroad between Egremont ferry and Manor Road slip by the company. No terms had been come to, and it was recommended that the opinion of Mr. North, solicitor, should be taken on the subject.

Right Of Way Dispute At Egremont

Liverpool Mercury
8th December 1877

A brick making company, whose workers are situated between the Egremont Ferry and the manor slip, having stopped the footway adjoining the sea wall, the Wallasey Local Board have apparently determined on vindicating the public rights, and on Thursday night, between six and seven o'clock, the obstruction was removed by them. Yesterday morning the brickmaking company re-erected the barrier, which was again pulled down yesterday afternoon on the authority of the local board. It is stated that on both occasions the services of the Wallasey fire brigade were called into requisition, and, having laid the hose along the wall, with a full pressure of water on, they were prepared, if necessary, to meet with a plentiful supply of cold water any attempt interfere with the performance of their duty. We understand that no resistance was made. The attempted obstruction has excited considerably feeling in the locality, and great satisfaction is expressed at the prompt and vigorous action of the authorities.

Storming A Barricade At Egremont

**Liverpool Mercury
10th December 1877**

The stupid and dangerous course adopted by the brickmaking company of Egremont in opposing by force the determination of the authorities to keep open the roadway abutting the sea wall north of the ferry resulted in a great popular demonstration on Saturday, accompanied by scenes which raised the liveliest apprehensions of a formidable riot.

On Thursday and Friday last the company erected barricades across the roadway, and these, as previously reported, were removed by the authorities. During Friday night, however, the company constructed two formidable barricades, protected by trenches filled with water, and made other preparations which unmistakably indicated that active resistance would be made to any attack upon them. The likelihood of a "row" caused an immense gathering of people in the neighbourhood early in the afternoon, and the number received large accessions as the fire brigade – in brass helmets and carrying their usual implements – mustered in the vicinity of the ferry between two and three o'clock. At this time Inspector Hindley and a body of fine stalwart policemen; while among the crowd were officials and several members of the local board.

Some formal requests to remove the barrier having been made to the brickmaker's and refused, the storming party of firemen gallantly rushed to their task, and vigorously assailed the first barricade with axes and levers. What with the trench and the state of the outworks, inches deep in a claysy puddle – their task was no easy or pleasant one, and it was soon rendered much more difficult and unpleasant by hissing jets of steam from pipes connected with the boilers in the brickworks, which were brought to play upon them. The firemen's response was cold water from the hose in sufficient quantity and force to speedily confound the enemy's politics; and though enveloped in steam they could be seen now and then plying axe and lever with the utmost vigour, despite numberless unfriendly attentions from the brickmen behind the palisadings. While this excellent public service was being done, some persons inside the works thought it a good joke to utilise the bricks which lay plentifully about them, and a shower of these dangerous missiles were directed against the attacking party. Amongst these were many person who, unfortunately, did not wear helmets, and they speedily betook themselves to a safe distance. At this critical juncture the police interfered with admirable promptness, and having "spotted" three or four of the men inside the works in the act of throwing the bricks, rushed in upon them and made them prisoners. This action, together with the intimation that such of the directors or shareholders who were egging the workmen on would, if they persisted, be dealt with in the same manner, as inciting to a breach of the peace, at once out a stop to the brick-throwing; and the upshot was the complete and speedy demolition of the barricades, amidst great cheering. The appearance of many of the besiegers and defenders, covered with clay from head to foot, was a sight not to be forgotten. Our reporter hears that the workmen arrested were taken to the lockup, and subsequently bailed out. Of course the affair caused intense excitement, and the brick throwing incident aroused loud cries of indignation, which might have easily resulted in serious damage of property, if not to limb, for there were hundreds of sturdy fellows who were ready, if necessary, to storm the works as well as the barricades, and give the instigators of the obstruction a thorough ducking.

All through Saturday night and yesterday a force was kept ready for immediate action should another endeavour be made to stop the road.

The Right-Of-Way Dispute At Egremont

Magisterial Compliment To The Police

Liverpool Mercury
13th December 1877

At the Wallasey petty sessions yesterday, before Messrs Chambres (chairman), Penny, Bouch, Kerford, Mann, and Bulley, the three men in the employ of the Wallasey Brick and Land Company who, as already reported, were taken into custody for participation in a riot at Egremont on the 6th instant, appeared to their recognisances. Their names are Charles Loder (manager of the company), John Fishwick and Patrick Boyd (labourers), all charged with riotous conduct, and the last named with assaulting Police Constable 162. Mr Wright, of the firm, Wright, Stockley and Becket, appeared for the accused.

From the full particulars of the occurrence which were published in the Mercury, it will be remembered that on Saturday afternoon, the 8th instant, an effort was made by the Wallasey Brick and Land Company to close to the public a piece of land about eight yards wide, running along the river wall on the Cheshire side from Egremont Ferry Pier to Manor Road or Maddocks slip, which had been used for many years as a footpath between the places named. The company had recently purchased the land in question, public interfered. On Thursday last the company erected a barricade to prevent the public walking along the river wall, but that night it was removed by someone opposed to its existence. A similar barrier was erected on the following day, but a similar fate awaited it, and it was removed that afternoon. In neither of these cases was there any disturbance or opposition. On Saturday, however, the barricade had been again erected by the company and more ingenious appliances brought to bear against its demolition. About three o'clock p.m. on that day another attempt was made to clear the obstruction, the Wallasey fire brigade under Mr. Leather, lending their assistance. A crowd of about 4000 persons collected, and somewhat dangerous proceedings ensued. Fortified with large hammers, picks, &c, the members of the fire brigade commenced the work of pulling down the barrier, but were compelled to desist for a time by the company's employees turning on steam from the works some distance behind into perforated iron tubes which had been placed on either side of the barricade. The police came upon the scene just in time to prevent a more serious disturbance, but, as it was, several stones and brickbats were thrown by men in the company's yard as well as by their opponents on the river wall.

The first witness now called was Inspector Hindley, of the Cheshire County Police, who deposed in the main to the facts as already published. When he saw the affair was getting serious, he ordered the policemen present to take anyone into custody who threw stones. Two of the men in custody, Boyd and Loder, were on the company's fence directing the steam from two tubes upon the people on the river wall. Witness handcuffed and took into custody the manger of the company (Loder). Police Constables 147, 162, 157, and 165 all gave corroborative evidence.

Mr. Wright submitted that the magistrates had no jurisdiction in the matter, inasmuch as it was purely a question of title to land. An action would forthwith be brought by the company against those who were the instigators of the occurrence, and he would like to say a few words to convince the bench that the company have exclusive rights over the whole of the land referred to. Mr. Wright then went on to explain that the company, early in the present year, bought the land in question, and by the agreement entered into were to pay for every yard of it, including the portion in dispute. The men from whom they purchased it claimed the freehold and fee simple of every portion of the land without the reservation of any right of way whatever. The company erected their works in due course close to the river wall without any desire to prevent the public walking along the strip of land to and from Egremont Ferry. The lapse of time, however, without any interference would give the public a right of way, and as the bench would be aware, for 18 or 20 years the wall had been there. If for 20 years the public had used the passage without the company asserting its rights, a right of way would be established there, and what they considered a most valuable part of their property – namely the river frontage for shipping bricks – would lapse from them. It was only after very mature deliberation that the company had come to the conclusion to assert its right, and they only intended to keep the passage closed for a day or two. The company offered the local board some time ago £2000 worth of land if they (the board) would construct a road 10 yards broad along the river frontage, reserving to the company the right to use it as they otherwise would be entitled to use it for their tramways upon lines level with the road. The local board, however, refused to accept the offer. Subsequently due notice was given to the public that the road would be closed, and as it was their only course, the company erected the barricades, with the result already known. The steam pipe referred to was not concealed at all, and notice was given before the steam was turned on. In conclusion, Mr. Wright quoted from Okes' Magisterial Synopsis, section 46, to show that the bench had no jurisdiction in the matter.

The Chairman said the magistrates thought they had jurisdiction in a case of riot like the present, but they would retire and consult their law advisor.

After a few minutes' consultation the magistrates returned into court, and, having taken their seats, Mr. Chambres, addressing Mr. Wright, said that they understood that the brick company contemplated building another barricade. Stronger than those which has been built, and they wanted to ask if there was any truth in that report.

Mr. Wright replied that there was no truth whatever in it; the company did not contemplate any such action. There had been a meeting of the directors of the company since the disturbance, and they came to the unanimous conclusion that, in the face of the violence offered, it would not be right for them longer to hold their own, as owners of the property, but would be forced into bringing an action against the trespassers.

The Chairman - Then as the representative of the company, you can assure the court that no further obstruction will be placed there till the legal rights of both sides can be ascertained?

Mr. Wright – Most certainly.

The Chairman replied that the bench were of opinion that direct excess of force had been used, and that the magistrates had jurisdiction. If it had not been for what had just fallen from the lips of the legal representative of the company they would have felt it their duty to send the case to the sessions for trial, where most likely a severe sentence would have been passed. As it was, the bench could not countenance anything in the shape of a riot. On the occasion in question, the magistrates thought, the police, under Inspector Hindley, had acted in a most admirable manner, and had done exactly that which the law required them to do. The inspector did not lose his presence of mind, but called to many of the people by name, and by that means put a stop to that which most likely would have ended in bloodshed. The bench were further of opinion that he did not use any excess of force, and that in putting handcuffs on the unfortunate person who was manager of the company (Charles Loder) he did what was perfectly right, because in the sight of 2000 or 3000 people he showed the supremacy of the law, and that it must be obeyed. The bench were exceedingly sorry for the three men brought before them, in one sense, but they could not reprobate too strongly their conduct from another point of view. They were acting as the agents of the company, the chairman of which was a member of the local board of health, and were advised by a legal man who was, unhappily, a member of the local board, and who was very recently chairman of that board; all of which circumstances aggravated the case. Those men were employed by the company to commit an excess of violence in what they considered to be an assertion of their rights. The court had, however, nothing to do with the rights on one side or the other, but simply to uphold the peace, which must be preserved. In regards to the defendant Fishwick, it was quite clear that he did not throw stones or brickbats, though he had one in his hand, which he dropped, happily for himself, on seeing the police. The defendants Loder and Fishwick would be bound over to keep the peace for six months – themselves in £100 each, and two sureties in £50 each. Patrick Boyd would be bound over in the same amount, and would, in addition, have to pay a fine of 20s and costs for his assault upon the police officer. In conclusion, Mr. Chambres expressed the hope of the bench that a case of that kind would never again occur in the parish.

◆ ◆ ◆

GANDY BELT WORKS GUTTED

Wallasey News

19th February 1927

The Gandy Belt Works, Seacombe, were completely destroyed by fire yesterday. Fortunately no lives were lost, but the financial damage is estimated at the huge sum of £250,000. This is, we understand, wholly covered by insurance. The fire was easily the fiercest and most destructive seen in Wallasey for very many years, the only previous outbreaks comparable to it being those at Buchanan's Flour Mills, and the New Brighton Tower.

At about ten minutes to four, the fire alarm in the works was sounded. Normally about 300 men and women are employed, but owing to slackness of trade, a proportion were on short time. Consequently, the building, which is well equipped with fire exits, were quickly cleared. Most of the people working on the ground floor made a hasty exit by the main gates to the works, opening out into Wheatland Lane; those on the upper storey, including most of the girls, descended the emergency escapes at the rear of the building, into Vernon's field.

Spread Quickly

Within less than half an hour of the sounding of the buzzer, the fire had made the most alarmingly progress. A strong breeze was blowing from the north-west; this fanned the flames to a terrific height and it was soon apparent that the middle of the building, from which the outbreak had appeared to start, was doomed. The middle of the back wall crashed down first, then the fire spread rapidly out towards each wing. The occupants of the houses on the left hand side of Vernon Avenue watched the progress of the flames with by no means unnatural anxiety. There is no space or entry between the backs of these houses and the works; had the wind been blowing in the opposite direction, nothing could have saved this property. As it was, the flames roared with terrific intensity a few yards from them, and the roofs of both the rooms of the works nearest to the avenue collapsed. So dangerous was the situation that tenants removed some of their belongings - including their pianos - out into the street.

In front of the works, in Wheatland Lane, a great crowd gathered at first, but in the narrow part of the road, just past the junction of St. Paul's Road and Wheatland Lane, the heat rapidly became unbearable, and the onlookers retired, leaving the field to the firemen and police.

No Water

At first there was great difficulty in getting any water from the hydrants, and even when a flow was started, it proved at many points quite inadequate to deal with the furnace that the heart of the building had become. The houses in Vernon Avenue were concentrated upon, and the firemen were successful in preventing the flames from getting a hold here.

It was from the waste ground at the back of the works that the full fury of the blaze could best be seen. The whole of the middle part of the wall had collapsed, the interior being revealed. This was a raging inferno. The flames leapt up in the air to a terrific height, and huge clouds of thick black smoke - oil smoke, apparently - were belched forth every minute or so. At frequent intervals, great thuds could be heard, which were attributed either to the bursting of oil receptacles or to the collapse of ceilings and floors. Gradually, the rooms at the very top of the building caved in; girder after girder came crashing down into the furnace below, and it became only a matter of time before the roof itself collapsed.

The Cause

The cause of the outbreak has not been officially stated, but it is believed to have been due to the fusing of a wire. The works are full of highly inflammable materials - oils for treating the leather belts, and so forth - hence the extraordinary spread of the blaze.

Walking Home

Thousands of workers were compelled to walk home owing to the trams being stopped. It was feared at one time that the overhead equipment would collapse and formers were placed across the road to keep the crowd out of danger.

Scenes After Dark

Although much abated in intensity, the fire continued long after dark, and the sky was lit up for miles around. Great crowds thronged the streets, and a barrier had to be put up in all the roads leading to the works, only police permitted to approach within thirty or forty yards of the building.

A Magnificent Spectacle

Viewed from the railway bridge at the bottom of Oakdale Road, across the full stretch of Vernon's land, the fire presented a magnificent spectacle. The walls stood up starkly against the glowing sky, encircling a huge floor of flame. Occasionally, great clouds of smoke were emitted. The fire smouldering for many hours into the night.

Shortage Of Water
(Official Explanation)

For at least twenty minutes after the arrival of the brigade, no water could be obtained.

When at last a supply was forthcoming it was almost inadequate to fill the hoses. It will be recalled that attention was directed to the state of the pipes in this district some eighteen months ago.

In September, 1925, Councillor Hall stated that the question of the water supply had been engaging the attention of the Gas and Water Committee.

As a result of an inspection they found 65 to 75 hydrants were "duds" and that the pressure in the neighbourhood of the Gandy Belt Works was insufficient to deal with a serious fire. The same applied, he said, to the Cottage Hospital, the Wesleyan Church in Claremount Road, and the convent at New Brighton.

Defective Pressure

Mr. J.B. Crowther, the Borough Gas and Water Engineer, stated last night that the Gandy Belt area was included in a number of districts which were to be dealt with for defective pressure, owing to the corrosion of the pipes. The area had not yet been tackled. The supply in the district had been off at periods during the week, but this only affected domestic supplies.

There was no reason, so far as he knew, why it should have

been impossible to obtain a supply of water.

Mr. Crowther added that the blaze spread so quickly that he thought that no amount of water could have made much difference to the ultimate result.

Praise For The Firemen

Within two or three minutes of the alarm being raised and the brigade called, Wallasey firemen were on the scene, and at work under the direction of the fire chief, Inspector Constable (Mr. D.L. Barry) and Chief Inspector Ormerod directed all the available policemen who had been rushed to the works.

At the outset it was realised that it was utterly impossible to save the works from destruction, but with the assistance of the Birkenhead Brigade, the firemen fought the flames from points at which the heat was terrific and almost unbearable, in their effort to avert the destruction of adjacent cottages. In several cases firemen had narrow escapes from being injured by glass and crashing debris but they continued their work with commendable coolness.

The fire was still smouldering at a late hour last night.

Tragedy Of Unemployment

Although nobody was killed, or even seriously injured, the fire will have had tragic consequences, apart from the actual destruction of the property. A large number of employees - including many who, it is understood, were to have returned to work on Monday, after being on short time for a prolonged period, will be thrown out of work. It will, of course, be many months before work can be resumed.

❖ ❖ ❖

THE SUSPECTED CHILD MURDER AT EGREMONT

Cheshire Observer

Saturday, 12th July, 1862

On Thursday afternoon the coroner for the district, H. Churton, Esq., held an inquest, adjourned from Wednesday, the 2nd instant, on the body of a male child, which had been found in a heap of night soil, collected from one of the Seacombe hotels, by the night-soilman, on the Monday previous, a fact sworn to in evidence at the previous inquest by a man named John Hodson. The only witness examined on Thursday was Samuel Wagstaff Smith, member of the colleague of surgeons, who deposed – I am the medical officer of the Wallasey dispensary, and on the 2nd July, in virtue of instructions, made a post mortem examination of the body of a male child, found amidst a heap of night-soil. The body somewhat decomposed and could not have been more than a few days old. It was not full-grown, but an eight-months' child. There was no external marks of violence about the body, except blood about the right ear : that the umbilical cord was about fourteen inches in length, somewhat shrunk, no way tight, and very dry; that it was rough at the extremities, as it torn, not cut.

On opening the chest I examined the lungs and found them

of a pink colour, which floated when immersed in water, even when cut into pieces, from which I inferred that the child had inspired slightly. There was evidently atmospheric influence on the lungs; the left side of the heart was full of black blood; all the other organs appeared healthy and natural. In answer to the coroner, the witness said, I do not think that the child could be said to be born alive; the lungs were imperfectly distended. Cases have occurred where prior to birth the child has breathed : it might have died during parturition; or the child's head, which naturally comes first, might have been alive, and then instantaneous death followed. The body was so fresh when I examined it that I do not think it could have been born more than three days.

On this evidence being given, the coroner addressing the jury said. From the statements now made by the medic I gentlemen, it is clear the case is at an end. He then reviewed the evidence, which he considered clear and highly satisfactory, that the jury could return no other verdict than that the child has been still-born. At first, remarked the coroner, there were many circumstances connected with the finding of the body calculated to arouse the suspicion of Inspector Rowbottom. In the hotel, adjoining the ashpit whence the body had been taken, a woman suspected to have delivered of a child : that the woman had somewhat suddenly left the service of the hotel-keeper, on the 28th May, and had gone to Liverpool, where she consulted a Dr. Waters as to her health, and afterwards was admitted into one of the Liverpool hospitals, from which she was dismissed on the 6th June. The jury, without retiring, returned the verdict – "Still-born."

At the conclusion of the inquest, and while remarking in very complimentary terms on the evidence given by Mr. Smith, the coroner said – Recently I had a very notable instance of the importance of correct medical evidence. In another section of the county I held an inquest on the body of a child found dead under similar circumstances, and on the same day the magistrates held a court, and had signed a commitment of the mother on the serious charge of murder, founding their procedure on the medical testimony given by a surgeon who had been examined before the court. I directed the jury to return the verdict still-born; and on this being told to the magistrates I was sent for. I showed to the satisfaction of the bench that the child had been stillborn, that the lungs being like jelly and adhering to the spine, could never have been distended, and the child could not have been born alive. I had the satisfaction of seeing the murder-commitment paper torn in pieces, and the innocent but unfortunate mother acquitted. So much for perfect and imperfect medical evidence.

In connection with the inquest we were much gratified that the coroner had one of the jurors give a donation to Mr. Smith, for the benefit of the funds of Wallasey dispensary.

◆ ◆ ◆

LANTERN PARADE AT WALLASEY

Liverpool Mercury

Tuesday, 1st September, 1896

The spirit of carnival has developed in this district to a large extent during the past few years, and the latest example, a lantern parade and fancy dress festival at New Brighton, Egremont, and Seacombe last evening, proved one of the prettiest gatherings of the kind which has been held. Fortunately for the success of the festival, the weather, which is, perhaps the chief factor to success in outdoor affairs of this nature, was favourable until the proceedings were well over, and the ladies and gentlemen in fancy dress who formed the procession, and the thousands of spectators who thronged the line of route, were enabled to enjoy the proceedings in comparative comfort. The object of the carnival was to help the funds of the Liverpool and New Brighton Lifeboat Institute, and numerous willing volunteers gave aid in various ways to make the festival a success. The start was made at dusk from the Horse Shoe at New Brighton Pier, and the procession was divided into sections, each of which was headed by a band. Among the several hundred cyclists who formed part of the procession, some exceedingly pretty, striking, and grotesque characters were to be noticed, while the members of the various harrier, athletic, and swimming clubs and minstrel troupes, who were indefatigable with their collecting boxes, were attired in every variety of fanciful and humorous costume. The hundreds of coloured lanterns and lights, with which the vehicles and cycles were adorned, gave a lively and picturesque appearance to the scene as the procession slowly made its way along the appointed route. The first section was led by Chief Superintendent Hindley, on horseback, a number of outriders, the local fire brigade, the 1st Cheshire and Carnarvonshire A.V Band, the New Brighton lifeboat and crew, drawn by five horses, on a lorry; the 1st Cheshire Bugle Band, and the chairman's, secretaries', and treasurer's carriage. The second section was headed by the Gleam of Sunshine Band and the ladies' committee carriage, the third by the Workshops for the Blind Band, and the fourth by the Moreton Brass Band. The route taken was along Victoria Road, Rowson Street, Seabank Road, King Street (Egremont), Brighton Street, Seacombe Ferry, St. Paul's Road, Church Road, Victoria Road (Seacombe), Liscard Road, Liscard Village, Rake Lane and Upper Brighton, back to the starting point. A feature of the procession, which showed good organisation, was the prompt start at the advertised time, and the avoidance of delays and stoppages which, as a rule, characterise undertakings of this kind. The tradesmen of New Brighton and Seacombe materially helped the success of the spectacle by a liberal display of bunting and coloured lanterns, and the discharge of fireworks.

Prizes were awarded for the best turnouts, both harriers and cyclists, as well as for the best collectors. These were as follows :-

Cyclists – Best Illuminated Machine: 1. W. Ridley (West Kirby), "Sultan"; 2. F. Gell (Liscard), "Eastern Prince." Neatest Costume: 1. B.Hands (New Brighton), "Japanese." Most Comic: 1. T.Smith (New Brighton), "Old Lady", 2. A.Medalf, "Irish Sailor." Most Original: 1. H.Silcock (West Kirby), "Neptune up to date." Neatest Character Dress (lady): 1. Miss Alice Crouch, "Italian Flower Girl."; 2. Miss. Carson, "Little Red Riding Hood." Best Tableaux: 1. R.Jenkins, "Winter," 2. T.Bell and E.Howard as

"Weary Willie and his Wife on the Road." Best Illuminated Tandem: 1 W. And A.Crouch, "Duke's Cameo"; 2. Brothers Soloman, "Darkies." A special prize was accorded to Mr. W.R. Richards for his representation of the famous Sussex cricketer, Prince Ranjitsinhji. The judges of the above events were Messrs. F.T Parry, R.R Ellis, J.Greetham, J.F Hughes, and F.H Smith. The harriers' turnout was none the less attractive, and competition in this respect was exceptionally keen. The following were the wards in regard to this particular section :-

Most Comic Harrier: H. Walker (Xaverian Darkies), "Negro Lady." Neatest Costume: J.P Breckenridge, "Louis XVI." Most Original Costume: 1. J.F Walker, "Light Railways"; 2. E.N.T Mitchell, "King Winter"; 3. H.Knight, "Tiny." Neatest Dressed Boy Under 14: J.A Salisbury, "Black and White." Neatest Dressed Girl Under 14: Francis Drew. "Gipsy." Neatest Dressed on Horseback: I.S.P Chambers, "Indian"; 2. J.H Scott, "Jockey." Neatest Dressed Marshall on Horseback: S. Lowe, "Hussar." Most Comical Dressed Marshall on Horseback: "Clown", F. Gibson. Special Prizes: Miss Phillipps, "Harvest"; Master A.E Walker, "Mornington Cannon"; J. Bushell, "Dick Turpin"; "Neopolitan." Miss Agnes Benson: "Negro Clown," M.M Robertson"; "Red Indian," A. Hulme; "Charley's Aunt," H. Hooton; "Acrobat," E. Battersby; "Dashing Cavalier," --- Colley; "Upside Down," E. Bagot, "Illuminated Premises" (extra prize), Mrs. Tate, 51 Brighton Street, Seacombe. Prizes were given to shopkeepers for special displays, and these were accorded to – 1. Mrs. Outram, Victoria Road, New Brighton; 2 Mrs. Dale, Brighton Street, Seacombe; 3. Mrs. Huxley, New Brighton Hotel. In connection with the affair, Old English Sports were held on the shore at New Brighton in the afternoon. The following were the results:-- Boy's race: 1. Claude Tregenze; 2. J. Leach; 3. J. Thornton. Girls Race: 1. Maud Jones; 2. Florrie Jones; 3. Alberta Clegg. Egg-and-Spoon Race: Margaret Harrison. Sack Race: 1 J. Daniels; 2. J. Leach. Donkey Race: Mrs Stephenson. Climbing the Greasy Pole: Thomas Hayes. The following were the chief officials of the parade :-- President, Mr. Charles Birchall; chairman, Mr. J.W Brien; vice-chairman, Messrs F.H Smith, R.B. Robertson, J. Greetham, J. Bennett, J. Ward Dale and R.R Ellis; honorary treasurer Mr. C. Huxley; and general honorary secretary, Mr. John F. Walker.

❖ ❖ ❖

THE WALLASEY PALS

Wallasey Chronicle

11th September 1920

On September 7th, 1914, the first detachment of recruits from Wallasey for the 13th Battalion of the Cheshire Regiment – the Wallasey Pals, the men who had rushed to the colours with the first flush of the war fever – marched out of the borough to the accompaniment of bands and cheering, flag-waving crowds. In the six years that have flown since that time much has been said and much has been done, but the River Mersey still flows past Seacombe Ferry and German ships that sail upon the breast fly the British flag! Some, but not all, of the men that marched away so cheerfully were back in Wallasey, and the lucky ones none the worse for their adventures. It was, therefore, a kindly but not expected act on the part of the Mayor (Alderman E.G. Parkinson, J.P) to entertain the survivors of that patriotic band with a little reunion on the anniversary of the first day of their odyssey.

On Tuesday evening they met round one table at the Marine Hotel, New Brighton, as the guests of the Mayor, and, while not forgetting their comrades who would never be with them again, they gave themselves up to the complete enjoyment of a happy evening spent in company with their old pals. There was a lot of reminiscing, as Dr. MacMillan put it, and much laughter over the recalling of incidents that have gone down in the history of the battalion, but despite the boisterous tone of the gathering, a mention of the men who had fallen always brought sympathetic silence.

The dinner, as the most arduous part of the evening, was disposed of first, and then commenced the musical programme, the items being interspersed with the speeches, mostly in a lighter vein.

Toast Of The Evening

The Mayor gave the toast of the evening . "The Guests", which only he and his friends at the head of the table could drink. He said they were there to be happy and to forget the horrors and privations they had been through. Those who had seen nothing of the front were very grateful to them as representing the returned soldiers. He would have liked to entertain all the returned soldiers, but that would have been impossible, and he thought it would be nice to remember the first batch of men who went away with light hearts, singing "Tipperary" and "Are we downhearted?"

"They were not downhearted, though no doubt they felt a little that way when floundering over their boot tops in mud. They could thank God that they had come through, and in all reverence remember those of their pals who had given their all (Applause).

Mayor Thanked

Ex-Regimental-Sergeant-Major R.M. McLachlan, who replied recalled the time of the battalions training on Salisbury Plain, which some liked and some did not. That was when they wore blue uniforms and white bands, and they did not know whether they were the enemy or what. (Laughter). The number of men present did not represent by one-eighth the number that left Wallasey six years ago, but, although there were so many absent, he thought that every department of the battalion was represented. On their behalf he thanked the Mayor for the kind way he was entertaining them (Applause.)

Ex-Sergeant-Major Keegan also recalled the time when good and high-spirited boys joined up to see that the country was right, and they were all pleased to see so many pleasant faces there when the Mayor had the honour of welcoming them home. They thanked him for the glorious time he was giving the boys of the Wallasey battalion. (Applause.)

Those Who Stayed At Home

Alderman Dr. J. Oldershaw, J.P., recalled the meeting in Messrs. Wilson and Wilson's salesroom when 150 men fell over themselves to join up, and then the scenes which led to their arrival at Chester. At the meetings of the Tribunal afterwards he often wondered if he had done the right thing in asking them to go, when so many others with lesser claims stayed at home, and he had often fallen on his knees by his bed at night and asked if he had done right in asking them to give their all for the preservation of the country. He felt it was the working of Providence to see so happy a re-union of the Wallasey boys who, without much pressing, joined H.M. Forces (Applause.)

The League Of Nations

The Mayor, in responses said he had only felt it his duty to invite them to a dinner as the boys who went from Wallasey on September 7th, 1914. He knew the British feeling that made them willing to fight for just a cause, but he thought it was now the duty of all to support the League of Nations, so that they had their children could live in peace and happiness. (Applause.)

The musical programme, which was arranged by Mr. Frank Weston of the Cosmo, Wallasey Village, went down exceptionally well, and included songs from Sergeant-Major Keegan and Private Liversake, Messrs. Margin and Kerble, two jolly singing boys from the Tivoli Theatre, New Brighton; Mr. George Hyam, the popular comedian from the Wallasey Hippodrome; Miss Madge Wilcox, Messrs. Bert Proctor, Tom Derbyshire and Ben Baker. Miss Gladys Simcoe and Mr George Freeman acted as accompanists.

◆ ◆ ◆

THE NEW "NELSON"

Wallasey News

23rd February 1935

There has been a veritable invasion of "The Nelson" Hotel at Grove Road, Wallasey, since the new building was opened to the public on Friday of last week. People have arrived not only from all districts of the borough but from distant parts of Wirral and Cheshire.

The reason for this steady trek to "The Nelson" is not far to seek. The old licensed house has been replaced by a palatial new building which may fairly be described as the last word in architecture of its kind and a real ornament to the neighbourhood. This really charming building must be inspected to be fully appreciated. The exterior and interior are examples of expert craftsmanship.

Viewed from the street the building strikes one as a modern gem of Tudor design. Built in stone, with Cotswold stone roofs and solid oak timbering as part of the construction, a pleasing impression is created to the passerby. The string courses have been embellished with fine carvings of various patterns. A very beautiful hanging sign has been erected on the front of the building with an exquisitely painted panel depicting Lord Nelson – a particularly pleasing example of the art of the craftsman, the panel enclosed in a frame of hand-forged iron work.

The interior is worthy of the hotel's outer aspect, and has the warmth and richness of a baronial hall. The decorative scheme has been carried out regardless of cost. The spacious lounge has been finished with a panelled ceiling and stone lined walls, with rubber flooring. Oak furniture and period curtains complete a pleasing scene.

A striking feature of the bar is a handsome stone fireplace extending from floor to ceiling, the carvings of which depict the arms of Nelson. Above hangs a magnificent reproduction of the "Victory" in colours, being an actual painting of the ship taken at Portsmouth. The gentlemen's smoke room, panelled in oak, is the last word in comfort.

The club-room upstairs is forty feet in length and twenty-two feet wide. It is oak panelled from floor to ceiling. The latter is also panelled in oak and embellished with carvings of Lord Nelson, Lady Hamilton and other period characters.

A feature of the whole building is the stained glass windows which shed a soft and veri-coloured glow upon the surroundings. In addition to the coal fires, without which the rooms would not be at their best, central heating guarantees warmth in every part of the building.

Ventilation is provided on a system which keeps the air clear of smoke without the necessity of opening windows. Pure air without draughts will add to the comfort of patrons.

No effort has been spared to provide drink under model hygienic conditions, The refrigerated cellar, under constant control, maintains the beer at an even temperature. The pipes, specially prepared from a substance guaranteeing purity and cleanliness, through which the beer passes up tp the bars, are easily detached for cleansing and inspection.

To the rear of the hotel tea gardens are being got ready in time for the summer season. Flower-beds and rose gardens are being laid out so that the rockeries and crazy pavements will be surrounded with flowers and the gardens equipped with dainty garden chairs. Special attention is being given to lighting and numerous modern artistic lamps are being erected. It will be possible to take tea and light refreshments under fairyland conditions throughout the day.

◆ ◆ ◆

TOWN LOSES HOSPITAL BATTLE

Wallasey NEWS

30th January 1981

Wallasey has lost its fight to keep a general hospital in the town when Arrowe Park opens in 1982. That news yesterday "bitterly disappointed" the town's MP and "infuriated" hospital campaigners.

The decision came despite a recommendation from Health Minister, Dr. Gerald Vaughan, who visited the town last year, that Wallasey's 93,000 people needed their own general hospital.

When Arrowe Park opens all Wallasey's hospital apart from Highfield in Mill Lane, will be phased out. Even Leasowe Hospital, which is the area's main arthritic unit, is expected to be shut down.

Wallasey will, however, get more services than it originally expected. A minor injuries unit it to be set up in Mill Lane, and at least 140 beds will be retained.

These will include 50 beds for observation and recovery cases, in addition to a geriatric unit, out-patient clinic, X-ray facilities and ante-natal clinic.

All surgical facilities will be transferred to Arrow Park.

The news is the climax of years of protest by Wallasey Hospital campaigners, who feel Arrowe Park is too far from Wallasey for it to be a viable hospital for emergency patients, particularly heart-attack and road accident victims.

Wallasey MP., Mrs. Lynda Chalker, who is Under-Secretary of State for Social Services, was shaken by the news.

"I am obviously bitterly disappointed," she said. "We have been forced to face the facts of medical opinion, the financial situation particularly in the Mersey Region, and the need to ensure the very highest standard of medical care."

What will infuriate many people is the fact that Heswall Children's Hospital is to be kept open, although this is in a unique position because it is run by the Liverpool Area Health Authority and not Wirral AHA.

Yesterday Coun. Jack Gershman, organiser of Wallasey's "Save Our Hospitals" campaign, said the news was "very disturbing."

"We are completely opposed to it and will use everything in our power to carry on fighting to the bitter end. It is in the Health Minister's final decision, then it is more important than ever that we make representations to him again," he said.

Private sources yesterday confirmed that the main opposition to Wallasey retaining its own general hospital has come from the medical profession.

The two tragedies at Victoria Central Hospital, involving Mrs Leah Leadbetter and David Yates, have led many doctors to believe that surgery should take place in the advanced hospital at Arrowe Park.

There was also the question of getting doctors to staff a Wallasey Satellite Hospital. The Area Medical Committee was concerned that any resources provided in Wallasey would take away facilities from Arrowe Park.

◆ ◆ ◆

NEW GROSVENOR BREWERY, SEACOMBE

Liverpool Mercury

Friday, 17th December, 1875

Mr. Paul Evans, the proprietor, has just reconstructed the Grosvenor Brewery, Victoria Street, Seacombe, which is one of the oldest establishments of the sort in Cheshire. This alteration was necessary. owing to the rapidly-increasing business of the concern. The "Grosvenor" is now one of the most compact breweries in the country, having been fitted up with all the modern appliances for the manufacture of the best article at the least possible cost. The new brewery, which is capable of brewing twice a day, has been erected by Mr. John Ellis, builder, Seacombe, from the plans and specifications of Messrs. Gregory and Haynes, brewery architects and machinists, Manchester. In celebration of the re-opening of the "Grosvenor," Mr. Evans entertained, on Wednesday evening about 60 gentlemen at dinner, at Mrs. Stokes's Seacombe Hotel. The company included Messrs, Wigan, W. Harbridge, J. Miles, W. Allen Thomas Ambler, W. Simms, W. Evans, H. Banks, John Fox, Ellis Davies, Thomas Smith, Mr. Grundy (Haddon Hall), A. H. Lease, Joughin Iveson, Dowdsworth, J. Wright, Whitehall Graham, &c. An excellent dinner was provided by Mrs. Stokes. Mr. Paul Evans, the proprietor of the Grosvenor Brewery, occupied the chair, and Mr. W. Allen, of Retford, the vice chair. The tables having been cleared, the chairman proposed the usual loyal and patriotic toasts, which were enthusiastically received. The Vice-Chairman proposed "success to the new Grosvenor Brewery," and in doing so remarked that Mr. Evans had spared neither expense nor trouble in making his establishment a model one, having fitted it up with all the most approved appliances for doing an extensive trade. He (the vice-chairman) knew something about brewing and, after looking over the "Grosvenor," he was bound to say that he never saw such a complete brewery in his life (Applause). The new brewery was capable of turning out treble the number of barrels of ale per week that could be manufactured at the old establishment; and, notwithstanding the increased facility for production, so compact was the new building and plant that it only covered the exact site of its predecessor. With regard to quality, it had been his pleasure that day to taste more than one sample of the ale produced at the "Grosvenor," and, speaking as a brewer, he had no hesitation in saying that he never tasted better ale in his life, and if Mr. Evans continued to brew an article of the same superior quality success was sure to attend his efforts. (The toast received with great applause). The Chairman, in acknowledging the compliment, thanked the company for their good wishes, and said he had no doubt that in time, with the assistance of those who had hitherto so kindly patronised him, he would be amply compensated for the expense and anxiety to which he had been put in the rebuilding of his premises. With increased facilities at his disposal for manufacturing, he hoped the number of his patrons would increase in the same ratio. In conclusion, he sincerely thanked his friends for their attendance that evening (Applause). - The toast of "The Patrons of the Grosvenor Brewery," proposed by Mr. W. Evans, was responded to by Mr. J. Wright and Mr. W. Harbridge of the Woodside Hotel. "The Trade, and its varied interests," and several other toasts, followed. The proceedings were enlivened at intervals by the excellent playing of Mr. Martin's efficient band.

◆ ◆ ◆

A MONSTRE WHEEL FOR NEW BRIGHTON

Liverpool Mercury

Saturday, 28th November, 1896

New Brighton, rapidly developing as a holiday resort, is to have a gigantic wheel which is to exceed in magnitude and attractions anything of the kind yet erected. The great wheels at the Chicago Exhibition, Earl's Court, and Blackpool, which have proved such money-making concerns, are to be utterly eclipsed. The top of the wheel will be about 350 feet high above the shore, and at various stages will have magnificent saloons and exhibition rooms. The site is admirably chosen, being the sea front now occupied by the New Brighton Palace, which has been purchased for this venture. An enormous number of people visit New Brighton every year. The Wallasey Ferry steamers carried to and fro 11,000,000 passengers, not counting season tickets. It is intended to provide for these vast numbers a sumptuous place of entertainment, and with this view the Palace will be entirely reconstructed and redecorated. The cost of the splendid freehold property, with foreshore rights, reconstruction of theatre and pavilions, and building the great wheel, will be about £130,000. One of the engineers employed in the erection of the Forth Bridge will superintend the putting up of the wheel. The splendid view of the Mersey, with its wonderful traffic of great Atlantic lines and other shipping, renders the site a singularly attractive one, and there can be little doubt that New Brighton as an up-to-date and healthy holiday district is about to rapidly progress. A company entitled the New Brighton Graydon Castle Great Wheel and Tower Company Limited has been formed to take over the whole of the property, and full details of the scheme are given in our advertising columns. The capital is £140,000 in £1 shares, and it is pointed out that if only 1,500,000 of the eleven million visitors pay for admission there will be a net profit of at least 50 per cent. The local authorities, it is stated, will carry out promenade improvements on the front, and a marine park, it is added, is to take the place of the contiguous waste grounds, and sand drives. As indicating the value of the great wheel as an attraction, and consequently as a source of revenue, attention is drawn to the earnings of the Earl's Court wheel, viz., £36,314 in six months and 29 days, and the recently erected wheel at Blackpool, viz., £15 3s. 10d. per hour during the first few days. In addition to the earnings of the wheel at New Brighton there will be receipts from entertainments and other attractions provided, and from the shops and restaurants along the front, estimated together at £16,000. The Palace is to be reconstructed and opened next season so that a considerable revenue will be secured during the building if the wheel. The whole of the shares are offered for subscription, the list closing on or before Tuesday next.

◆ ◆ ◆

NEWS IN SHORT 3

New Lock-Up

Liverpool Mercury
Friday, 30th June, 1843

At the Cheshire Quarter Sessions, held at Nether Knutsford, on Monday last, on the motion of I.W. Harden, Esq., J.P., seconded by Henry Winch, Esq., J.P., the handsome sum of four hundred pounds was voted by the county towards the erection of a suitable lock-up and constable's residence for the populous and flourishing townships of Poulton-cum-Seacombe, Liscard, and Wallasey. We congratulate our neighbours in Cheshire on their prospect of now speedily obtaining what has been so long sought for.

St. Paul's Church, Seacombe

Liverpool Mercury
Friday, 15th October, 1847

This place of worship was consecrated on Tuesday last by the Bishop of Chester. The church was crowded, and many could not obtain admittance. Amongst those present were the Revds. Messrs Tobin of Egremont; Philip, of St. Nicholas; Jones, of St. Andrew's; Stewart, of St. Bride's; Hampston, of St. James's; Pollock, of St. Mark's; Davies, of St. Paul's; Fenton of Wavertree; Dr. Byrth, of Wallasey; and several clergymen of Cheshire locality, &c.; also. G. Grant, H. Wynch, George Crump, H. Ripley, and others, Esquires. The usual ceremonies were solemnly gone through, the Bishop taking a large and zealous part. Dr. Byrth read prayers. For the text, his Lordship selected the latter clause of the 2nd verse, 9th chapter 1st Corinthians :- "The seal of mine apostleship are ye in the Lord." The choir was conducted on the occasion by Mr. Lewis.

Splendid Laburnum Tree

Liverpool Mercury
Tuesday, 30th May, 1848

There is now to be seen at Mr. Meadows's, Poulton-cum-Seacombe, (the Manor House), a beautiful Laburnum tree, so rich in size of flower and leaf, that it is admitted, by all who have seen it, to surpass any tree of the kind hitherto grown in this part of England. It is about twenty feet in height, and the branches overspread a circle of about that diameter. The leaves are larger than those usually produced in this species of decorative shrub, and it is scarcely possible adequately to describe the abundance, size, and brilliancy of the bloom. It hangs in gently-tapering pendants, so thick on every branch, as almost to hide the leaves, or at least to outshine them, forming, as it were, a chandelier of nature's fashioning, which the most skilful lapidary, had be precious stones of the same hue, would fail to accomplish. The pendants are from fifteen to eighteen inches in length, and in such clusters as to weigh down the branches. It is remarkable that this tree, planted originally about seven years ago, on another site, was blown out of the ground by a gale of wind four years since, and was transplanted, at hazard, to its present position, near the mansion. From the manner in which it has unexpectedly flourished, the arboriculturist may perhaps derive a hint for experiments in transplanting. The bloom is not yet full, and it is not improbable that it will yet average several inches more in length, with corresponding volume.

Conflagration At New Brighton

Liverpool Mercury
Friday, 26th September, 1851

On Tuesday evening last, a fire, attended with considerable loss of property, broke out in the livery stables of Mr. Wilkinson, near the Albion Hotel, New Brighton. It is not known how the fire originated, but at about eight o' clock it was discovered that the stables were in flames. Every exertion was immediately made to suppress the spread of the fire. Intelligence having been conveyed to the police station at Birkenhead, the engine and fire brigade were dispatched to the scene of the conflagration, and though they used every effort, the fire was not subdued until one o'clock the following morning. Four or five of the stables were totally destroyed. One horse was severely scorched, and a great number of fowls and a quantity of straw were burnt. The flames were distinctly seen from Woodside. The stables are insured, but not the stock, and the damage to the latter is estimated at £50.

Notice -- Purse Found

Liverpool Mercury
Friday, 20th July, 1855

Found, a few weeks ago, in Seacombe, a PURSE, containing money; and on the sandhills at New Brighton, a Brown SABLE VICTORINE. The owners may have the same on giving a proper description and paying the expense of advertising, &c., on application to Chief Constable Thomas Scambler, Liscard; or at the offices of the Wallasey Local Board of Health, Church Street, Egremont.
July 19th, 1855.

Wallasey Police Court

Liverpool Mercury
Wednesday, 22nd October, 1856

John Evans, landlord of the Jenny Lind Hotel, New Brighton, was charged with having four men and one woman in his house drinking between three and five o'clock on Sunday, the 12th instant. Police Officer Mason proved that one of the parties was a near resident, and he had a glass of ale before him. The bench considered the case proved, but the house being a well-conducted one inflicted the mitigated penalty of 5s. and 8s. 6d. costs. -- Robert Dawson, Trafalgar Hotel, North Egremont was charged with having three men in house drinking on Sunday, the 12th inst, at a quarter-past eleven o'clock in the morning. Fined 5s. and 8s. 6d. costs. -- Margaret Edwards, beerhouse keeper, New Brighton, was brought up by Police Officer Mason, for having three gentlemen sitting in the parlour. Mrs. Edwards said that they were travellers from Lancashire, and had had refreshments. Dismissed. -- Benjamin Davies, of the Swansea Arms, Seacombe, charged by Police Officer Mason with having his door open on the morning of Sunday, the 12th instant, and two men drinking, was ordered to pay the costs of the court, it being the first offence. -- William Davies, of Liscard, beerhouse keeper, was charged by Police Officer Mason with refusing to admit the police, and having two men in the back premises, they being neighbours. Admonished, and ordered to pay the costs of the court. -- William Ball, of the Sebastopol beerhouse, Wallasey, was charged by Police Officer Mason with having five persons in his house drinking, at 20 minutes past four o'clock on Sunday, the 12th instant, knowing they were not travellers. Cautioned, and to pay the costs, being newly in the business.

Egremont & New Brighton Ferries

Glasgow Herald
Friday, 25th May, 1860

The Wallasey Local Board of Health hereby offer the following PREMIUMS for the TWO most approved PLANS, accompanied by ESTIMATES for improving the existing Landing Places or constructing new Landing Places at the above Ferries, so as to render them in all respects convenient for Passenger Traffic, and, as regards Egremont Ferry, for Goods Traffic also, namely --

For the First best Plan for each Ferry...£50
For the second ditto...£25

The Plans selected are to remain the property of the Board.

Plans to be sent to the Offices of the Local Board, 1 Church Street, Egremont, near Birkenhead, on or before the 1st day of July next; and further information may be had, if required, on application to the Chairman of the Ferry Committee of such Board; or to the Undersigned, at his office, 3 Courtyard, Liverpool.
By Order.

T.K. HASSALL
Clerk to the Board.
May 17, 1860.

Wallasey Ferries Notice

**Liverpool Mercury
Thursday, 26th June, 1862**

The recently constructed PIER at New Brighton, in Cheshire, forming a splendid Esplanade of 1,000 feet, at the entrance of the river Mersey, is now Open to the Public, Free of Charge, by order of the Wallasey Local Board.

Braithwaite Poole, General Manager
Head Offices, Egremont, Cheshire, June, 1862.

Caution To Swearers

**Liverpool Mercury
Saturday, 12th March, 1864**

At the Wallasey Police Court, on Thursday, before Mr. T.Holland, Thomas Evans, Little Brighton, was brought up on a warrant (having failed to appear on summons), charged with having used obscene and blasphemous language on board one of the Wallasey ferry boats on the 22nd ult. The case was proved, he was fined £1 and costs, or 14 days' imprisonment.

The New Brighton Pier Bill

**Liverpool Mercury
Saturday, 14th May, 1864**

Yesterday this bill came before Lord Redesdale's committee in the House of Lords, and, being wholly unopposed, was passed. It will now be sent without delay to the House of Commons, where it will be read a third time after the Whitsuntide recess, and then returned to the House of Lords to receive the royal assent.

This bill, of which a synopsis was given in the *Mercury* when it was originally introduced, contains 58 clauses and a schedule. Its object is to construct a pier and works at New Brighton for public recreation and other useful purposes. The bill proposes that the Wallasey Local Board should be authorised to join in the making of the pier and works, and that the company, which it is now proposed to incorporate, should be authorised to sell or lease, and that the Wallasey Local Board should be authorised to purchase, or take on lease, the proposed pier and works. The 4th section incorporates Mr. Harold Littledale and others whose names are not given into a company, to be called "The New Brighton Pier Company," with a capital of £30,000, in 3000 shares of £10 each, and with power to borrow on mortgage £10,000. Clause 17 describes the works to be made as follows :- "A pier or quay, to be wholly situate in the parish of Wallasey, commencing at or near the eastern end of Victoria Road, in New Brighton, in the said parish, at a point about 100 feet north-east of the north-eastern corner of the Ferry Hotel, and projecting into the foreshore or bed of the river of the Mersey, in an eastwardly direction, for a distance of 900 feet or thereabouts, with a head to the said pier 500 feet in length, or thereabouts, with an angle therewith." By the subsequent clauses, the working plans are to be submitted for the approval of the Board of Trade, the pier and works are to be completed within three years from the passing of the act, shipowners are to be answerable for any damage done by their servants, powers are given to lease the rates and tolls, and the company are authorised to erect so much of the pier and works herby authorised to be constructed as may be required by the Wallasey Local Board for the purpose of their ferry at New Brighton. The schedule to which this act refers authorises the company to charge the following rates and tolls : - For every person who shall use the pier for the purpose walking for exercise, pleasure, or any other purpose, except for embarking or disembarking, for each and every time a sum not exceeding 2d.; for every Bath or sedan chair taken on the pier, for each and every time not exceeding 6d.; and for every perambulator 2d.; and by the 28th section the company reserve to themselves the right to grant to persons using the pier pass on such terms, and for a period not exceeding twelve months, as may be agreed upon, provided that in granting such tickets no preference shall be given to any particular person.

Wallasey Petty Sessions

Liverpool Mercury
Thursday, 14th May, 1868

These sessions were held yesterday at the Courthouse, Liscard, before Mr. J.C. Ewart and Major Chambres. William Singelhurst, of Moreton, who has an office at No. 12 Union Street, Liverpool, was summoned to show cause why he had not paid £7 7s., with 2s. 9d, interest to the Wallasey Local Board, being his portion of the expense of erecting privies to three iron houses in the parish of Wallasey. Me. Ewer, law clerk to the local board, supported the summons; the defendant was not in attendance. Mr. J.T. Lea, surveyor to the board, proved that the work had been done, and the magistrates made an order for the payment of the amount claimed, with costs. -- James Minnis, a shoemaker, living at Liscard, was summoned for having assaulted Eliza Neville, a respectable-looking middle aged woman. The complainant, who resides next door to the defendant, saw on the 6th instant a bucket at his (defendant's) door. Finding that it was a bucket she had missed some time previously, she took it into the house, but she was also followed by Mrs. Minnis, who demanded it back. Some words were exchanged between the parties, and ultimately the defendant seized the bucket and struck the complainant on the head with it. For the defence, Mrs. Minnis and her sister were called, and they deposed that the bucket belonged to the defendant, and that the attack was fist made by the complainant. The defendant was cautioned, and ordered to pay costs. -- Two young men, named Thomas Cainan and Thomas Upton, were summoned for galloping on horseback on Sunday evening, the 26th ultimo. The magistrates considered it a very dangerous practice, and fined the defendants 20s. and costs, or in default of payment to be imprisoned one month.

Cheshire Quarter Sessions

Cheshire Observer
Saturday, 6th July, 1872

Pleaded Guilty. Mary Farley, Seacombe, charged with stealing 1s. 10½d. the property of Mary Fletcher, at Liscard on the 18th June. Seven months in prison, and five years in a Reformatory.

Wirral Licensing Sessions

Liverpool Mercury
Friday, 30th September, 1881

The adjourned licensing session for the hundred of Wirral was held yesterday, at the County Hall, Birkenhead, the magistrates on the bench being Lieutenant-Colonel King and Messrs. G.B. Kerferd. T.R. Lee, W. Hope, L. Mann, and Captain Molyneux.

The "black list" was first dealt with. Thomas Monk, of the

Seacombe Ferry Hotel, was fined 20s. and costs, on the 20th of August, for having his premises open in prohibited hours. Mr. Moore supported the application for the renewal of the license, stating that the hotel was conducted by a limited company, of whom Mr. Philip Eoerle and other gentlemen were the directors, and Mr. Monk's name was merely continued as the holder of the license until next transfer day. The license was renewed, as were the license of the Thomas Baker, Egremont Ferry Hotel, Liscard, fined 20s. and costs on the 20th of August for having premises open during prohibited hours. The following beer license was also renewed -- James Smith, Oddfellows' Arms, Seacombe.

New Application

William Proffitt senior, builder, applied for a spirit license to a house at the corner of Ashville Road and Oakdale Road, Seacombe.. Mr. Wilkinson supported the application, and said that no other public house could be built on the estate. The nearest public house to the applicant's premises was 800 yards distant, and there were only two cottage beerhouses, which were quite inadequate for the wants of the neighbourhood. Mr. Proffitt also applied for a beer and wine license, to be consumed on and off the premises. Inspector Dutton was called to give evidence as to the character of the applicant. The witness said he had not seen Mr. Proffitt for 25 years. He was then a shoemaker, and he might have been transported since for what witness knew (Laughter.) Superintendent Egerton said he did not consider the applicant a fit and proper person to have a license. On the previous day he was fined 5s. by the Wallasey magistrates for being on licensed premises in prohibited hours, but the information was withdrawn. Witness had also seen Mr. Proffitt figure before the Wallasey bench at the instance of the local board of the district, for substituting bad for good material in the building of houses, and so on (Laughter.) Lieut-Colonel King intimated that the magistrates were unanimous in refusing all Mr. Proffitt's applications, and said that Mr. Wilkinson had done his best to whitewash the character of his client. (Laughter.)

Thomas Philip Nevin applied for a wine license to the Plough Inn beerhouse, Poulton. Mr. Thompson supported the application, which was granted.

Fatal Accident To A Master Carter

Liverpool Mercury
Friday, 9th June, 1882

An inquest was held yesterday, at the Abbottsford Hotel, Seacombe, before Mr. Churton. coroner, on the body of William Bridgewater, master carter, who resided in Wheatland Lane. On Wednesday afternoon the deceased was seated in front of the buffer of a railway waggon in Birkenhead Road, at the docks, and was in the act of getting down, when his foot slipped and he fell upon his back on the line. One of the wheels of the waggon passed over him, and his left shoulder and arm were crushed in a shocking manner. He was immediately conveyed to the Seacombe Cottage Hospital, where he was attended by Dr. Byerley, Dr. Craigmile, and Dr. Clarke, but he never recovered from the shock, and died at twelve o'clock at night. During the inquiry, the coroner and some of the jurymen animadverted on the reckless and foolish custom of men riding on the buffers of wagons. A verdict of "Accidental death" was returned. The deceased was 59 years of age.

Wallasey Petty Sessions

Liverpool Mercury
Thursday, 22nd June, 1882

Before Messrs. G.B. Kerferd, R. Lowndes, And L. Mann

Brutal Assault On A Sister-In-Law - James Dennis, a labourer, was brought up on remand, charged with unlawfully wounding Margaret Walker, his sister-in-law. It appeared that the parties lived at Seacombe, and that on Saturday night week the prisoner's wife and the prosecutrix, and in a passion seized a jug and struck her a violent blow on the head. The prosecutrix was rendered insensible, and she was taken to Seacombe Cottage Hospital, where she remained a week suffering from her injuries. The magistrates considered it a brutal assault, and committed the prisoner to jail for four months, with hard labour.

Wounded With A Teacup - William Reynolds, a joiner, was charged with unlawfully wounding Hannah Ireland, the wife of a flatman belonging to Seacombe. On Saturday, the prosecutrix and the prisoner's wife quarrelled. The prisoner interfered, and struck the prosecutrix twice with a teacup, inflicting a wound four inches long. The prosecutrix was taken to the Seacombe Cottage Hospital, where the wound was stitched by Dr. Craigmile. In his defence, the prisoner stated that the prosecutrix first struck him, and that he merely pushed the teacup against her to prevent her striking him a second time. Witnesses were also called to prove that the prosecutrix had been drinking during the day and had been quarrelling with his neighbours. The magistrates ordered the prisoner to be imprisoned for two months with hard labour.

A Turbulent Widow - Mary Allison, a widow, was summoned for wilfully damaging a door in the house occupied by Mr. Craig, at Upper Brighton, the manager of the Wallasey tramways, and also for assaulting Mrs. Craig. Mr. Danger appeared for the defence. It seemed that on the 12th inst. the defendant was a passenger in one of the tramway cars from Seacombe to New Brighton, and had with her her little girl. She refused to pay a fare for the girl, who, she said, was under age. The guard, however, insisted upon being paid for the girl, and took her to the manager's house. The defendant then became very violent, and struck Mrs. Craig a blow in the face. She also damaged a door. The magistrates inflicted a fine of 5s. and costs in each case, besides ordering the defendant 15s. for the damage to the door, making £2 2s. altogether.

Wallasey Cemetery

Liverpool Mercury
Tuesday, 8th August, 1882

To Asphalters

The Wallasey Local Board require TENDERS for ASPHALTING FOOTWALKS (about 3470 yards superficial) at the New Cemetery, Rake Lane, Liscard.

Specifications can be seen at the office of the architect, G.E. Grayson, Esq., 31 James Street, Liverpool.

Sealed tenders, addressed to 'The Chairman of the Cemetery Committee' and endorsed 'Tender for Asphalting Footwalks', to be left at my office, Church Street, Egremont, Cheshire, before Five o' clock in the afternoon of FRIDAY the 25th inst.

The Board do not bind themselves to accept the lowest to any tender. By order --

T. SOMERVILLE JONES
Clerk to the Board
Public Offices, Egremont, Aug. 5, 1882

The Proposed Infectious Diseases Hospital In Wallasey

Liverpool Mercury
Monday, 26th February, 1883

At the usual monthly meeting of the Wallasey Local Board, on Thursday, the following resolution will be submitted by the Works and Health Committee:- That the recommendation of this committee, passed on the 16th ult. and confirmed by the board on the last inst., to purchase 2½ acres of land in Mill Lane belonging to the governors of the Wallasey Free Grammar School, on certain conditions, be rescinded, and, in lieu thereof, that three acres, or thereabouts, of such land be purchased on the conditions named in a proposal made to the board by Mr. James Smith, of Dalmorton House, Upper Brighton, and, also, on condition that the Local Government Board approve the same as a site for a hospital for infectious disease. Mr. Smith proposal referred to as follows:- "That the Wallasey Local Board purchase three acres, or thereabouts. of the land belonging to the governors fronting Mill Lane, and make an approach to the back land. Mr. Smith to purchase the remainder of the land belonging to the governors, say 10 acres or thereabouts, for £2500, and present it to the parish (through the local board), on condition that the board lay out the land as a suitable recreation ground, draining, levelling, and, in future, maintaining it in efficiency according to the usual regulations of public parks." It will be proposed that the best thanks to the board be accorded to Mr. Smith for his generous offer, as embodied in the above-named proposal.

A Polluted Well At Wallasey

Liverpool Mercury
Monday, 1st October, 1883

At the Wallasey Petty Sessions on Saturday last before Mr. W.T. Jacob and Captain Molyneux, the adjourned application made on the previous Wednesday by Mr. Somerville Jones, clerk to the Wallasey Local Board, for an order to close a well belonging to Mrs. Alice Meadows, from which the tenants of the Boot Inn and adjoining two cottages, Wallasey Road, Liscard, were supplied with water for drinking and domestic purposes, was again heard. Mr. Jones stated that the well was polluted as to the prejudicial to health, and that the families living in those houses had been attacked by typhoid fever. He stated that, in the meantime, the water had been analysed by Dr. Campbell Brown, and submitted his certificate, which stated that the use of this water for drinking or domestic purposes might tend to spread the disease. Drs. Watson and Cannell, who attended the patients, as well as Dr. Craigmile (the medical officer of health), proved that the water from this well was used by the persons who had been attacked by the fever. The magistrates made an order that the pump be forthwith discontinued and removed, and the well made into a "draw well," to be in future used only for livery purposes.

Shocking Fatality To A Boy At Liscard

Liverpool Mercury
Wednesday, 2nd July, 1884

An inquest was held at yesterday at the Wellington Hotel, Liscard, before Mr. Churton, coroner, on the body of George Arthur Welsh, six years of age, whose parents reside in Seaview Road. It appeared that on Friday evening last the deceased was playing close to a newly made lime-pit at Liscard, when he fell into the pit, and was burnt all over the body in a very severe manner. He was taken home and attended to by Dr. Cannell, but death ensued on Sunday morning. The jury returned a verdict of "Accidental death."

Sad Bathing Fatality

Cheshire Observer
Saturday, 13th August, 1887

A sad bathing accident occurred at New Brighton on Sunday morning, resulting in the drowning of a young man named Alfred Heap. It appears that the deceased and two other youths were seen bathing in the Mersey at the Magazines, New Brighton, about eight o'clock on Sunday morning, by PC Wainwright, who was on duty near the place. The officer saw the deceased go underwater as if he were drowning, and he shouted to the other lads to go to his assistance, but they apparently did not hear him, as they took no notice. The body did not rise to the surface. The deceased, who was about 18 years of age, was a son of Sergeant Heap, of the Cheshire Constabulary. formerly stationed at Wallasey, but now at Hyde. The unfortunate youth had been in the office of Mr. A.C. Kent, clerk to the county magistrates. at Abbey Street, Birkenhead, for five or six years, and was a young man of much promise and greatly respected by all who knew him. It was low water at the time of the accident, and the deceased was a good swimmer, but the place where he was drowned has the reputation of being dangerous, and has been the scene of several similar fatalities. Deceased resided in Liscard.

Wallasey Petty Sessions

Liverpool Mercury
Thursday, 20th August, 1891

The Obstructions of New Brighton Shore --- William Wilkinson, Tollemache Street, New Brighton, was fined 10s. and costs for obstructing the foreshore at New Brighton by placing there an ice cream and ginger beer stall on Saturday 1st August. There was a small number of similar information's, but the summonses were withdrawn on a technical objection, and test summonses will come before the court at a later date. The point at issue was whether the obstruction occurred above or below high water mark.

Prosecution For Cruelty --- Joseph Jones, of Albion Street, Upper Brighton, was summoned for causing a mare to be worked whilst in an unfit state for work, owing to lameness; and Robert Jones was summoned for working the animal. The cases were proved by Inspector Osborn, of the RSPCA. – Joseph Jones was fined 5s. and costs, and Robert Jones was ordered to pay the costs – 4s. 6d.

Death of Major Chambres

Liverpool Mercury
Monday, 28th August, 1893

The announcement made on Saturday morning of the death of, at the age of 74, of Major William Chambres, which occurred on Friday night at his residence, Wallasey Grange, Grove Road, Wallasey, was received with deep regret by his large number of acquaintances in Liverpool and the Cheshire suburbs. The deceased gentleman was a member of the firm Messrs. William Chambres and Co., stock brokers, North Western Bank Buildings, 6 Dale Street, Liverpool. Of late years he had not entered prominently into the public life of the city; but for six years he was a member of the City Council, having in 1874 been elected an alderman in the stead of Mr. J.G. Morris, who resigned. Major Chambres had not previously been a member of the Council. On several occasions he was asked to accept the mayoralty, but declined the preferred honour. He was a magistrate of the city, his name having been placed on the commission of the peace in 1877. He was also a justice of the peace for Wirral, his appointment dating back to 1867. In that capacity his services were frequently given at the Wallasey Police Court, as he was always ready to take duty if occasion required it. Up to two years ago, when his health began to fail, he was chairman of the licensing bench. As a volunteer officer, Major Chambres was widely known, and held in great esteem, both by his brother officers and by the rank and file of the corps with which he was connected. He held his commission in the New Brighton corps of the Cheshire and Carnarvonshire Artillery Volunteers, from which he retired some years ago with the honorary rank of major. Among other positions of a public nature that the deceased had worthily filled was that of Deputy-Lieutenant for Cheshire. He was also one time a member of the Wallasey Local Board, was a member of the Committee of the New Brighton Convalescent Home and a Governor of the Wallasey Grammar School. In religion he was a consistent supporter of the Established Church, and in politics he was a staunch Conservative. Charities in the district where he lived received generous help at his hands, and in Wallasey, in the parochial affairs of which place he took a warm interest, his genial disposition and kindly manner rendered him popular amongst all parties. When the news of his death was made known, flags were hung at half-mast on the Wallasey ferry boats and at the Seacombe Stage. At the Liverpool Town Hall the flag was also half-mast, out of respect to his memory, and also to the memory of ex-Alderman Nicol, who pre deceased him only a few hours. In addition to his more immediate business connections, Mr. Chambres was a director of various insurance companies.

Wallasey Police Court

Liverpool Mercury
Thursday, 24th September, 1894

Robbing A Child - A woman named Eliza Nolan was charged with stealing 2s. 8d. from the person of Sarah Anne Andrews, a child living at Liscard, on 22nd inst. The girl was returning from an errand on the day in question, and when in the Warren Drive the prisoner stopped her, spoke to her, and stole the money out of her pocket. The accused had previously been convicted of thieving, and she was now sent to jail for two months with hard labour.

Theft From A Well-Known Volunteer Shot - A stylish-dressed young woman named Kate Ellis, aged 21, living in Folly Lane, Wallasey, was charged with stealing a gold watch and two medals, value £8, the property of John Jackson Marr, electrical engineer, 35 Church Street, Egremont. Mrs Marr stated that the prisoner had visited her house several times, and was there on Tuesday, 11th inst. The watch was at the time on the mantelpiece in one of the bedrooms, but the following day it was missed. The prosecutor stated that on the 16th inst. he saw the medals safe in their cases. The medals were those of the Scottish Twenty Club, and had been won by him. Further evidence showed that, on the 17th inst., the prisoner pledged the medals for two guineas at the shop of R. H. Reid, pawnbroker, 10 Mount Pleasant, Liverpool, and had stated that her husband had won them in connection with the Scottish Twenty Club. She afterwards pledged the watch at Messrs. Parley and Sergeant's, London Road, Liverpool, giving the name of Mary Lee, Gladstone Road, Liverpool. Prisoner pleaded guilty and the father of the accused stated that he was greatly surprised at what had come to his knowledge. His daughter had always borne a good character, and he did not what had prompted her to commit such an act. The Chairman, after consideration, said the bench had been unable to find extenuating circumstances in the case, and they felt compelled, very reluctantly, to deprive the prisoner of the advantages of the First Offenders Act. She must go to jail for one month. The accused was removed below crying bitterly.

Fire In A Seacombe Dwelling House

**Liverpool Mercury
Thursday, 24th August, 1899**

At 10.10 p.m on Tuesday, the Seacombe fire brigade, in charge of Maguire, and the Liscard brigade, in charge Superintendent Haworth, were summoned to an outbreak of fire in the dwelling house 132, Wheatland Lane, Seacombe, occupied by John Dunn. It appeared that in the front bedroom the body of a three-year-old child was laid out, surrounded by lighted candles, which are supposed to have ignited the window curtains and set fire to the room. The firemen found the compartment well ablaze, and they managed to carry away the corpse before it was burnt. The police took the body to the mortuary. The furniture in the room was destroyed, the damage amounting to £20.

Licensing Sessions

**Liverpool Mercury
Friday, 8th December, 1899**

The following transfer of licenses were consented to :- Boot Inn, Wallasey Road, Liscard, from Thomas Joseph Phillips to

Henry Wright, 22 Central Park Avenue, Liscard; Nags Head, Rake Lane, Upper Brighton, from the late Thomas Biggs Roberts to Mary Ann Roberts, widow; Prince Alfred Hotel, Church Road, Seacombe, from Thomas Jones to Eliza Mary Jones, spinster. The magistrates consented to alterations being made at the Farmers' Arms, Moreton, and the Plough Inn, Moreton, and refused to allow alterations to the Boot Inn, Liscard; No. 7 Union Street, Egremont and the Stanley Arms, Seacombe.

Vessels Fired At

Wallasey NEWS
8th August 1914

There were great excitement at New Brighton on Thursday morning about seven o'clock, the booming of the battery guns making a terrific noise. Hundreds of people hurriedly dressed and rushed to the promenade, where it was found that a large sailing vessel had failed to answer the signal from the battery, and shots were being fired across her bow, thus compelling her captain to drop anchor. A similar incident happened the previous day with another vessel.

According to the regulations boats have to pass through the examination anchorage and be examined by the examining officer. No vessel must be navigated or be at anchor between sunset and sunrise seaward of a line joining the Seaforth Battery and New Brighton Pier, except she be entering or leaving port.

Poulton Bridge To Be Tolled Free

Wallasey NEWS
6th July 1935

A final move has taken place in the attempt being made by Wallasey Corporation, jointly with Birkenhead Corporation, to free Poulton Bridge of tolls.

A meeting of representatives of both authorities, at which Councillor C.McVey (Birkenhead) presided, was held at the Town Hall, Wallasey, on Thursday afternoon and terms tentatively agreed to by the local authorities concerned with the Merseyside Dock Board, were finally approved.

It was also decided to approach the Ministry of Transport for a grant towards the cost.

The cost of making Poulton Bridge toll-free has not been made public, but we understand that the terms are considered satisfactory. Birkenhead is to pay sixty per cent of the total cost when the final figure has been ascertained.

Old Rectory Gutted By Mystery Fires

Wallasey NEWS
4th January 1975

Two mystery fires almost completely destroyed the old rectory of Saint Hilary's, one of the town's oldest buildings, over the weekend.

The seventeenth-century stone house was completely gutted by a blaze on Friday night. Two days later a second fire caused further damage to wooden interior infrastructures.

Nobody was injured in either of the fires. The rectory has not been inhabited for some years, and was being used for storage.

It was one of only seven buildings in the town listed by the Department of the Environment as being of historical interest.

Break-Ins

Sources in the Fire Brigade say they have "no idea" as to the cause of the blazes but that there had been recent break-ins by youth

Built in 1632, the old rectory has not been occupied by a resident rector since 1940's.

The present rector, Canon Digby Thomas, said that the church had no immediate plans to restore the building.

"What happens to it now is really up to the Department of the Environment," he added.

◆ ◆ ◆

BRIGHTON STREET FIRE

Wallasey News

Saturday 7th February 1929

The disastrous fire which resulted in the loss of three lives and injuries to a man and his three children, in Brighton Street in the early hours of Tuesday morning, was the most tragic in Wallasey for many years.

It is made still more poignant by the fact that one of the victims, Mrs. Groves, wife of William Richard Groves, the occupant of the upholsterer's shop, 188, Brighton Street, leaves three young children, the eldest being only four years of age.

The other victims were

Miss Rose O'Connor (86) and her niece, Miss Mary Linden, middle-aged, who were suffocated.

Mr. Groves and his three children were burned about the face and hands, the eldest child being the most badly burnt, and all were detained at the Central Hospital.

The outbreak which developed with fierce intensity was first discovered by Mr. Groves before 4.30 a.m., and he raised the alarm. Even then the flames had begun to sweep upwards, and he rushed from the room with his children, expecting Mrs. Groves to follow. He had got two of the children safely through the shop and into the street when he was found near the door by Police-Sergt. Collings, who immediately went into the shop and rescued the third child from the foot of the stairs, which were blazing furiously. As the sergeant carried the child out of the shop the stairs collapsed, and on his return he found the flames had been driven across the approach to the upper rooms. Undaunted, the officer attempted to find another way to the women trapped in their bedrooms above the shop, but after smashing a kitchen door at the rear of the premises he was beaten back by the flames and had to abandon his brave attempt.

FIREMEN BAULKED.

When the foremen arrived, they also were baulked by the flames, which, fanned by the wind, swept upwards, and at one point cut through the roof, lighting up all the neighbourhood. It was then utterly impossible to enter the bedrooms, though several attempts were made, and it was only after the firemen had battled with the outbreak from extension flames at the front and rear of the house for some time that a search could be made and the full extent of the tragedy revealed.

Mrs. Groves was found suffocated under the bed, in the back bedroom; Miss. O'Connor was dead in bed in the front room, where she, too, had been suffocated, and Miss. Linden was on the floor at her bedside.

Mrs. Groves was partly dressed – a fact which rather substantiates a suggestion that she hesitated to follow her husband in order to put on some clothes, and was trapped by the flames while doing so.

The bodies were covered with sheets and lowered from a bedroom window by a lifeline, and afterwards taken to the Seacombe mortuary.

ICICLES ON LADDERS

As the firemen battled with the outbreak they had the further hardship of the water freezing and forming icicles as it washed down the ladders. Fortunately, there was quite a strong force of water from the hydrants, and there was a no difficulty from

OLD NEWS OF WALLASEY

this source.

Some idea of the intensity of the outbreak and the rapidity with which it developed was given to a "News" representative by Mr. Eddas, a dairyman who occupies the adjoining shop.

"The first I heard was a cry of 'Fire'," he said, "and I thought at first it might be in by our building. I found it was not, and on looking through the bedroom window I saw a man in his shirt and trousers screaming out 'Fire'. He seemed to be almost demented with grief. Then I saw two police officers, and I went out. The whole of the building was a mass of flames, and burned like a furnace. It seemed certain that my shop and another on the other side would be destroyed, and I gathered what loose money I had in the shop. The brigade were faced with what seemed a hopeless task, because the flames were fierce and burnt through the first floor with amazing rapidity, lighting up the whole of the district. The blaze lasted altogether about an hour and a half, and the firemen did wonderfully well to save the adjoining shops, which, fortunately, were divided by a three brick wall."

Though there were no actual eyewitnesses of the attempted escape of the victims of the exception of Mr. Groves, graphic stories were told by neighbours of the scenes immediately following the discovery, and an extraordinary fact was revealed. This was that the occupants of Messrs. Priestly's, photographic premises opposite, were awakened two hours before the outbreak was discovered by a police officer who told them he could smell burning which seemed to have its source on their premises. A search was made immediately, and as a result it was thought that the fumes came from an oil stove in the house. Two hours later the household was again awakened, but this time by the cry of "Fire," and they found Mr. Groves in the street crying out "My wife's in there. Help, help." It was then seen that the shop and the rooms above were ablaze. On running out they saw Mr. Groves in a grief-stricken state, banging his fists on the hoarding. He was taken into

Miss Priestly's houses, and the children also were cared for, their burns being dressed and the four afterwards taken to the hospital in the ambulance.

Fire Two Hours Before

The children were at first sheltered in the watchman's hut at the corner of Clarendon Road, where the Corporation watchman, Mr. Edward Horseman, very kindly looked after them and provided the two children with bread and butter and tea.

Everything in the shop and the bedrooms was destroyed, part of the roof fell in, furniture was burned and broken, and a motor cycle in the back was wrecked, its tyres being burned off and the bodywork charred and twisted.

OFFICIALS AND THE FIRE

When a "News" representative sought an official statement on the tragedy and its cause he was told that the cause had not been established, and that the only person able to give any information of what occurred in the building immediately after the discovery was the husband of the youngest victim, William Edward Groves, who is still in Central Hospital with his three children. He has not yet been able to make a complete statement on the occurrence, but we understand he had stated in hospital that he thought his wife was following him. When he attempted to return again to the bedroom he was prevented from doing so by the barricade formed by the blazing staircase. The police statement of the tragedy showed that Sergt. Collings and Police Constable Swetnam were on duty near the corner of Tobin Street, when they heard the shout of "Fire".

They went to No. 188, Brighton Street and found the whole premises one mass of flames. As Sergeant Collings went through the door part of the staircase collapsed. He succeeded in rescuing one of the children from the burning house.

The father, Mr. Groves, had already escaped from the burning building with his two other children, who had been taken to a neighbour's house, all having been more or less badly burned.

When the fire brigade arrived, in charge of Inspector Nicholson, the flames were so fierce that it was utterly impossible to enter the building, although repeated attempts were made.

When at last the firemen did enter the premises they found the old lady, Miss Rosie O'Connor, dead in bed in the front bedroom over the shop. They also found the old lady's niece, Miss Mary Linden, and Mrs. Groves lying dead on the floor near the bed. They had, there is little doubt, died from suffocation, and their bodies were badly burned after death.

Apparently the fire had started in the back kitchen, and it was probable that nearby was a store of upholstery, and that this had been ignited and caused the furious flames, which ascended to the upper rooms and travelled right through to the roof. Part of the roof of the back bedroom had ultimately fallen in.

A statement afterwards made by Sergt. Collings said that the shop was a mass of flames when he arrived there and found Mr. Groves near the door with two of his children, shouting something about his wife being inside.

SUGGESTED CAUSES

Several causes of the outbreak have been suggested, but no reliance can at present be placed on any of them. One is that a neighbour heard the sound of an explosion, apparently caused by gas; another is that a lamp had been left burning to keep the pipes free from frost, while the "News" was credibly informed that, the previous night some rubbish had been found burning at the rear of the premises and had been stamped out by Mr. Groves. Whether they smoldered and broke out again later is not known.

INQUIRY PROCEEDINGS TAKE FOUR MINUTES

The inquest proceedings were opened by Mr. J.C. Bate, the West Cheshire Coroner, with a jury on Wednesday afternoon, and lasted four minutes, only evidence of identification being taken.

Mr. Alfred Edward Kelly, of 49 Rocky Lane, Anfield, Liverpool, identified the youngest victim as his daughter, Mrs. Emmelina May Groves (25), and the others as Miss Rose O'Connor (86) and her niece, Miss Mary Linden (51).

The Coroner told the jury that Mr. Groves would not be the chief witness, but he was in hospital and would not be available for three weeks. The inquest would therefore be adjourned until February 13th.

NOTHING KNOWN ABOUT VICTIMS

Very little is known about the victims of the fore, as Mr. Groves and his family came to live in Wallasey less than nine months ago. Until then they had lived in Liverpool, Miss O'Connor being a distant relative of the family.

◆ ◆ ◆

WALLASEY MEN IN NORTH SEA BATTLE

Wallasey NEWS

10th June 1916

There were a few Wallasey men on the ships of the cruiser squadron which gallantly challenged the German Fleet [Jutland]. On *H.M.S. Indefatigable* were two lads – Richard James Fenby, son of Captain George Fenby, of 57 Merton Road, Liscard, and James A.D. Bent, the son of Mrs. Lolley, of 2, The Grove, Seacombe.

Richard Fenby was an old boy of the Manor Road Council School, and had only been to sea since last June, when he joined the *Powerful*, but was afterwards transferred to the *Indefatigable*. He was seventeen years of age. James Bent was sixteen years of age, and intimation has been received that he must be regarded as dead. His father is serving on *H.M.S. Slefoy*, and he has a brother on *H.M.S. Theosis*.

On *H.M.S. Defence* were two local shipmates, Gunner Watkin Lythgoe, of 3 Balmoral Road, New Brighton, and Norman Brown of 2 Summer Hill, New Brighton.

Oakdale Bowler's Thrilling Experience

Stoker Fred Spicer, of 108 Ashville Road, Seacombe, in a letter to his father, wrote of the thrilling experience he had passed through whilst serving on *H.M.S Porpoise* (torpedo boat). He writes: "I don't know how our ship got through it all so lucky.

There were four of us – the *Porpoise, Ardent, Tipperary* and *Fortune*. We met some German cruisers, and as far as I could see our ship was the only one to come through safe. It was the *Fortune* that saved us, for a German battleship was just about to fire a broadside at us, when the *Fortune* came up and whilst maneuvering for position to fire a torpedo she received the broadside that was intended for us. She was lifted clean out of the water and exploded, making a lot of smoke. The German caught us with a couple of shells putting two of our boilers out of action and bursting a torpedo, killing two and wounding two of our men. We also had our main steam pipe blown away. We managed to get to port safely, and we will soon be ready to have a go at the enemy again. I had the pleasure of seeing a few German ships go under."

Stoker F. Spicer is, Mr.J. Ryan informs us, Oakdale's youngest club member, and he has the congratulations of all his club chums on his lucky escape.

A Warrior Survivor
Seacombe's Lad's Luck

On Wednesday morning Mr. J.C. Jones, a survivor of the *Warrior*, which suffered severely in the naval battle, arrived at his home, 42 Geneva Road, Seacombe. Save for the slight reaction after the tremendous nervous strain of the engagement he was in the best of health.

The *Warrior*, which came up when the great battle cruisers were already at grips, was hotly engaged for half an hour. She was so severely damaged by shell that she then withdrew from the fight and indeed would have been sunk altogether but for the timely help of the *Warspite*. The story of the gallant attempt by a channel steamer to tow the disabled cruiser to port is well known, and how eventually the *Warrior* had to be abandoned and her crew transferred. Her casualties had been heavy, for out of a crew of seven hundred odd more than eighty had been killed and nearly fifty wounded. Among the survivors was J.C. Jones, a lad of eighteen, who was said to be youngest of his rating on the ship.

His mother first knew he was unharmed by a telegram she received on Saturday morning saying he was quite safe and asking her not to worry.

On his return home he was naturally reluctant to speak of his terrible experiences, and simply remarked it was wonderful how he came out of it.

Mr. Jones, who was educated at the Higher Elementary School, Vaughan Road, joined the Navy some twelve months ago.

Killed On The "Black Prince"

David McConochie, the eldest son of Mr and Mrs McConochie, who was 22 years of age, was killed in action on board *H.M.S. Black Prince*. His parents live at 45 Green Lane, Liscard. He was a member for some years of the 22nd Battalion Liverpool Boys Brigade, Beech Street.

◆ ◆ ◆

WALLASEY'S "PRE-FAB" DWELLERS HAVE "NO COMPLAINTS"

Wallasey CHRONICLE

28th September 1946

Opinions of a cross-section of Wallasey's "pre-fab" dwellers, collected by the Wallasey Chronicle yesterday, reveal that on the whole there are "no complaints," after the first few weeks of occupation.

Wallasey residents have viewed the unusual structures only from the outside and have wondered what the inhabitants think of their new type homes.

Yesterday Chronicle reporters chose, at random, occupiers of the estates in Lancaster Avenue, Poulton Road, and Borough Road, Seacombe, and invited them to express their views. The unanimous verdict has been "perfect!"

Drying Difficulty

The only criticism received, and this housewife begged it to be stated that she was most certainly not complaining, was that there is a difficulty in drying clothes.

The recent wet weather made it impossible to hang washing

out of doors and although the heating arrangements in the pre-fabs are excellent for room-heating purposes, they do not throw out enough heat to dry clothes.

This is a real difficulty when it is remembered that most dwellers have at least one child.

"Dreaming"

Mrs. Walmsley, 25 years old wife of ex-navy man Mr. H.F. Walmsley of 272 Poulton Road, mother of a four-year-old daughter and a 10 months old son, told the Chronicle:-

"I sometimes have to pinch myself to make sure I'm not dreaming. A house of my own, room for the children to play! After so long in furnished rooms, this is just heavily."

It was Mrs. Walmsley who feels the pre-fabs would be better fitted with a lower more open firegate for drying purposes.

Mr and Mrs Walmsley were bombed out of Burnside Road and have in furnished rooms ever since. This little "heaven" as she calls it, is her first real home since she was 13 years of age.

Mrs F Lonsdale, wife of a trimmer, mother of 11 months-old Frieda and 6 years-old Marjorie said, "I just can't find words to say how lovely these houses are."

Mr Lonsdale, ex-King's Regt., wounded at Cassino, demobbed in February spends most of his spare time on his plot of garden in front of the house. Bulbs are his chief problem at the moment but he shares his wife's sentiments as regards their new home.

Notice To Quit

One couple with one child, occupying a "pre-fab," told the Chronicle they had had notice to quit their new home, within a few days of occupying it.

Reason, stated the housewife, was that when her application for a house was made three years ago, she was occupying rooms in her mother's house in overcrowded conditions. She moved later to a small house in the Seacombe area, but owing to the condition of this house, she and her husband accepted the offer of a "pre-fab" from the corporation. Neighbours, she alleges immediately complained. And the authorities, according to her, have issued notice to quit the premises.

Three Airmen

Visiting Lancaster Avenue site, a Chronicle reporter called upon three housewives whose husbands all proved to be former members of the R.A.F. demobilised within the last 12 months.

Mr R Fisher, one of the first tenants to move in, whose address is actually 2 Wimbledon Street, said, "I know pre-fabs have been called for everything in other parts of the country: but they really are marvellous."

She has two small children, a boy in his second year and a girl aged 6 months.

Garden Fences

The only "snag" she could think of was that as garden fences had not yet been erected children made rather a nuisance of themselves by playing round between the houses. Already one of her windows had been broken by children throwing stones.

"When we first came, sightseers bothered us," she added, and the first Sunday there was a procession of people walking around the houses and peering in at the windows."

Formerly uncomfortably cramped in a boarding house bed-sitting, the Fishers now find they have "plenty of room," and "every convenience."

They were a little worried about the attitude the authorities might adopt towards their full-sized Alsatian pet; but permission to keep him was grated without question and he now sits at the kitchen door with an air of complete satisfaction.

Indoor Washing

Mrs J White, who moved into No. 12 at the opposite end of Wimbledon Street 10 weeks ago, said that she was "perfectly happy" in this "first home of my own." She had two small children, and had formerly lived with her parents.

Her washing had to be done indoors, in the kitchenette where the washing machine was fitted, but that caused no inconvenience so long as windows were kept open walls did not become unpleasantly steamed.

At present "everyone" was using her "garden" as a public footpath and schoolchildren were a particular nuisance: but she did not intend that comment as a complaint because the nuisance would surely be eliminated as soon as the Council erected garden fences.

Mrs D McFarlane, of 36 Lancaster Avenue, whose home is in the third row of prefabs from the Wimbledon Street "front," and at whose door stands a single evergreen – the only flower in a barren wilderness of yet untended gardens – said that her husband (who has 6 years R.A.F. service to his credit) was "doubtful about coming" as it promised to be "too much like returning to camp life." His fears had, however, been unnecessary: her neighbours were friendly, but there was no "camp atmosphere."

The prefab was a marvellous change from living with her two baby boys in one room and sharing a kitchen with other people, and the prefab kitchen was a dream.

She wished, however, that something could be done to stop the children roller-skating down the ramp leading into Urmson Road for the noise was disturbing and frequently woke her children in the evening.

◆ ◆ ◆

WHEATLAND LANE RE-DEVELOPMENT

Wallasey NEWS

7th December 1963

Demolition of more than 60 houses in Beaconsfield Road, Servia Street and Bosnia Street marks the beginning of the first stage in Seacombe's next big re-development scheme.

Meanwhile another large scale rebuilding plan for Seacombe is emerging. The plan, considered by the Housing Committee on Thursday, envisages a service traffic road from a point near St. Paul's Church, up to St. Paul's Road, down Wheatland Lane, and down Kelvin Road to the Dock Road. Land at present partly occupied by the Plaster Board works and the Berwick toy factory, in Birkenhead Road, would be zoned as an industrial area.

Houses, maisonettes and flats are included in the plan on sites to the rear and to the north of the Gandy Belt works.

On the Beaconsfield site will be erected a hostel for the aged.

The scheme for the Demesne area, prepared by the Borough Architect (Mr W.P. Clayton) covers approximately four acres and comprises Brighton Street, Beaconsfield Road, Servia Street, Bosnia Street, Tabor Street, Shaw Street, parts of Demesne Street and Ellis Street.

The number of houses in the area listed for demolition as unfit for habitation was 126, but the order includes houses which it is essential should be demolished to make way for the new property.

The existing property involved extends from No. 17 to 33 Brighton Street, and No's 4 to 40 (omitting the premises of Chronicle Motors) the whole of Shaw Street and the even numbers of Ellis Street.

Present plans for the development of the area include a two-form entry junior school to replace the existing Riverside School. Among the buildings to be demolished are a public house in Demesne Street and the old post office in Brighton Street. It is not proposed to include any shops in this re-development area.

◆ ◆ ◆

POLICE GET A 'MOVE ALONG THERE' ORDER AS THE STATION CLOSES

Wallasey NEWS

27th January, 1973

The wallpaper is faded in rectangular patches where large pieces of office furniture have stood. In some of the deserted rooms, old-fashioned telephones are to be seen. Solid oak desks are stacked in twos in the passageways. On a window-ledge a forgotten potted plant is going yellow.

The dust is already setting on bare parquet floors, behind the locked front doors of the old Wallasey Police Station in Manor Road [corner of Queen Street] - locked after 70 years, for good.

For at the weekend, Wallasey Division of the Cheshire Constabulary completed moving house into a brand new Police station further up the road. Nearly 200 Police pensioners, serving officers, and former officers, said farewell to the old building on Monday night at a special party.

Mr. W. Kelsall, deputy Chief Constable of Cheshire, officially handed over the keys to Mr. H. St. C. G. Gasking, Wallasey Magistrates' Clerk.

And if those old walls could talk ...

Chief Insp. Donald Clarke, who joined Wallasey Police in 1947, reminisced about one of the most more unusual incidents that have taken place in the old building's.

Semi-Conscious

"One day we were busy in the front office with three prisoners, and suddenly we heard a commotion outside the shutter. A taxi driver backed up into the office carrying a semi-conscious man.

He said, "Help me, there's another two out there!" The prisoners ran out and assisted with carrying them in. It was a Liverpool taxi driver who had seen the men in the water at New Brighton."

In the old building, the Magistrates' Court and associated offices still flourish, and will now have room to expand. Downstairs, the room vacated by the CID, photographers, constables and officers, will be taken over by the probation service, though some parts of the building, such as the cells and the Police kennels, may be hard to find a use for.

The station was built in 1900, as the headquarters for Wirral division of the Cheshire Constabulary. Before then, a court house and Police station were housed in a building in Liscard Road, now the Continental Bingo Club. It was built shortly after 1845.

With the incorporation of Wallasey as a borough, in 1910, the town took control of its own Police Force. Ten years later, the Council bought the Concert Hall for £20,000 as overflow accommodation for the Police. In 1940, a new wing on the main station was opened by the Earl of Derby.

Civil Defence

During the war, the cellars, suitably fortified, were used as a Civil Defence control unit. In 1967 Wallasey Police again became part of the Cheshire Constabulary.

Another of Chief Insp. Clark's anecdotes runs as follows:

"Detective Constable J.J. Fearon, attached to the traffic Department, was sent to an incident in Seabank Road, where a workman sitting in a workman's tent had discovered a snake. He succeeded in putting it in the boot of his car and driving in to the rear of the Police station. When he arrived, he opened up the boot and the thing jumped out. It has never been seen since."

Somewhere, in the gloomy foundations of the old Police station, there lurks, perhaps a giant anaconda - supporting on his sinewy body the entire Police station, as Atlas does the world.

Was this the real reason for the move to the new building - plate glass, tiled floors, modern wood fittings, and freedom from ferocious reptiles?

◆ ◆ ◆

THE DIRT, THE NOISE, THE CLOUDS OF DUST, THE PLAGUE OF CHILDREN

Wallasey NEWS

22th January 1966

As progress comes to Tudor Avenue – with pick-axe and bulldozer, and the sound of and fury of houses crumbling at their onslaught – clouds of dust and grit settle on those homes that have been spared the first sacrifice for the new tunnel.

Those residents who have not had to move out and seek sanctuary elsewhere, while appreciating the need for a new tunnel, are finding much to complain about in the activities of their new neighbours, the demolition gangs. The dirt and the din of demolition, the grit, the noise of heavy lorries and crashing walls, the plague of children, and of scavengers.

'Great Inconvenience'

"We have lived here for thirty-eight years. I know progress can't be stopped but it's a great inconvenience," Mrs. Jean Miller told a "News" reporter this week as she watched the workings on the ventilation shaft.

Mrs. Miller, who lives with her husband, and 17 year old son at 13 Tudor Avenue, said; "We haven't been told anything officially. Some say we will be down within two or three years bur meanwhile we must learn to live with a big workings at the bottom of the road.

"Children think that our houses have also been dispossessed and throw stones at the windows. I have to leave the electric light burning all night."

'Dirt Settles Everywhere'

Mrs. Mary Galvia, who has two small children and has lived at 8 Tudor Avenue for four years, said: "We get all the dirt from the workings. It settles everywhere on the furniture and walls, even on the baby's clothes while they are airing.

"It will probably get worse once the houses are pulled down, as there will be dirt from the river."

"Of an evening we are plagued by children playing amongst the rubble of the demolished houses."

Mrs. Margaret Walker lives at 19 Tudor Avenue with two children, a boy aged 5 and a girl aged 2. She said: "The tunnel is a good idea but the workings are causing us much inconvenience.

"We have lived here for over five years and were thinking of selling the house but can't do so now. We have been offered no compensation, not even a reduction in rates."

'Disgusting'

Mrs Joyce Abbott has a one-year-old son and has lived at 11 Tudor Avenue for three years. "The tunnel is all right but the dirt and noise we are expected to put up with is disgusting.

"It is not even peaceful at night, with children breaking windows and scavengers routing about in the rubble.

"We have been told very little, officially, about the future."

Mrs. Joseph Smith, a retired grocer, who has lived at 31 Tudor Avenue for three years, and formed an action committee to oppose the building of the ventilation shaft, commented; "It is a shame what they are pulling down. Good houses are demolished while shabby property is allowed to remain. I think it is disgusting.

"There is dirt and dust everywhere and I suppose work will go on for years."

Miss Joyce Hatton, aged 17, a telephonist with the G.P.O. in Liverpool, who lives at 29 Tudor Avenue said: "I have lived in Tudor Avenue all my life and it's upsetting to see so much of it coming down. Why couldn't they have pulled down some of the houses on the promenade?

"There is dirt everywhere and my mother is kept busy with dusting. It even gets on to my tape recordings.

❖ ❖ ❖

THE NEW BRIGHTON TRAGEDY: PART 1

Spicer - Before the Magistrates.

Liverpool Mercury

Tuesday, 27th May, 1890

Felix Spicer, aged 60, described as a seaman, was yesterday brought before the magistrates at the Courthouse, Liscard, charged with the wilful murder of his son, William (aged 13 year old and two months) and Henry (aged 3 years and eight months), by cutting their throats at New Brighton on Sunday morning. He was further charged with having attempted to murder Mary his wife. The magistrates were Captain A.M Molyneux, Mr James Smith, and Mr W. Heap, and Colonel Hamersley, chief constable of Cheshire, occupied a seat on the bench. It being generally known that Spicer was to be brought up, there was a large attendance of the general public. After some ordinary trivial cases had been disposed of, Spicer was placed in the dock. He is a short, thick-set man, with scanty white hair, and full moustache beard and whiskers turning from sandy to grey. Throughout the proceedings, a policeman being by his side, he stood in the dock with his left hand on the rail, the fingers nervously and incessantly beating a tattoo, whilst his right hand hung lifelessly by his side. His aspect was that of a pre-occupied man, and only occasionally he betray a keen sense of interest in what was going on. The magistrates' clerk read over the formal indictments, and when he came to the end of the first one, charging the prisoner with having "feloniously, and of malice aforethought, killed and murdered- one William Spice", the prisoner interrupted him, saying with emphasis, "I deny it, sir". The clerk went on with the reading without further interruption.

Superintendent Hindley stated the case. The prisoner, he said, had been in New Brighton something like 18 years, during which time he had known him as keeping refreshment rooms. Some short time ago he lived in Windsor Street but he was sold up, and then went to live at Richmond Street. Since he had been in Richmond Street, his wife had had a refreshment room, a lock up place, near New Brighton Ferry, and there appeared to have been some dispute between them in consequences of her refusal to allow his name to be put over the door. After the dispute the wife slept at the refreshment room, the prisoner stopping at Richmond Street. On Saturday night last he went to the refreshment room after it had closed, knocked at the door, and asked to be admitted. She refused him admittance and went to bed, but about three o'clock in the morning she was aroused by the smashing of the windows. She jumped up, and, seeing the prisoner, she slipped her skirts on and made a rush to get out through the broken window. The prisoner attempted to prevent her, slashing at her with a knife, and inflicting several severe wounds. She ultimately succeeded in getting into the street, and finding shelter in a neighbouring house. Her nose was cut nearly through, her throat was cut across, and her hands were badly wounded in trying to ward off the blows. She was now in the hospital, doing as well as could be expected. The police went to the house in Richmond Street, where they apprehended the prisoner, and they afterwards found that two of the children who slept there had been murdered in bed. A doctor was called, and he would state that, to the best of his knowledge, the children had been dead about three hours. It was only proposed to offer such evidence as would justify the bench in granting a remand for eight days. A woman named Fraser, who lived at Richmond Street, would be called and would prove that the prisoner was in the house on Saturday night. It would also be proved that the prisoner's bed, was not occupied that night, and Mrs Fraser would tell the court that she heard the children screaming and the prisoner going about in the house. He thought this would satisfy their worships that his request for remand was a reasonable one.

Annie Fraser, wife of Archibald Fraser, 17 Greetham Street, Liverpool, was then called. She said she did not live with her husband, but had for some time been living with Mrs. Spicer as waitress, at Richmond Street, New Brighton. Mrs. Spicer also kept a Refreshment Room at 3 Bickley Parade. Witness had been at the refreshment room on Saturday last, and left shortly after eleven o'clock at night to go to Richmond Street, where she slept. She arrived at the house about quarter to twelve, and saw the prisoner and the nurse girl, Mary, in the kitchen. The prisoner asked her where she had been, she replied that she had just come from the refreshment room. She saw he was in a very bad temper, so took no further notice of him, but said simply "Good night" and went upstairs to bed. She slept in a little room at the top of the stairs on the first landing, just opposite the front door. The nurse girl, who slept in the same room, went upstairs five minutes before her, and was undressing when she went up. Witness had commenced to undress when the prisoner called "Annie, I want you. Will you come and rub my shoulders?" She replied "Yes, certainly", and went downstairs and rubbed his shoulders. After which she bade him goodnight and went to bed. He bade her good night, and said he was going to sit up for the lodger, referring to a stranger who had engaged a bed at the refreshment room that day. Witness was suffering from indigestion, and passed a restless night, but was not disturbed by any noise. About break of day she got up and partly dressed herself and sat down on the side of the bed, and immediately after she sat down she heard the voice of the youngest deceased, Harry, cry out as though troubled in his sleep, and then a shuffling noise, as though his father, who had been in the habit of looking after the children since their mother had stayed away, was going to him. She could not say which room the person whose footsteps she heard went into. She afterwards lay down on the bed in her clothes and fell asleep, but had not slept long when she was awakened by the opening of the scullery back door, and heard some one, apparently with slippers on, run swiftly upstairs and down again, as though he had run up to fetch something. The person, whoever it was, was not upstairs as much as a minute. About three minutes or so after that she heard a loud knocking at the front door, and then some one outside her bedroom door said "we want you". She opened the door and saw Mr.Storey and Dr.Ross, Dr.Bride's assistant, coming upstairs, and one or two policemen in the lobby. She never saw the prisoner from the time she went to bed. Mrs.Spicer had not been in the house for a month or five weeks. Witness left her that night at the refreshment room. Mr.Spicer usually slept in the front bedroom. Witness went into that room on the Sunday morning and saw that the bed had not been used. Mr.Spicer was expecting a lodger, and the lodger had not turned up, and she did not think that Mr.Spicer had been to bed at all. He had told her that he was going to sleep on the sofa.

Supt Hindley --: Can you give the bench any ideas, from your own knowledge, why Mrs.Spicer did not go to Richmond Street to sleep? Yes; when Spicer came home from sea he wanted to take possession, and Mrs.Spicer naturally objected. --: When did he come back from sea? In September I think, and Mrs. Spicer has kept him ever since. --: Was there any unpleasantness about this? Not then. He was right enough until last Easter. He and his wife were quite friendly until two or three days after Easter, when they had words about the refreshment room being put in Mr.Spicer's name, but they did not have a real quarrel until the following Monday. On that day Mrs. Spicer went to town, and whilst she was in town he took the money. When she returned she saw the money on the shelf where he had placed it, and she took it up and put it in her pocket. Mr.Spicer said, "leave that there" and she said "no, it doesn't require two to take money here." Then they had some words, and Mrs.Spicer asked witness quietly, without Mr.Spicer hearing, if she would go up to the house and send her bed down, saying she did not wish to go home with him. She sent a girl down with the bed, and Mrs.Spicer had slept at the refreshment room ever since. The bed was kept in the daytime in the kitchen under the dresser, and made up at night in the refreshment room. The slippers produced were Mrs.Spicer's

The prisoner, on being asked, if he wished to put any questions to the witness, replied quietly, "no, sir".

Alfred Short, a clerk, was the next witness. He said he occupied a front room on the ground floor at Richmond Street, as a sitting and bedroom. On Saturday evening he went to bed at a quarter-past eleven o'clock, leaving the prisoner in the kitchen sitting on the sofa, and William, the elder of the two deceased children, sitting on a chair beside the sofa. Witness bade him good night and went to bed, leaving with him at his request, as he generally did, his watch, so that he might know the time in the morning. Witness soon went to sleep, but he was awakened shortly afterwards by a little alteration between Mr.Spicer and Mrs.Fraser. He heard Spicer speak very loudly to her about being late, but he did not hear her reply. He went to sleep again, and heard nothing more until he was awakened by two policemen coming into his bedroom in the morning. He got up and dressed himself, and heard Mr.Storey say - "he has murdered his two children". He went upstairs with Police-constable Potts (204), and, going into the back bedroom where the children slept, saw them lying, one at the foot and the other at the head of the bed, with their throats cut. They were both dead, and there was a great quantity of blood about - in fact, the place was like a slaughter house.

F.Potts (P.C 204) stated that he was on duty in Rowson Street, New Brighton, about five minutes to four o'clock on Sunday morning in company with Police-constable A.Jones (301), when a young man came up to them, and, in consequence of information he gave them, they went to the refreshment room, Bickley-parade. Finding no one there they went to Richmond Street, accompanied by Mr.Storey, whom they saw coming from the doctor's. Mr.Storey and he stayed at the front of the house whilst Constable Jones went to the back. Having obtained an entrance, Jones opened the front door and let them in. Jones arrested the prisoner, and Storey and witness went upstairs and found the two deceased boys in the back bedroom on the second landing. They were both dead. Witness remained there until the arrival of Dr.Rose and Police-sergeant Cooper. Mrs.Fraser gave him two letters (produced) in the lobby of the house about six o'clock that morning. One was in an envelope, unopened.

Sergeant Samuel George Cooper said he called at the police station, New Brighton, at 25 minutes past four o'clock on Sunday morning, and saw the prisoner there in custody of Police-constable 301, and from what the Constable said to him he went to Richmond Street. On his return, about six o'clock, he examined the prisoner, and found blood stains on both his shirt wristbands and partly up the sleeves. There were also blood stains on the knee of his trousers and down each trouser leg - mostly on the right knee and leg - on the breast of his coat, and on the back and front of a pair of sand shoes which he was wearing.

The articles were produced, and caused a sickening sensation.

On the usual question -- "Have you anything to ask this witness"? being put to the prisoner, he replied -- "They are not bloodstains, sir, it is red paint on the shoes".

The Clerk to the Magistrates -- You will, of course, have an opportunity of speaking for yourself later.

The Prisoner -- Yes sir; very good.

The Chairman -- Your case will be remanded until the 2nd June at ten o'clock in the morning.

The Prisoner -- I would like to have a little assistance to defend me. I have no means at present.

The Clerk -- You get assistance on the trial.

The Prisoner -- I would like to have it now if I could get it. I could explain lots of things to you. There are some letters there which would explain the whole of it.

The Clerk -- You had better not say much now. Have you no money?

The Prisoner -- No

After a consultation with the clerk, the magistrates, through the chairman, said -- We have no power to meet you in any way at this stage.

The prisoner was then removed.

The New Brighton Tragedy

The Yorkshire Herald
Wednesday, 28th May, 1890

An inquest on the victims of the New Brighton murder was opened yesterday. Mr. Caurton, coroner, commented on the conduct of Colonel Hamersley, Chief Constable, in removing the prisoner to Walton Gaol, and not allowing him to appear at the inquest. The Coroner said he will write to the Home Secretary. The Inquest was adjourned till to-morrow. It was stated that at the time the prisoner married Mrs. Spicer he had another living wife.

Funeral of The Victims.

Liverpool Mercury
Thursday, 29th May, 1890

The funeral of the two victims of the murder at New Brighton on Sunday last, William and Henry Spicer, took place yesterday at Wallasey Cemetery, Rake Lane, Liscard. The interest naturally taken by the inhabitants of the district in the shocking event was the cause of a large assemblage of spectators at the house in Richmond Street and at the cemetery. Steps had been taken by a number of gentlemen, including Mr. Henry Spencer (the foreman of the coroner's jury). Mr. James Boughhey, Mr. John Bailey, and Mr. Berriman, to raise by public subscription to buy a grave in the cemetery, defray the expense of the burial, and temporarily maintain the remaining children. The funeral procession, consisting of a hearse and three mourning coaches. left the house about half-past three. The coffins were covered with wreaths and crosses sent by sympathising neighbours and friends, and each bore an inscription recording the names, date of death, and ages of the boys. The chief mourners were the sisters and brother of the deceased - namely Gertrude, Annie, Ethel, and Thomas Spicer. Mrs. Fraser, the waitress at Mrs. Spicer's refreshment room, occupied the one of the carriages with two of the children, and the attendance included most of the members of the coroner's jury and several New Brighton tradesmen. The burial service was conducted by the Rev. John H. Gwyther, pastor of the Congregational Church, Rice Lane, Liscard.

The New Brighton Tragedy

The Dundee Courier & Argus
Friday, 30th May, 1890

Additional information was taken by the Cheshire Coroner yesterday in the case of the murder of two children by Felix

Spicer, their father. Mrs. Spicer, who was terribly injured on the morning of the murder, said they were not married. He took her at sixteen under promise, and when the first child was born she pressed him to marry her, but he laughed at her in her shame and misery. A few days before the tragedy he told her landlord they were not married, and from that day she determined no longer to live with him, a declaration which brought about last Sunday's tragedy.

The Inquest was again adjourned.

A Sad Story

The North-Eastern Daily Gazette
Thursday, 30th May, 1890

Yesterday at the adjourned inquest on the two children murdered by their father, Felix Spicer, at New Brighton, Cheshire, the mother, who was terribly injured, in her encounter with the accused, gave evidence. She said prisoner took her from home under the promise of marriage when she was 16. Though she pressed him to do so, he never married her. She had seven children by him. She kept him by means of the refreshment rooms. He was of ungovernable temper, and had recently told her landlord that they were not married, which caused her to determine no longer to live with him. He then begged her forgiveness, whereupon she wrote the following to him "You told Mr. Wright I was not your wife, you mean, contemptible scoundrel. Did you think of my tears (her first child) I begged you to marry me out of my shame, and you laughed at me? But I have waited, and the day has come. I can tell everyone my tale, for I hated you since the day you laughed at me. I don't regard my name now. Why should I? Now everybody knows; but there is one thing I want you to know - the gallows before another night under the same roof as you. I will neither see you or be annoyed by you. You can remain in the house as long as you keep away from me. I will see the rent paid, but remember that I shall never change as long as I live".

The woman was much affected whilst giving her evidence. The case was adjourned till next Wednesday.

The New Brighton Tragedy

Manchester Times
Saturday, 31st May, 1890

A shocking tragedy was enacted early on Sunday morning at New Brighton. Mary Spicer carries on the business of a refreshment house keeper in Victoria Road, where she resides, and her husband resides in Richmond Street, the wife, it is said, having refused to live with him. On Saturday night Spicer assisted in putting his five children to bed, and between two and three o'clock on Sunday morning he cut the throats of two of them whilst they were in bed. Spicer then went to the Victoria Road house, where he attempted to murder his wife. She, though terribly cut about the arms and face, effected her escape by jumping through the bedroom window, her husband making a similar leap. The crash of glass brought the police to the spot, and they pursued the murderer and captured him in his house in Richmond Street. The police, on entering the house, found the sons, William and Henry. lying dead, with their throats cut from ear to ear. Jealousy is suppose to have been the cause of the tragedy. The house in Richmond Street is let to lodgers, all of whom were sound asleep when the police entered on Sunday morning and apprised them of the murder of the two children.

Felix Spicer was brought before the Wallasey (Cheshire) magistrates on Monday and was remanded till Monday next.

At New Brighton Police Station on Tuesday morning, before Mr. C.W Tibbits. deputy-coroner, there was opened an inquiry into the cause of the death of William and Henry Spicer. The first witness called was Annie Fraser, who lived at the house where Spicer resided. She spoke of hearing Spicer walking about the house on the morning of the murder. Mrs. Spicer had lived with her husband at Richmond Street till the week after

Easter Monday, when she went to 3, Bickley Parade, where she carried on business as a refreshment house keeper. There were six children, all of whom were living at Richmond Street, except the eldest, who was at Cardiff. Spicer himself had formerly been a ship's cook. Mr. and Mrs. Spicer were on comfortable terms till the week after Easter. At that, however, a quarrel took place, Mrs. Spicer saying her husband had no right to touch the money at the refreshment place, as she was mistress there. The next day Spicer said he would show her who is master, but he did not offer to assault her in any way. He was a very passionate man. She saw Spicer on Saturday evening when she went up to Richmond Street for something. He then told her to ask Mrs. Spicer if he might go down to the rooms that week, and she sent word back that she did not want him for that week, nor did she ever want to set eyes on him again. On Saturday night witness got into the house at a quarter to twelve, when she found Spicer sitting in the kitchen. He was perfectly sober, but was in a bad temper. About daylight, feeling restless, she got up and sat by the window. The two deceased children slept in the room adjoining witness's, and Spicer slept in a room by himself. While witness was awake she heard someone go into the children's room, but did not pay much attention to the circumstances, as Mr. Spicer had been in the habit lately of looking after the children. Afterwards there was a loud knocking at the front door. Some persons were let into the house, and she was told the children were murdered. Police constable 204 (Potts) deposed that he received information of the murder of the children. At the time prisoner was arrested it was not known that the children were murdered. He was taken into custody on suspicion of having wounded his wife. He was very cool, was sober, and did not offer any resistance. He said to Jones, "I have done nothing". -- Mr. Churton, the coroner, who had entered the court in the course of the inquiry, asked : "Is the prisoner here"? -- Sergeant Cooper : "No". -- Mr Churton : "Why not"? -- Sergeant Cooper : "He has been sent to Walton". -- Mr Churton : "For the last forty years I have never held an inquest without having the prisoner present, and for the simple reason that he is afforded an opportunity before the coroner of making a statement which he cannot do before the magistrates. His mouth is closed there. It is a strange thing that he should be sent away. I shall take certain steps myself this evening in regard to this matter". -- Dr. F.W.F Ross stated that he was called about 4.15 on Sunday morning, and went down to Richmond Street, where he found the children William and Henry lying on a bed. They were dead, and the wounds which had caused their deaths must have inflicted by a very sharp instrument. -- In reply to the Coroner, a policeman stated that no instrument had been found. -- The inquest was afterwards adjourned.

With regard to Mrs. Spicer, it may be stated that though terribly injured by the knife with which her husband attacked her, the injuries are not likely to lead to fatal results, and it is expected by next Monday she will be able to give evidence.

Interview With The Prisoner

The Dundee Courier & Argus
Monday, 2nd June, 1890

On Saturday. Alfred Short, who lodged in the house of Felix Spicer, the man charged with murdering his children at New Brighton, had an interview with Spicer in Walton Gaol. When asked about the crime, prisoner said, "I know nothing about it, so help me God. I washed little Harry, and kissed him and put him to bed, and bade him good night, bless his little heart". Here the prisoner wept bitterly. "Willie", he continued amid his sobs, "went to bed about about half-past eleven. I wished him good night, and know no more of either of them. I am as innocent as you are". Again his sobs interrupted his statement and when he became calm he continued -- "I am remained in the kitchen until three o'clock in the morning, when I went down to the refreshment rooms of my wife. The knife I used to the woman was my clasp knife, which was taken possession of by the police. In further conversation, the prisoner said he would not tell a lie to hurt any soul breathing. He referred to his love for the children, and said the woman had brought it all upon herself by refusing to forgive him. At parting he he told his visitor to tell his wife that he forgave her. He sent his love to her, although she had been very cruel to him.

The New Brighton Tragedy

The Sheffield & Rotherham Independent
Monday, 2nd June, 1890

On Saturday morning the police renewed the search for the knife used by Spicer in the murder of his two children and the attack on his wife last Saturday. After pulling up the flooring of the various rooms, search was made in about a cooking stove, when the knife was found in one of the flues. It bore ample evidence of the crime. The police have also ascertained the whereabouts of the missing lodger., who will be called at the adjourned inquest next Wednesday.

The trial was fixed to commence at ten o'clock, and although the courthouse is situated away from a busy thoroughfare, there was a large crowd outside. The public were admitted to the back part of the court, and a fierce struggle ensued on the part of the crowd which endeavored to squeeze itself into a "gallery" capable of accommodating only one hundred persons. Spicer, who had been in weak health in the last few days, was brought from Walton Jail and driven in a cab to the court. He looked careworn, but seemed to follow the proceedings with an intelligent interest, keeping his eyes fixed on the witnesses, and occasionally be consulted with his solicitor. Owing to some remarks in an interview published in a Liverpool paper, the chairman made a statement hoping that such statements would not again be published. Mrs. Spicer, who was accompanied into court by her sister, a resident of Cardiff, gave a clear account of the terrible struggle she had had with the accused, and two witnesses who had watched the affair from their windows supplemented her testimony. The lady, who wore a dark ulster and veil, was deeply affected, and when the question was put to her, "have you been to Richmond Street since", she replied "no", and then burst into tears. Her wrists were still covered with bandages, and as she leaned on the solicitors table, at which she was seated while giving her evidence, a plain gold band was observable on the third finger of her left hand. Her depositions having been read over to her, she signed her name "Mary Palin". The bench then remanded the accused until Monday next, and refused a request made by Mr. Moore that for convenience in consulting for the defence the prisoner might remain in Liscard, and not be removed to Walton. A number of persons remained outside the court house until after five o'clock, when the court adjourned, and witnessed the departure the cab which conveyed Spicer back to Walton Jail.

Maria Fearon, aged 15 years, stated that she was the nurse-girl employed by Mrs. Spicer. She repeated her evidence as to putting the children to bed on the night of May 24. After going down to the refreshment rooms witness returned to Richmond Street and gave the prisoner his supper, but he said he could not eat any. Witness went to bed about twelve o'clock, and soon after Mrs. Fraser, who had had some words with Fearon, also went to bed. By Superintendent Hindley : She heard no arrangement made as to which beds the children were to occupy. While Spicer was in the kitchen a man came in, and Spicer said, "I'm very sorry, old pal, I have no room for you to-night;" at the time returning the man's umbrella. The man went out with Spicer, and she did not see him again. She had not seen him before. Spicer had told her that four lodgers coming that night.

Mr. Moore, at the close of the witness's examination-in-chief, said that as he understood the examination of the various witnesses would not finish that day he proposed to adjourn his cross-examination. It was most desirable that after hearing the evidence he should have an interview with the accused, and go through the evidence line by line. He had had an interview with the prisoner that morning, and received an outline from him, and it was a very long business.

James Thomas Lea, architect and surveyor, produced plans of the house Richmond Street, New Brighton, and refreshment room, 3, Bickley Parade, and the surrounding streets. The distance between the two places was 325 yards.

Dr. Frederick William Forbes Ross, in partnership with Dr. Bride, and practising at Victoria Road, New Brighton, gave evidence similar to that given at the coroner's inquiry with reference to the position and conditions of the bodies of the children found at Richmond Street after the murder. He said the knife shown to him by Sergeant Cooper, on Saturday, might probably have caused the wounds on the bodies. They were caused by a cutting instrument. The knife shown to him was a short one, with a brown wooden handle, and a blade nearly four inches long, and there were blood stains and soot on it. When he arrived at the house the children had been dead for about an hour. By Superintendent Hindley : Subsequently, he saw the prisoners clothing. The shirt had blood stains on the cuffs, and there were a few spots scattered across the breast and body. He saw the shirt on Spicer within half an hour after he had examined the scene of the murder, and it was decided that it should be taken off him. He did not examine the shirt sufficiently to say whether the blood spots were on the front of the shirt. He went to the prisoner, and asked to look at hands. He told Spicer he had washed them, and the reply was, "Indeed sir, I have not washed them this morning." Witness then said, "you lie, Spicer" and asked the officer to turn up his cuffs. The policeman did so, and witness found that both wrists and a portion of the arm were smeared with blood, and there was a waterline showing where the washing process had stopped.

Superintendent Hindley -- Did you notice any cuts on his hands?

Witness -- There were no new cuts which could have caused this blood.

The Superintendent -- Could this blood have got on the shirt if he had had his coat on?

Witness -- Possibly, but I do not think it could have got on the body of the shirt.

The Superintendent -- Did you notice blood anywhere else?

Witness -- Yes, on the latch of the back gate of Richmond Street, on the kitchen floor, and also on the inside of the handle of the scullery door. I looked for blood outside, but did not find any. The bloodstains found on the handle need not have been visible to the eye; they might have been left there by a clumsily-washed hand. He tested for the stains chemically. He applied the same tests to the prisoner's clothes, which were handed to him by Sergeant Cooper, and found fresh bloodstains on all the garments. Some of the stains on the shirt were quite fresh. At the same time the sergeant showed him a piece of wood which had been sawn to leave a sort of handle, and on this was blood, half dried. A bloody hand had grasped the handle so that the blood had gone into the wood. This piece of wood was lying on the pavement in front of the window the prisoner was said to have smashed. He found this wood about 20 minutes after he had left the children. He had seen the wife just before this, and found her in a state of shock, pale and exhausted, at Mr. Bailey's. She was slashed across the bridge of the nose, but the hemorrhage was ceasing. There was a wound on her right-hand palm, and one on the left forearm.

The Superintendent -- Would the amount of blood the wife lost be sufficient to account for the amount of blood on the prisoner's clothes?

Witness -- I don't think so. I do not think it would account for the blood on the right knee of the prisoner's trousers. I had found stains on the head of the bed, showing that there had been blood smeared by a knee in three places. On examining the prisoner's trousers at the police station I found there was a stain on them just below the right knee. It was quite moist, and had soaked through, and had soaked through the cloth, marking the prisoner's knee.

John Bailey, grocer, 4 Victoria Road, New Brighton, stated that about 20 minutes to four o'clock on the morning of the May 25 he was awakened by his wife, who told him she heard someone screaming. He got out of bed, and went to the window, which overlooked Victoria Road. He saw Mr. and Mrs. Spicer, whom he knew by sight, on the parapet in front of Bickley Parade. They were struggling together. He was kneeling with both knees on the lower part of her body. With the left hand he seemed to grasp the hair of her head, and with the right hand he was working away across her throat. He saw the prisoner's closed hand go up and down each time, and it seem to have been arrested by Mrs. Spicer each time he seemed to strike. He could not say whether the prisoner had a knife or anything in his hand. Witness raised an alarm by shouting "murder", "police", and blew a whistle. This had no effect, so he called to Spicer by name, saying "Spicer, this is too abusive". He received no answer, and Spicer did not look up, but continued in the same position. Witness left the window, and put on some clothing, and went out into the road. Spicer and his wife were on their legs, the latter standing at the back the cabmen's shelter, and having her back towards the river. The prisoner was on the north-east angle of the shelter, nearer to No. 3 Bickley Parade. Seeing the prisoner make an attempt to run after her the witness called to him "Spicer don't do that; you must not do any more". Witness called to Mrs. Spicer to run into the house as the door was open. She hesitated for a moment, and then started. She went into the house, and witness followed and closed the door. He did not see the prisoner again. She was bleeding dreadfully from various parts of the face and arm - in fact, she was a ghastly sight. He did not see a knife of any sort in the prisoner's hand.

Francis Storey was the next witness called, but before he commenced the magistrates left the bench for a few minutes, and on returning to the court :

The Chairman said : The attention of the bench has been called to some remarks in one of the Liverpool newspapers of this date. They wish to say that they think in the interests of justice some of the remarks should not have been made, and they hope that nothing of this kind will be said again. At the same time, they wish the witness to know that they have nothing to be afraid of if they tell the truth; and if any threats are made to them they should communicate at once with the police, who will see that they are protected.

Mr. Moore -- I am unaware of any threats having being used, directly or indirectly, either by my client or myself or my friends.

The hearing of the evidence was then resumed.

Mr. Storey said he was a general dealer, at 3 Victoria Road. On May 25 about quarter to four o'clock in the morning, he was awakened by hearing screams and a cry of "murder", "police". He got up and went to the bedroom window, and saw a man and a woman struggling on the parade. While putting on some clothes, with the intention of going down, he heard more shouting from next door, and on going to the window again he saw the woman running up the road with the man after her. As he passed under the window witness saw a short knife blade in his hand. Witness had the impression that the knife was rounded off at the top. The man caught up to the woman outside Bailey's window and grasped her about the shoulders. He had the knife in his hand raised. Witness saw no more as he hurried from the window to get dressed as he considered the matter had become very serious. Mrs. Storey soon after told him the woman had got into Bailey's and was safe, so he did not hurry downstairs, but on again looking through the window he saw the prisoner, whom he then recognised, go to Mrs. Spicer's house and smash the window with a plank of wood. Having committed the damage he put the piece of wood down by the side of the parapet and then entered the refreshment rooms through one of the broken windows. Witness came downstairs and went into Mr. Bailey's house, where he saw Mrs. Spicer, and on coming out he informed the police as to the direction in which Spicer had gone. He afterwards accompanied the police to Richmond Street, and while they were in the parlour the prisoner walked from the kitchen, and was arrested by Police constable Jones. When they got outside the house witness told Constable Potts he had better go and see if the children were all right, and he did so. Sergeant Cooper afterwards showed witness blood stains on the frame on the window at Bickley Parade, through which the prisoner had entered. There was a pool of blood where the struggle had taken place.

Gertrude Annie Spicer, aged eight years, living at Richmond Street, repeated the evidence she had given before the coroner, the principal point being that during the night on which the murder was committed she heard her brother cry. She called out "what's the matter, Harry"? and someone whom she thought was her father, replied "Go to sleep".

Mrs. Spicer was then called, and it was with great difficulty that she could compose herself to give her evidence. She said her name was Mary Palin. She had known the prisoner for 17 years. She was 32 years of age, and lived with him at Richmond Street. They had had seven children. The prisoner came back in September after a nine month's voyage. He had not been to sea for 15 years prior to that. She slept at Richmond Street until the week following Easter, when she commenced to stay at the refreshment rooms. She did this because of something the prisoner had told Mr. Wright. The witness repeated the evidence given before as to the dispute Spicer and she had on Monday after Easter with regard to the money received at the refreshment rooms. She told him he had nothing to do with business, and this seemed to annoy him very much. He said he would let her see whether he had nothing to do with it. He pulled off his coat and knocked about the things in the place, and she called in Police sergeant Whitchurst, to whom she showed her tenant's agreement. The sergeant told him she had the power to put him out, and after that he became very quiet. She then had a bed brought down to the refreshment rooms. She did so not because she was afraid, but because she thought it might save a quarrel. She had not intended to stay more than the night, but she decided to stay longer because of the prisoner going to the landlord. After this, Spicer sent messages and notes asking her to come back and begging her pardon.

Letters written by the prisoner to the witness were then put in. In the first one read the prisoner addressed her "my dear Polly", and asked that "by the great God forgive me, and do not always cast me out with a broken heart. Do forgive me. Have mercy on me, and I will make every amend in my power. Have mercy on me, have mercy on me. As a good girl give me some proof of your friendship. Yours for ever, F. SPICER". On the back of this sheet in the handwriting of Mrs. Spicer was the reply - "You are too late, and you need not to try to see me. The door is locked, and once for all I will not be annoyed by you. I shall not see you". A letter written by Spicer on May 19 last, and the reply from the witness (which have been published), were next read, as also a letter written by the prisoner to Mr. A. Wright saying that it was a great trial to him, as, being the founder of the business, that more favourable consideration had not been shown to him. He added that he was afraid Mr. Wright had been misinformed about his affairs, and he asked for Mr. Wright to reconsider his decision so that he can work in the rooms in amicable way, which he gave his honest word should be peace and love. He closed by saying "I am, now broken-hearted." The next letter put in was addressed to the witness and was as follows :- "I will call down tonight about nine o'clock. I hope you will consider my feelings and forgive me, and make it up and shake hands. I am a broken man. For God's sake and have pity on me. - Yours for ever - F.SPICER".

The witness, continuing, said she believed he came down on the night after the letter was written. They had a conversation, and she refused to make the quarrel up. On the night May 24 the prisoner came to the refreshment rooms about half-past ten o'clock just as she was locking up. He knocked at the door, and she asked who was there. He called out to her to open the door, but she replied that she could not as she was undressing. He bade her good night, and she returned the wish. He then repeated "Good night girl" and walked away. In the afternoon of that day she made an arrangement with a gentleman who wanted lodgings, and referred him to Richmond Street. Before she went to bed the girl Fearon came down to the refreshment room and returned to Richmond Street. This would be about half past eleven o'clock. The witness described the attack on her as follows : Early the next morning, when it was quite daylight, I was awoke by the crash of glass. I jumped out of bed and saw Spicer through the window. He had his arm through the side window feeling for the key of the door inside. I put on some clothes and my slippers. When Spicer found there was no key he broke another window. I jumped up on to the partition and tried to get through the window, and in doing so overbalanced him on the other side. He leaped on to me and held me down. He had a white handkerchief or piece of linen in his hand, and it spelled of brandy or some kind of spirits. He was trying to get it on my face. I got it out of his hand. He had nothing else in his hands. I saw him try to get something out of his right breast pocket, and I thought it was a revolver. I saw it was something brown. I had screamed murder when I first jumped out of the window, and he kept saying "you scream murder, you scream murder, but you won't scream murder, you - wretch, in a minute, when I have done with you". By this time I saw it was a knife he had got out of his pocket. It was not a clasp knife. I had seen the knife before, and it has been shown to me by Sergeant Cooper. Spicer struggled for some time, and I held on to his coat sleeve and kept guarding off the knife. He aimed all the time at my throat, and I drew my skirt around my neck with the left hand, using the right hand to ward off the knife. I was obliged to hold on to the blade for some time, and I kept asking him to spare me for God's sake and for the sake of the children. My right hand was cut through holding on to the knife. My left hand was injured with the glass. I could not tell when my face was cut; I found afterwards that I was cut and bleeding.

Mr Solly -- How did you get away from him?

Witness -- I can hardly say. I knocked the knife out of his hand, and that gave me the opportunity for escaping. I looked around and saw the neighbours in the window. I ran up past Mr. Bailey's, and then came back and got on one side of the cabmen's hut, and Spicer was on the other side. I was dodging him round the hut. Mr. Bailey came to his door and called me to his house, where I entered. Spicer had walked away towards Bickley Parade. The cut on my nose was done by Spicer, I think, when I was escaping. After I knocked the knife out of hand he stooped to pick it up, and then it was I managed to escape.

By Superintendent Hindley -- I had heard nothing about four lodgers coming to Richmond Street before prisoner called at the refreshment rooms. I cannot say how the prisoner was dressed. He certainly had on a coat of some description, and was not in his short sleeves. He wore a cap, and the coat was a long one, I think. I had heard Mr. Bailey call to the prisoner, who turned round and, using foul language, told him to go in. I remember the prisoner on coming home, after his discharge from the Claremont, producing the knife, and saying it only cost 4d., but that it was worth half a-crown, and it would cut all the throats of New Brighton. I am not certain he said "cut the throats", it might have been "would settle all in New Brighton". This occurred before Christmas. He kept the knife in a box used for odds and ends.

Mr. Bailey, recalled, said that when he saw the prisoner on the Sunday morning he wore a kind of short overcoat. He had a peaked cap on his head, and slippers on his feet.

Mr. Storey, recalled, said the prisoner wore a blue coat and a 'cheese-cutter' cap.

The Bench decided to remand the accused until Monday next.

Mr. Moore said the date would suit him. There was a good deal to be done in the way of seeing the prisoner, and he asked the bench not to send the prisoner to Walton, but to retain him on the court premises.

The Chairman -- We have decided to remand the prisoner to Walton. They have every accommodation there for you to have consultations.

The New Brighton Murder

Liverpool Mercury
Thursday, 5th June, 1890

The fund which was started for the benefit of Mrs. Spicer and her children some few days ago is still open and Mr. John Bailey, Victoria Road, is the honorary treasurer. Part of the money which has been received has been used to defray the expenses connected with the funeral of the children. Mrs. Spicer has expressed her gratitude for the kindly interest that has been taken in her.

Committal of The Accused

Liverpool Mercury
Tuesday, 10 June, 1890

Yesterday, at the Wallasey Police Court, Felix Spicer was brought up on remand charged with having murdered his two sons, William and Henry Spicer, and also with having attempted to murder Mary Anne Palin, at New Brighton, on the morning of Whit Sunday, the 25th of May.

Mr A.T Wright, a member of the firm of Messrs. Wright, Becket & Co., solicitors, Liverpool, under whom the tenancy of the premises Bickley Parade was held. He said that on the 2nd May the prisoner called at his office and asked that he might have the tenancy of the premises, 3 Bickley Parade, which were at one time let to Mrs. Spicer. The prisoner had been a tenant of the shop until about Christmas 1888, and at that time had asked to have the premises taken off his hands, and as he could not pay all the rent he authorised witness to take the fixtures for the amount due. Spicer, at his last interview with witness, about Easter, urged that he should be allowed to resume the tenancy. He mentioned that Mrs. Spicer was not his wife, but displayed no ill-feeling against her. Witness told him that he was quite satisfied with Mrs. Spicer's tenancy, but if it was more satisfactory to him he would tell Mrs. Spicer to call at the office. Witness wrote to Mrs. Spicer, who called on the following Monday, and the result of the interview, together with other inquiries, was that witness wrote to the prisoner stating that he had heard Mrs. Spicer's story, and did not propose to make any change to the tenancy. He advised Spicer to seek employment elsewhere, and not to interfere in the business in any way.

Walter Edward Banning, a lamplighter [said] on Whit Sunday morning, about 2.15, he had heard the crying of the baby at the house in Richmond Street. On going to the front door he heard a light shuffle, as of feet, in the lobby, and that he heard a voice, but did not hear what was said. He again heard the child's voice, but, thinking it was a baby crying, went away.

Mrs. Fraser, the witness at the refreshment room, was recalled, and repeated a portion of her evidence, already published. In cross examination by Superintendent Hindley, witness said that about a week or a fortnight before the murder the prisoner asked her how she got into the refreshment rooms in the mornings - if she had a key. She replied that Mrs. Spicer let her in, and that she had no key.

Joel Fitton, iron turner, 82, Wild Street, Derby, said that on the night of the murder he was staying at 5 Victoria Road, New Brighton, which is nearly opposite 3 Bickley Parade. About half past three in the morning he was awakened by his boys knocking at his door. In consequence of what they said he ran downstairs to the sitting room window. From there he saw the prisoner and Mrs. Spicer struggling. Witness noticed a knife on the floor, which Spicer was trying to reach. Mrs. Spicer got away and went across the road to Mr. Bailey's and Spicer went towards the rooms. The knife witness saw on the floor looked something like a shoemaker's knife, and would be four or five inches long. He could not swear that the knife produced was the one he saw, but the knife had a dark handle. After the struggle Spicer went inside the refreshment room through the front window and witness heard the sound of running water, which gave him the impression that the prisoner was washing his hands. He then came out and went towards the shore, and turned along the lower parade.

Mary Ann Palin, known as Mrs. Spicer was recalled [and] was shown the knife produced by the analyst, which she recognised as the one with which the prisoner had attacked her on the night of the murder.

Charlotte Myers, wife of John Myers, 6 Richmond Street, New Brighton, said she kept a lodging house. On the night of the murder she saw the prisoner in Richmond Street about 20 minutes to eleven. After some conversation, the prisoner told her that his house was full of lodgers, and asked her to accommodate anyone who might turn up. She went home, and about eleven 'o clock Spicer, accompanied by a gentleman, called, and Spicer told her that he had brought a gentleman for the night. The lodger stayed in the house all night, and got up about seven o'clock. He paid for his bed, and left without having breakfast. She had not seen him since, and did not know his name. -- By Superintendent Hindley : She would of known if any one had left the house during the night because she had put second lock on the door, and it could not have be shut from the outside

Thomas Frederick Cooke, a plumber, 3 Belmont Road, New Brighton, stated that on the 31st May, he was assisting to search the premises of 3 Bickley Parade. In the cooking range, between the upper plate and the oven flue, he found the knife produced, and handed it to Constable Jones. The knife must of been put there through the manhole.

[In relation to Alfred Short interview with Mr F. Spicer at Walton Jail, see Monday 2nd June: Sheffield & Rotherham News article]

Mr Moore to Mr. Short : This interview occurred on the 31st May at Walton Jail?

Witness : It did sir

Mr Moore : Was there any warders present?

Witness : There was one warder present, head warder, present.

Mr Moore : Had you an order from the Prison Commissioners to see the prisoner?

Witness : No sir.

Mr. Moore : Had you on the 26th May, been examined and given evidence along with other witnesses?

Witness : I had sir

By the Bench : My interview took place in consequence of a letter received from the prisoner. I had not previously written to him.

This concluded the evidence., and the formula of charging the prisoner was then gone through. In reply to the magisterial caution on the first charge, that of the murder of William Spicer, the prisoner, acting on the advice of his solicitor, replied that he was not guilty, and that he did not want to call any witnesses. He made the same reply to the second charge, that of the murder of Henry Spicer, adding that he would reserve his defence. In reply to attempting to murder Mary Ann Palin, he said he was guilty of the assault on her. He was then committed to the assizes at Chester on three charges.

The New Brighton Tragedy

Manchester Times
Saturday, 14th June, 1890

The inquest on the victims of the New Brighton murder was resumed at Seacombe on Wednesday. The Coroner, in his address to the jury, again complained strongly of the action of the Home Secretary in refusing the prisoner to be brought into the Coroner's Court. The jury, after a short deliberation, returned a verdict to the effect that had been wilfully murdered by their father. Felix Spicer, now in custody in Knutsford Gaol.

◆ ◆ ◆

THE NEW BRIGHTON TRAGEDY: PART 2

Trial At Chester Assizes

Liverpool Mercury

Friday, 1 August, 1890

Yesterday, at the Chester Assizes, before Mr. Justice Stephen, who presided in the Crown Court, Felix Spicer, rigger, 60 years of age, was brought up charged with having, at Liscard, on the 25th May, 1890. feloniously, wilfully, and of his malice aforethought, killed and murdered William Spicer; further, with having, at Liscard , on the 25th May, 1890, killed and murdered Henry Spicer; and further, with having, at Liscard, on the 25th May, 1890, attempted to kill and murder Mary Ann Palin.

Mr D.L.V Colt Williams and Mr Malcolm Douglas prosecuted; and Mr Edmund Burke Wood, at the request of his lordship, defended the prisoner.

In his opening statement, Mr Colt Williams said that as the prisoner was arraigned before them on the serious charge of wilful murder he felt sure he might ask the most careful attention of the jury. He needed not to point out that the charge was a grave one, the most grave charge which could be found against any person, but what made it even worse than such cases sometimes were was that the prisoner was charged with murdering his two sons. He (learned counsel) would have to occupy their attention for some time in giving a short account of the family life of the prisoner implicated before going on to the facts of the case upon which the prosecution relied. There was no direct evidence, everything being circumstantial, and it would be his duty, aided by his friend, Mr Douglas, to connect the prisoner step by step with the murder. However averse they must be to find a father guilty of murdering his own child he believed that if the jury considered the case proved they would say so in their verdict. The prisoner was a man about 60 years of age, a seafaring man, be being described as a rigger, and having also gone to sea as a cook. He had lived at New Brighton for about 17 years, and there had lived with him, a woman named Mary Ann Palin, who had always been looked upon as his wife, but who had never really been married to him. They had seven children, the eldest boy, who was about 14, being away at the time of the murder; William, whom prisoner was charged with killing, two little girls, one aged eight and the other six; the little boy Henry, who was also murdered; and a little baby. One of the seven children died some years ago. Prisoner and Palin kept a refreshment room at 3, Bickley Parade, and some time ago, owing to prisoner pecuniary difficulties the tenancy was transferred to Palin at the prisoner's request, but before Easter this year he seemed to be put out about the arrangement. He went to the rooms and kicked up a disturbance, till Palin called in a constable, showed him the agreement, and had the prisoner warned not to interfere with the management. The rooms consisted of a one-storeyed place containing a restaurant and a kitchen. The house in Richmond Street was an ordinary one, containing a kitchen and bedroom, in which the children and servant slept.

Shortly after Easter week there seemed to have been some quarrel between the prisoner and Palin, as he went to the refreshment rooms during the absence of Mrs Palin in Liverpool, who had gone there to see a Mr Wright. Some money was taken during the absence of Palin, and when she returned words seemed to have taken place with regard to the taking of the money. Palin made use of words to the effect that one was enough to take the money, and then practically told him that he had no business in the place. That appeared to have made the prisoner very uncomfortable, and subsequently he wrote a letter to Mr Wright, agent of the landlord, telling him that Palin was not his wife. Correspondence ensued, in which Palin refused to sleep any longer at Richmond Street, and had her bed taken to the Restaurant, where she afterwards slept. The tenour of the correspondence was that prisoner wished her to return, but she replied upbraiding him for betraying her by saying she was no longer his wife, and for having disgraced her. The letter also mentioned about his promise to marry her before the first child was born. There was, undoubtedly, a desire on the part of the prisoner that they should make up the quarrel, but Palin, feeling that she had been so much injured by the prisoner telling Mr Wright that she was not his wife never went back, but continued to sleep at each night at the rooms. The children repeatedly went to the rooms, but returned to Richmond Street to sleep. Mrs Palin conducted the business of the restaurant, but on Saturday, the 24th, prisoner, suggested he should be allowed to help in the business which would be transacted in the course of the coming Whit Week. Palin sent a message to him saying that she did not require that assistance, and that she would not have him near the rooms. As there was an intimation made that four lodgers were going to Richmond Street, Palin said the children must not be disturbed as to their sleeping accommodation. Why the prisoner wanted all the children to sleep together the learned counsel did not know, and why he should have said that four lodgers were coming when they never did come was a matter of conjecture. As a matter of fact, there was an empty room in the house that night, and yet when a lodger came he was told there was no room to spare. It might be suggested that the stranger who stopped at the house of the neighbour, Mrs Myers, that night, and who had never been found, might by some chance have gone back into Richmond Street and murdered these children, but he (learned counsel) should show that that was perfectly impossible, for Mrs Myers would tell them distinctly that she heard this lodger go to bed, and after he had gone to bed there were two locks upon the door which she herself locked, and that it would be impossible for any one to go in or out without her knowing it. The prisoner never went to bed that night and he said that he was going to stop up in order to wait for this hypothetical lodger who never came. The person who saw him last that night was Mrs Fraser, with whom he had at first some words because she arrived from the prosecutrix's shop so late, but who afterwards at his request rubbed his back, as he complained of rheumatism. She would tell the jury that during the night at about daybreak she heard a cry coming from the little boy Harry, followed by a shuffling noise, as if somebody was going about in slippers. She did not pay much attention, because she knew that the prisoner was in the habit of going to the bedroom of the children and soothing them if they were disturbed. Again the little girl Gertrude, who was sleeping in another room, heard her little brother Harry cry out. She opened the door, and asked what was the matter, whereupon a voice which she supposed to be that of her father, said "go to sleep". The child cried out again, and she then heard the same voice exclaim, "shut up". A lamplighter who was passing heard the pitiful cry of the child proceeding from the house of the prisoner, and he heard a noise as of a man shuffling along the passage. The evidence would show that the accused was in the habit of wearing sandshoes down at the heels, and therefore if he was walking about he would so in a shuffling manner. Mrs Fraser heard someone go out, and shut the scullery door after him, and again she heard the same shuffling noise, as of some one going swiftly up the stairs then down again. It was suggested it was the prisoner. He had gone out of the house after having murdered these children, and having gone down to Bickley Parade, he came back through that scullery door, on the handles of which there were blood stains. It was also suggested that previous to the arrival of the police he drew down the blind in the kitchen.

The theory of the prosecution with regard to what took place after this was that having cut the throats of the children he went into the backyard and took from it a piece of wood which he had been shaping a handle to a day or two previously, and with that went down to the rooms and smashed the windows. Palin would say that she awakened by the hearing of a smash of glass. She then saw the prisoner putting his hand through the window and feeling for the key in the door. He must tell them, however, that prisoner had previously asked from Mrs Fraser how entrance was gained in the morning to the rooms where Palin slept, and Fraser told him that she went down in the mornings and Palin opened the door for her. On the window which prisoner put his hand through and where Palin saw him feeling for the latch there were found smears of blood, and this was material, because when examined immediately after his arrest prisoner's hands were perfectly free from all cuts and scratches. Counsel went on to speak of the assault on Palin, but said but he said he would not specify the particulars of that, as it was not before them, but he must tell them that Mrs Palin jumped out of the window into the street, and there Spicer attacked her. He had got her on the ground, he took a knife from his coat pocket, and the analyst would tell them that the pocket had bloodstains on it, thus bearing out the theory of the prosecution that there must of been blood on the knife before the attack on Palin. The knife he used was one which Palin had seen him handle previously, and he had told her that it would "cut the throats of all New Brighton". After the assault the prisoner went back into the rooms, and one of the witnesses would prove that while he was in there was the sound of running water. There was a lavatory in the rooms, and soon after prisoner's arrest it was noticed by the wash marks on the prisoner's hands and wrists that he had recently washed his hands.

After leaving his wife he went up to Richmond Street, where he was soon followed and arrested by the police for the assault on his wife. After his arrest one of the constables went up to the bedrooms, and in one of them found the two children with their throats cut, and their heads almost severed from their bodies. The learned counsel went on to describe the position in which the children were found, and of a pool of blood on the bed in which some one had evidently been kneeling. There was found on his knee immediately after his arrest wet blood marks, the knee of his trousers being soaked in blood. One of the little boys was lying where he had been sleeping and was dead. That would be shortly after four o'clock and the doctor was of the opinion that the two children had been dead about an hour, and that would coincide with what the prosecution said, that the prisoner, having murdered these children, went down to Bickley Parade. One of the witnesses would state that he remarked that Spicer had murdered his children. Spicer immediately replied "I know nothing at all about it". But he made no secret of the fact that he had made the attack on Palin. When at the Police Station, and charged with the murder, he denied having interfered with the children. There were also marks of blood on the prisoner's coat and shirt sleeves, and from that it would appear he was in his shirt sleeves before he left the house, and afterwards put on his coat. At the request of Spicer the lodger named Short went to see him at Walton Gaol, where he had related a story of what had taken place. He again denied murdering the children, confessed to attacking Palin, and said "I used my clasp knife to her". The prosecution would show that was untrue, because that knife was found upon the prisoner, and that there was no marks of blood on it. That was not the knife that Spicer had murdered the children with, and with which he attacked Palin, but the proper knife that had been used was discovered hidden in the flue of the kitchen range at Bickley Parade. Prisoner admitted having remained in the kitchen up to three o'clock in the morning, his excuse being that he was waiting for a lodger, who never came. Therefore, the only man about the house when the murder was committed was the prisoner. On the 23rd, or the day before the murder was committed, the prisoner was heard by his next door neighbour walking up and down the yard, and he was heard to exclaim in an angry voice, "they shall see they shall not have it all their own way". On the same evening someone was heard sharpening the knife upon the windowsill of the back window of Richmond House. The following morning there were marks upon the sill, and the knife, which would be produced, would show signs of having been recently sharpened but; whether it was sharpened that night or not the prosecution did not know. Those were the facts of the painful case, which would require the strictest proof by the prosecution. Prisoner seemed to have been fond of the children, and on the night of the murder assisted in putting them to bed. Therefore it might appear an extraordinary thing that he, being so attached to his children, should have murdered them in the cold blooded way in which it was alleged that he did.

Mary Ann Palin, after some formal evidence had been given, stated that she was 32 years of age, and had lived with the prisoner since she was 16. She had seven children, of whom four were still alive. On the 24th May last the eldest boy was from home. The next lad was nearly 13, the next was a girl of eight, another girl was six, and there was a boy aged three, and a baby. Witness had resided at Richmond Street with her children up to April last. She took in lodgers at the house, and carried on business as a refreshment house keeper at 3 Bickley Parade. The prisoner had not followed his occupation since she had lived with him. He went one voyage while they lived in Cardiff, and last year he went for a nine months' voyage. Up to September 1888, the tenancy of the Bickley Parade rooms was in the prisoner's name and it was retaken by her 1889 in the name of Mrs Spicer. He came back in September 1889, but did not disprove of her having taken over the rooms. Up to about Easter last she lived on good terms with him at the house at Richmond Street. She and the prisoner slept in the large front bedroom, and the children slept in a double-bedded back room - three in one bed room and two in the other. As a rule the children slept together. This continued till Easter, when the prisoner came down and assisted in the business. On Easter Monday prisoner was locked up for the non-payment of the poor rate which was owing. Witness paid the rate, and prisoner came back, and she agreed he should stay at the house, as he was owing more money, and was afraid there were more warrants out for him. He stayed a week at the house. She had no disagreement with before Easter. It was after that that the disagreement took place. He stayed away from the refreshment rooms for a week. He came to the rooms on the Monday following Easter week. Witness had been to Liverpool that day, and when she came home she found him a little worse for drink, and asked what money had been taken. He pointed to money lying on the shelf. Witness took a few shillings off the shelf. Prisoner asked her what she was doing, and she replied that she was taken the money. Prisoner said "leave it there; don't be in such a hurry". Witness said "oh, it does not take two to look after the few shillings here". Prisoner then began finding fault with the trades people she dealt with. Witness said she would deal with whom she liked. Prisoner said that he should let her know whether she should or not. Witness said that the prisoner had nothing to do with the business. Prisoner then went home. When witness was preparing the dinner next day, prisoner walked into the shop and took his coat off. He said, "you told me I had nothing to do with this place, but I must give you to understand there is no Mary Spicer". The girl Fraser was present at the time. Up to then she had been known as Mrs Spicer. She then said, "if there is no Mrs Spicer, so much the better for me". She gave him to understand that she would not have him coming there and conducting himself in an unpeaceable manner. In consequence of what she said he became violent, and kicked a chair across the floor. She sent for a constable, and when he arrived she showed him the agreement respecting the shop. She was quite agreeable for Spicer to come to the shop and be master of everything except the money. She had a bed taken down to Bickley Parade, where she slept until the 24th of May.

The children came down to the shop for their food, and she sent the prisoner's meals to Richmond Street, and also what money he sent for. Fraser was in her employ as a waitress, and slept at Richmond Street. Witness did not see Spicer for a week after the letter produced, which was in the prisoner's handwriting. She could not say when she received it. She did not think it would be in Easter week. The letter was as follows :- "Richmond Street, 15/5/90. My dear Polly - I trust you will take my lot into consideration and pity me, and by the great God forgive me and in nowise cast me out, with a broken heart. Do forgive me. Have mercy on me. I will make every amends in my power. Have mercy on me; have mercy on me: give me some hope of your friendship. May God turn your heart to forgive me. Yours forever, F.SPICER". On the back of that letter witness scribbled the following answer, and sent it to him :- "you are too late, and you need not try to see me. The door is locked, and once for all I will not be annoyed by you. I shall not see you". She also received the following letter from the prisoner :- 19/5/90, "my dear Polly - in the name of the heavens, have mercy and pity on me. If you will allow me to see and shake hands with you and make it up. Don't keep me in this desponding state. Forgive me, forgive me, for God's sake and my own. I have not slept these four nights thinking of you. Make it up with me. Let not our wrath go down with this day's sun. Have mercy on me. I will call tonight at nine. Don't refuse me a hand shake in the name of God. I beg you will not be cross with me. I am still for ever yours. F.SPICER". She also received a letter from him which he said - "my dear Polly - I will call down to-night. I hope you will consider my feelings and make it up and shake hands with me. I am a broken man. For God's sake, have pity on me. Your's for ever F.SPICER". In reply she sent the following letter - "Mr Spicer, this is in answer to yours. You dare to ask me to make it up. You must be mad to think I shall ever speak to you again, much less make it up. You told Mr Wright I was not your wife. You mean, contemptible scrub, did you think of my years when, before Felix was born, I asked you to marry me out of shame. You laughed at me, but I have waited, and the day has come, I can tell everyone my tale now. Don't think it was for a liking of you I waited for. I hated you ever since the day you laughed at me, but I don't regard my name now. Why should I, now everybody knows. There is one thing I want you to know, that is the gallows before another night under the same roof as yourself. I will neither see or be annoyed by you. If you force your presence on me I shall have you removed. You can remain in the house for as long as you keep from me. I will see the rent paid, but I will never change as long as I live" - POLLY.

Witness had taken the rooms from Mr Wright. It was in consequence of an interview with Mr Wright that she wrote the letter. The following letter was put in, and read by Mr Crompton. clerk of the assizes :- "Richmond Street, New Brighton, 8/5/90. Dear Sir, I am in receipt of your note, and am sorry, after the friendly advice you gave me, that you have thought fit to write as you have. It is a great trial to me, being the founder of the business, and your tenant so long, that you have not given me a more favourable consideration. I am afraid you have been misinformed about my affairs. I beg and trust you will reconsider your decision in my favour by getting Mrs Spicer to allow me to work in the rooms in an amicable way, in which I give you my honest word there shall be peace and love. I am near heart broken by this blow. I trust you will forgive me. With this appeal believe me to be, yours sincerely, F.SPICER. To A. Wright. Esq, 17 Water Street. Liverpool".

On the night of the 24th the prisoner sent the girl to her, saying he expected four lodgers that night, and the children were to be removed to the back room from the front room where they usually slept. She sent back word that they were not to be removed, and he was only to take the one lodger that she had sent up during the evening. She sent up the person she referred to to Richmond Street earlier in the evening, and he returned in half an hour saying he had taken a bed. She saw the prisoner at the restaurant windows the night before the murder, when he said, "Good night, Polly" or "Good night, girl" and then walked away. She made up her bed in the restaurant nightly, and removed it for the day time, when Fraser left the premises. She put out the lamps, and subsequently she was awakened by a great noise, caused by the smashing of glass. She afterwards saw prisoner make a desperate smash at the same pane of glass which was near the door. She fell through the window right into his arms, both prisoner and herself falling to the ground, witness being on her back. She shouted out "Murder!" and he said "You shout murder you - wretch. You won't shout that when I've done with you". Whilst she was on the ground he kept knocking her head down and making for her throat. He had nothing in his hands then, but she saw the handle of a knife sticking out of his breast pocket. He took this out of his pocket and attacked her with it. It was a knife he had shown her before, saying in a jocular way that "it would cut the throats of all New Brighton". The knife produced was the one in question, and with it prisoner had tried to cut her throat. When he attacked her her nose, forehead, and arms were cut, as was also her hand where she tried to hold the knife by grasping the blade. Finally she knocked the knife out of his hand and managed to run away behind the cabmen's shelter, and afterwards she got into the house of a Mr Bailey, just opposite. She thought prisoner had a long tweed overcoat on, and it was in one of the pockets that she saw the knife. She knew prisoner was in the habit of carrying a clasp knife, but the one that was produced was not that with which he attacked her.

In cross examination the witness said she first made the acquaintance of prisoner at Cardiff in 1873. He had made voyages, but did not know that he had ever been a voyage to Calcutta of that he had had a sunstroke while there. In one of the letters she wrote to the prisoner she meant she never had an opportunity of maintaining herself and the children, and "a day would come" when she would do so and have nothing more to do with him. After the manner in which he had treated her she had come to the conclusion she would not under any consideration live with him again. Witness, continuing, said "of course if he had offered to marry me I should have only been too glad". At this point the witness broke down.

Mr Wood : With respect to his appeals to you stating that he was broken hearted and that he was miserable and ruined, you treated those as nothing?

Witness: No sir. I have received those kind of messages before when I left him, and when I went and forgave him and went back to him, he even on the first night attempted to strangle me, and that was after he had pleaded as in this case.

Continuing, witness said she sent a man up to Richmond Street on the night before the murder as he wanted lodgings.

Re-examined by Mr Colt Williams : It was before the child Felix was born that prisoner promised to marry her. Had he ever promised to marry you?

Witness : Had he ever promised to marry me? Yes, he had repeatedly.

Continuing, witness said it was at Blackpool that prisoner tried to strangle her. She left him for some time after that, and went to live with her sister in London.

Mr Colt William : During the times you lived in New Brighton had you ever serious quarrels?

Witness : Yes. I left him several times, but he always implored me to go back.

John Bailey, grocer, Victoria Road, deposed to be awakened on the night in question by hearing of cries of "murder". He found prisoner and Mrs Spicer struggling on the ground, and told to her to run into his house. She did so, and he followed her and closed the door.

Francis Storey, another neighbour, and Joel Fitton, corroborated.

Police Constable Frederick Potts stated that his attention, and that of Police Constable Jones, was called to a disturbance in Victoria Road. They went to Richmond Street in search of the prisoner, when Police Constable Jones took him to the police office, whilst witness went upstairs and found the two children on the bed with their throats cut.

Police Constable Jones corroborated, and deposed to finding a knife which had been recently sharpened and was covered in blood and concealed in the kitchen range.

The medical evidence of Dr Forbes Ross, as to the nature of the injuries, was taken next. He said that one of the wounds to the throat of the younger victim appeared to have been an abortive attempt at cutting it. After this wound was inflicted, and before the fatal wound was given, the child might have shouted. He saw the prisoner after examining in the children. He wore a black coat, on the breast pocket of which were blood stains, his sandshoes being also spotted with blood. His trousers were saturated, and his hands had been washed, leaving a "watermark" of blood smears on the forearm. Both handles of the back door were stained with blood.

Annie Fraser, waitress at Mrs Spicer's restaurant, who slept at prisoner's house on the night of the murder, said she remembered hearing one of the children make a choking noise, followed by a shuffling of feet and the sound of doors being closed. Somebody then ran upstairs and down quickly. She thought nothing about it at the time

Cross examining by Mr Burke Wood : She had always found prisoner to be most affectionate towards his children.

Martha Fearon, another waitress, corroborated as to the prisoner's kindness to his children, when cross examined by Mr Burke Wood.

Alfred Short, Clerk, of Richmond Street, said that on the 24th of May he went in at ten o'clock in the evening. Spicer, his son, and the waitress were in the house at the time. Witness did not hear anything during the night except an altercation between prisoner and Mrs Fraser at twelve o'clock. He had an interview with the prisoner at Walton Jail on the Saturday following the murder, when he said "I washed Willie and kissed him put him to bed, bless his little soul. I am as innocent as you are"

Cross Examined by Mr Burke Wood : When he said "bless his little soul" he was very much affected and wept.

Witness had never seen a more kind man to his children. He was like mother and father to them. He sent the message to his wife, "Tell her I forgive her all she had done for me, but she has been very cruel".

A lamplighter named Bannng stated that just before daybreak on the morning in question he was performing his duties in Richmond Street when he heard a "pitiful child's cry".

A woman residing next door to prisoner stated that between nine and ten o'clock on the night of 24th May she heard the prisoner say he would "let them know who is master here". Later in the night she heard him sharpening a knife on the window sill.

After consultation with the judge and defending counsel, Mr Colt Williams decided to spare the little girl Gertrude Spicer the painful ordeal of giving evidence against her father.

At this stage the court adjourned, the counsel for the prosecution indicating that their case could be finished that day. The court rose at ten minutes after four.

Trial And Sentence

Liverpool Mercury
Saturday, 2 August, 1890

Yesterday, before Mr Justice Stephen, at the Chester Assizes, Felix Spicer appeared again in the dock charged with the murder, at Liscard, on the 25th May, of his illegitimate sons, William and Henry, and the attempted murder of Mary Ann Palin, their mother. Mr D.A.V Colt Williams and Mr Malcolm Douglas, in continuing their case for the Crown, called Police Sergeant Cooper, who gave lengthy evidence as to the examination of the Richmond Street and Victoria houses, the bloodstains and other inculpating traces he found there and on prisoner's clothes and hands. He said that when charged with the offence prisoner said "I know nothing about it. I have done no murder".

Mr William F Lowe, county analyst, was next called, and gave lengthy evidence as to the nature and position bloodstains upon the piece of timber used by prisoner to batter the windows of the Bickley Parade restaurant, upon his clothes, shoes, knife, and in various parts of the house.

Dr Theodore Fendell, medical officer at Knutsford Jail, was next called, and stated that the prisoner had been under his care since his admission to Knutsford Jail on the 11th June. During prisoner's incarceration witness had had constant opportunity of observing him, and had found that his health had been good, there being nothing at all wrong with him mentally.

Cross examined by Mr Burke Wood : Witness had heard that prisoner's sister had been in Colony Hatch, and prisoner had told him that he had had a sunstroke.

That would not modify his statement at all as to the mental condition of prisoner; he could only form an opinion from what he had noticed himself. the prisoner showed no sign of insanity, or even of mental aberration.

This was the case for the prosecution. Mr D.A.V Colt Williams, in summoning up for the Crown, gave a lengthy review of the incriminating evidence. He said he understood that Mr Burke Wood intended to call no witness on behalf of the prisoner, so it became his duty to address the jury in as few words as possible. As he had intimated in his opening address, that case was one of such great gravity that he was sure they would pardon him if he detained them for more then a few minutes in doing so. On that occasion he had also told them that it was a case of completely of circumstantial evidence, and that they would require at his hands a strict proof of every step in the case; he submitted to them with some confidence now that he had so proved the case that there could be no reasonable doubt in their minds that the prisoner at the bar was guilty of the terrible crime with which he is charged. It might be that some attempt should be set up to show that because a sister of prisoner's was said to have been at one time insane, and because it was suggested that prisoner himself had once had a sunstroke, that he was insane at the time he committed that act. On the other hand they had the evidence of Dr Fendell, who had observed prisoner since June the 11th, that he was not a man of unsound mind. Therefore his submission on behalf of the Crown was that this case was made out without any shadow of a doubt, and that he was justified in asking them, after weighing his friend's and his lordship's remarks, to find the man guilty of the offence with which he was now charged.

Mr Burke Wood then rose to address the jury for the defence. He said that in this case a great burden had been laid upon the shoulders of all connected with the trial, and upon no one in a greater degree than upon himself. He was bound to say that Mr Colt Williams had conducted the case for the Crown most fairly, and had not exaggerated in the least degree the importance and solemnity of the inquiry. A great responsibility rested on them, the jury had by their verdict, and he, perhaps, by his conduct of the case, the life of the prisoner at the bar upon their hands. He did not say this with a view to asking them to take a merciful view of the case, but simply to give their verdict according to their oaths and the evidence laid before them. He dared say they noticed that on the previous morning when they came into the box he took the precaution, and used the right he possessed, of challenging several gentlemen, and they went out of the box. He did so not from any doubt that they would not have displayed as great an amount of intelligence and fairness as any in the box, but simply because he thought it better to have twelve strangers than any who came from the neighbourhood where the tragedy occurred. It was hard for any person to divest his mind of impressions that he had formed. Perhaps the result of conversation - perhaps the result of reading newspaper reports, and there was no doubt that the press of Birkenhead and its more important neighbour, Liverpool, spread far and wide an account of the tragedy at New Brighton and it was impossible pretty nearly that people should talk about a thing of that kind without forming some impression on their minds as to the guilt or innocency of the prisoner. Therefore, he earnestly asked the jury to try to come with a clean sheet, as it were, of mind to consider the evidence of that day and the day before. His friend, Mr Colt Williams, in opening the case, had told them that the case he had to submit was one entirely of circumstantial evidence, and that he had no direct evidence at all, and that if they did not think this evidence sufficient to satisfy them, they should say so by their verdict. That was just what he should have expected them to do. He was sorry to have to go into particulars of the married life of the prisoner and Palin, but there was no doubt that he had wronged her, and had not done what he owed to her by marrying her. It was possible that he was not in a position to marry her at the time, because he had a wife already. However, they had lived together for a number of years, quarrels frequently occurring, but not with any serious result till in April last, when they finally separated. He must call their attention to the dreadful state of misery under which the prisoner laboured in consequences of this quarrel with his wife, who refused to live in the same house with him any longer. He wrote imploring letters requesting a reconciliation; but they were received with scorn. With regard to prisoner's statement that he could not receive a lodger on the night of the 24th because he had four men, and was full up, it had been stated that these four men were all a myth, and that this statement was only a part of his scheme to kill the children. Was it not possible that these men, whom prisoner said he had seen with women on the same night, had gone to some less respectable haunt for the night? At all events it seemed as likely as that the whole story was a myth invented by prisoner. Having pointed out that there was nothing peculiar in prisoner not retiring on the night in question, when he had a sofa prepared downstairs, he said that the testimony as to the prisoner being kind to his children was unanimous. Fearon appeared to have been a new arrival at prisoner's house, but even she had had time to how tenderly he brought them to be washed by her, and afterwards carried them upstairs and put them to bed. There appeared to have been the bright spot in that man's life - that was his love and affection for his children, and whatever Mary Ann Palin might have to say about his treatment of her, she had no occasion to make a single complaint of his treatment of her children. Annie Fraser said he was extremely kind to them; Maria Fearon described the way in which he performed those many little functions which a careless man might have relegated to the nursemaid, with the tenderness and kindness of a mother rather than the qualities of a father. The lodger also said he never saw anyone so kind in his life, and confirmed the opinion that he was like a mother rather than a father. He then referred to the evidence as to the discovery of blood stains in the house, and emphasised the fact that though prisoner was said to have done downstairs with the clothes reeking with blood, only one small stain was found on the banister. It would be an insult to deny that prisoner went down to Bickley Parade - the evidence was too strong and unanimous on that point - but if an assault of the nature described was committed upon Palin by prisoner, it would be a fair and reasonable conclusion to draw that the blood found on his clothing had flowed from her hands as she was on the ground by prisoner. Again, evidence had been given to this effect that the blood stains on the handle of the piece of wood used by prisoner to batter in the windows in Bickley Parade were wet when it was examined after the assault. He contended that if the stains were imprinted at Richmond Street, by the time he had walked to Bickley Parade and assaulted Palin the stains would have had time to dry. At all events this was not improbable solution of the case. He strongly urged upon the jury the fact that the lodger, who came in at seven o'clock on the morning of the crime, had not been examined by the counsel for the prosecution, and said that in view of the widespread newspaper reports he could not have failed to hear about the occurrence. In reference to the interview in Walton Jail he said that sometimes when prisoners made statements there was something or other held out, or it might be supposed that there was something held out; but in that case it was entirely a voluntary statement to a man whom he had sent for, and therefore entitled to more respect at the hands of the jury than many communications of a similar character. He said, "I know nothing, so help me God. I washed little Harry; I put him to bed. I bid him 'Good night', and kissed him - bless his little heart. Willie went to bed afterwards; I wished him 'good night' and I didn't go upstairs afterwards. I am as innocent as you are". That was a statement made to an independent man, and he would ask them to attach some importance to it. These children appeared to have been the idols of his life almost - these children whom he was charged with killing. A great lawyer, Lord Cope, described murder as being when a man of sound memory and discretion killed a human being. Did they believe for one instant that that man "murdered" his children? He was obliged to say he dared not leave any stone unturned in the duty that he had to perform on behalf of the prisoner; and therefore, though he submitted that the evidence for the prosecution consisted of a chain of evidence that was faulty and undefendable, he must omit no point that told in prisoner's favour. He could not help saying that if that man - he said this under his lordship's direction - if this man went into the room where those children were sleeping, very likely when he had the intention of going down and attacking the mother, and breaking into her premises, knowing that he was going to do the mother grievous bodily harm or to murder her, and that it would be impossible to escape - if he went into their room to take a last look at them, he submitted that if he went back into the room with merely the innocent intention of seeing his children, they would say he was not guilty of the murder of those children if, when his mind was so clouded with the trouble he had been in and the contemptuous replies to his appeals by his wife, this man, maddened with the thought of it, had his mental faculties so obliterated that he put an end to the children by cutting their throats. He asked the jury to ask themselves whether he was at that time a man of sound memory and reasonable sense, and said that if they thought not, he would ask them to say that a verdict of manslaughter would be all that could revert against that man. He was under his lordship's direction when he summed up the case to them, and he had no more to add on behalf of the prisoner. He had done what he thought was his duty, and according to his advice what he could do, and he only asked them to remember one thing - that they were not trying prisoner for the attack on Mary Ann Palin, and the savage assault he made on her, but simply for the crime of murder.

His Lordship said it was now his duty to sum up the evidence in the case to which they had listened so long and so patiently, and, before he got to the evidence he would make one or two remarks upon some general topics which had been alluded to by the learned counsel. Mr Colt Williams had told them, and Mr Wood repeated, that that was entirely a case of circumstantial evidence. He (the Judge) totally denied that anything popularly called circumstantial evidence was evidence at all, or should be given in evidence, and he should be right at the proper time, and place to show, by going through the various rules of evidence established in that country, that what was generally called circumstantial evidence with no evidence according to the distinctive rules of the country. That, however, was not the place to deliver a lecture upon legal topics, and he would pass over the expression with this single remark that, whether they liked to call the evidence circumstantial or not, the question was simply whether it satisfied them beyond all reasonable doubt that the man was guilty of the crime charged against him or not. He had also one other general remark to make upon the suggestion with which Mr Wood concluded his evidence - for it was possible there might be a conviction for manslaughter in that case if they thought that at the time he entered the children's room he had not the intention of cutting their throats. He told them that they could not consistently with law give any such verdict - the whole of the evidence in the case either proved that the man voluntarily and wilfully put his children to death by cutting their throats - which was murder - or that he was not guilty of any crime at all. They would, however. observe that something was said about the phrase "malice aforethought". It was undoubtedly true that to constitute murder there must be malice aforethought; but those were most unlucky words and were almost always misunderstood. Unless one knew how they should be technically interpreted one could not know what they meant. It was generally said that there most be premeditation - that was not so; if a man decided upon a sudden temptation to kill a person and did kill that person without provocation, if he did that, it was as much murder as if he had meditated it for a year and made every preparation for it. With regard to the words "malice aforethought" they had been better defined by Lord Chief Justice Holt than any he had ever read, and he had read a great quantity - "he that doth a cruel act voluntarily doth it of malice prepense". If the act was a cruel one and it was done voluntarily, that was what was meant by malice aforethought. So the whole matter really came to this - whether they thought that this mean voluntarily did the cruel act of cutting the throats of those children. That was the one subject which they had to inquire into, and he should address his summing up entirely to matters which threw light upon it. They had heard the evidence of a day and a half, and he did not think anytime had been wasted upon it. It seemed to have been very fairly given and very properly put before them, and now he would consider how the matter stood. There was no doubt at all that the prisoner and his wife did lead a most unhappy life, and that unhappiness seemed to have lasted for a considerable time. Mr Wood went back as far as 1873, when he said that the prisoner led Palin astray. Mr Wood suggested that he might have been married before and that that was the reason why he did not marry Palin. That might be so, but he could not ask the jury to pay attention to such suggestion. It was entirely strange to the matter they were now trying, and it never could be that a man could excuse, or justify, or extenuate one crime because another hung upon it. He might just make this one remark, though it was more in the nature of a moral observation than anything else, that was, that if prisoner had done that justice to the woman which he certainly owed her, if he had married, she could not have testified against him, and the fact that he did not think proper to marry her had been strangely avenged, and he was there on his trial for his life because he did not do that justice to the woman which he certainly ought to have done. Referring to the evidence as to prisoner's general affection for his children, he said that love for children was in a great measure the reflection for love of wife, and that a loss of affection for the wife would naturally cause a loss of affection for the children. That kind of kindness was quite consistent with something entirely different if a violent passion interfered. The counsel for the defence had impressed very strongly upon the jury that it was a suspicious fact that the lodger who came to the house in Richmond Street early on the morning of the day on which the crime was committed, must have known all about the occurrence from the newspaper. That was quite possible : but, strange as it might appear to lawyers, people hated to be called as witnesses, and he was not quite sure that he should not himself. (A laugh). People would get in their own houses, and say it was the place of the police to find them out, which made it very difficult to procure them as witnesses. Alluding to the evidence with respect to the blood stains, his lordship said that with the exception of the wounds on the woman's arm there was absolutely no accords whatever to be given of the blood which stained every single garment worn by the prisoner. He was speaking in reference to the suggestion with regard to prisoner's insanity, and remarking that the evidence went directly in opposition to the theory that he was of unsound mind.

Mr Burke Wood said it was very late in the case, but he had just learned from Dr Ross that prisoner was a sufferer from insomnia. His Lordship said it was indeed very late in the day, but directed that Dr Ross should be recalled. Dr Ross then stated that Mrs Palin had mentioned to him on one occasion that prisoner could never go to sleep, and bitterly complained of it in the same night. Insomnia, he continued, was sometimes a form of melancholia.

His Lordship : Have you ever observed any signs of melancholia about prisoner?

Dr Ross : No; but I thought it only fair to mention this.

His Lordship, remarking that the evidence did not very materially bear on the prisoner's state of mind, concluded his summing up, and the jury retired at exactly a quarter to two.

At ten minutes to two they returned into court.

The Clerk of Arraigns - Gentlemen of the jury, do you find the prisoner, Felix Spicer, guilty or not guilty?

The Foreman (in a low voice) - Guilty.

The Clerk - You say that he is guilty of murder, and that is the verdict of you all?

The Foreman - It is.

The Clerk - Felix Spicer, you stand convicted of willful murder. What have you to say why the court should not give you judgment to die according to law?

Prisoner - I am not guilty of the murder of the children, my lord. If I had worked on my own evidence I could prove that. I gave Mr Wood some papers as you suggested. He has them now, and if you read them you would exonerate me. There is proof where lodgers have been to the house, and paid an amount on deposit, and every action I have done during the week. If you were to read these papers it would prove you, my lord.

The Judge, assuming the black cap, said - Felix Spicer

Prisoner - Yes, my lord

The Judge - You stand convicted of wilful murder, and that under circumstances as horrible as I ever knew a murder to be accompanied with. As to what you say about Mr Wood. I can only tell you this, that Mr Wood, at very great labour to himself and at the sacrifice of much valuable time, has defended you with admirable skill and judgment.

Prisoner - Yes, my lord, I will admit that; but if you had read these papers, or if I had defended myself, I think you would have given me a better verdict.

The Judge - I cannot believe that Mr Wood has not read your papers.

Prisoner - There is marks of blood on the stones where I cut my hand with the glass.

The Judge - That is exactly what Mr Wood tried to persuade the jury, but they did not agree.

Prisoner - There is the money the lodgers gave me on deposit to come into the house where I stopped after half-past twelve to let them in. When I went out in the morning, all the doors were open, and I did not wake until 20 minutes past three.

The Judge - You have had the opportunity of saying all that, and you have had a very careful counsel to say it for you. The jury have come to the conclusion that you are guilty of wilful murder, and for my part I entirely share the same opinion. The matter is no longer in my hands in any way. All that remains to me is to pass upon you the sentence of the law.

Sentence of death was then pronounced in the usual way.

The prisoner, who displayed some agitation, was removed from the dock.

Interview With Spicer

Liverpool Mercury
Thursday, 14 August, 1890

Since the trial and conviction of Felix Spicer for the murder of his two children at New Brighton, circumstances have, it is stated, come to light bearing on the suggestion that the condemned man was insane at the time that he committed the deed. Spicer has a brother living in Birkenhead, and a half-brother, two sisters, and other relatives living in London. "Some of his London relatives," says a correspondent. "had expected to be called at the trial at Chester to give evidence as to the insanity which has from time to time manifested itself in the family, and the fact that they were not is said to be due to the late hour at which Mr Burke Wood was instructed, and that he was not then in possession of the information, which has now come to light. The important points bearing on the case are that one of Spicer's sisters has been confined in Colony

Hatch Lunatic Asylum as a epileptic idiot, suffering from exalted delusions and impressions. She had been in the asylum two or three times. Her son has also been confined both in the Colony Hatch and Hanwell institutions as an epileptic subject to violent outbursts and delusions. Another sister's daughter has been in the asylum, and is at present being watched by Dr Dunlop, of St. Pancras' Workhouse. It is further stated that a half sister of Spicer's lived with him for some time at New Brighton, and was subject to attacks of violent passion. She was of weak intellect, and in that condition of mind generally described as "soft". Spicer's brother's son also lived with him some time ago at New Brighton, and while there he one morning took up the carpet, cut the fringes off all the fire rugs, and trimmed all the rugs in the houses. He subsequently joined the Salvation Army, and became subject to religious mania, his peculiar conduct being on one occasion brought to the notice of the Birkenhead police magistrate. He afterwards went to London, where he one day cut down all the trees in his mother's back garden, because, as he said, they blocked the way to heaven. Yet another sister of the condemned man attempted to hang herself behind a parlour door, and she was cut down only just in time to save her life. She was of weak intellect, being particularly subject to suicidal mania.

Yesterday afternoon the same correspondent had a conversation with Mrs Cannon, a niece of the prisoner, who lives at Kentish Town, London, and who on Tuesday, along with her husband, visited Spicer in the condemned cell at Knutsford. The interview took place in the presence of the governor of the jail and two warders. Her account is as follows: "I noticed, first of all, that he had aged very fast. He asked after every one belonging to him, particularly his eldest son, Felix, who is an apprentice in a newspaper printing office in Cardiff, and whom he expressed a desire to see. He was most pleased to see me, as I was the first to visit him since he was condemned. I did not speak to him about the trial or the murder. I only told him to pray and look to his Maker. His own family all say that he must have been a mad man at the time when did the deed". Asked whether anything in the nature of insanity had ever been noticed in Spicer himself, Mrs Cannon said - "There have been fits of aberration at times. While I was there he spoke about his wife, and in order to distinguish her called her by her own name, Mary Ann Palin. He told me to go to New Brighton and see her, and ask her to come and see him. I said I would do so. (Mrs Spicer, otherwise Palin, who was present during the narration, said she intended to see him.) He further said that he could get very sleep. His appetite was pretty fair, and he got all that he wanted. The 20 minutes allowed for the interview had then expired, and they left. Spicer crying bitterly. Mr Cannon confirms hi wife's story as to Spicer's changed appearance, and said he looks like an old man of about 90. He never saw a man alter so in his life.

Execution Of Spicer

The North-Eastern Daily Gazette
Friday, 22 August, 1890

The final preparation for the execution of Felix Spicer (60), a rigger by trade, for the murder of his two children at New Brighton, were effected last night. Spicer, since he received sentence of death, had been confined in Knutsford Prison, the county gaol of Cheshire. Berry, the executioner, arrived at Knutsford from Bradford shortly after four o'clock yesterday afternoon, and immediately proceeded to the prison for the purpose of inspecting the necessary apparatus. The scaffold, which is the one used on the two previous occasions, was erected in a small building especially set apart for execution. Mr J. Cullimore, Under Sheriff, arrived at the prison last night in order to see that perfect arrangements had been carried out, and the executioner, in accordance with his instructions, took up his quarters for the night within the precincts of the prison, where he was supplied with sleeping accommodation.

A last effort had been made to restrain the last dread sentence of the law from being carried into effect, but with no result. A telegram was received yesterday by the authorities of the gaol from the Home Office, stating that the Home Secretary, after carefully perusing the evidence, and consulting with the Learned Judge who heard the case, saw no reason for interfering in Spicer's case with the due execution of the sentence of the law. Spicer himself has not denied committing the crime, but asserted at the same time that if he had so he was mad at the time. Up to the last he was exceedingly penitent, and paid marked attention to the ministrations of the prison chaplain, the Rev. W.N Truss, who paid him a visit late last night. Spicer has hardly varied in weight during his incarceration.

On The Scaffold

The chaplain entered the condemned cell shortly after six this morning and administered the Holy Sacrament. Spicer appeared very penitent, though when breakfast was brought Spicer did not touch it, and as the hour of his execution approached he seemed in danger of collapsing altogether. Berry, the executioner, entered the cell shortly before eight, and completed the pinioning process, which was undergone by the doomed man in a somewhat mechanical manner. On the way to the scaffold, which was the same as that which Richard Davies, the Crewe parricide, was executed, Spicer appeared rather faltering, but when he got out of the cell he revived considerably. When he had taken his place on the scaffold and the cap was adjusted on him he said "Good morning" to those present, and added in feeble tones, "I was mad if I perpetrated the crime. My poor dear children, May God bless and keep me, a miserable sinner". The bolt was then pulled, the body disappeared, and death seemed instantaneous. Spicer was 11 stone, 11 lbs, in weight, and 5 feet 4 inches in height, and he received a drop of 5 feet 2 inches. Representatives of the Press were admitted to witness the execution. Instructions were issued for the destruction of the rope with which Spicer was hanged immediately after the execution. The mode in which the rope is now supplied is that the High Sheriff, who is responsible for the carrying out of the execution, purchases the necessary length from the governor of Newgate Prison, who is authorised by the Home Office to sell it. This relieves the hangman of any responsibility as to the rope being unsuited for the purpose.

In accordance with the wish expressed by Spicer during an interview with some of his relatives, Mary Ann Palin, otherwise known as Mrs Spicer. declared her attention to close her refreshment rooms at New Brighton today to show her respect for Spicer, even though he had so cruelly wronged her.

◆ ◆ ◆

Printed in Great Britain
by Amazon